Early American Tokens

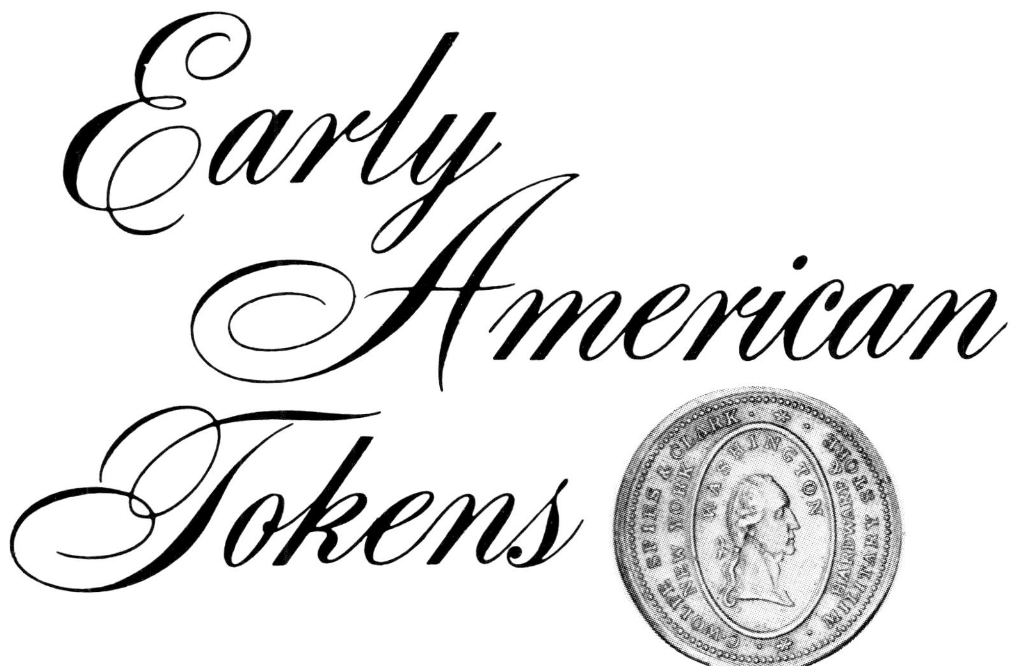

by Russell Rulau

A Catalog of the Merchant and Related Tokens
of Colonial and Early Republican America from 1700 to 1832.

Special Consultants:
- George Fuld
- Robert A. Vlack
- Byron Johnson
- David Schenkman
- Q. David Bowers

Second Edition

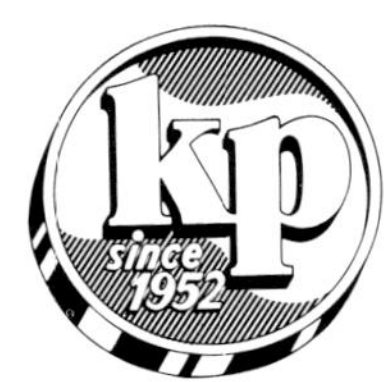

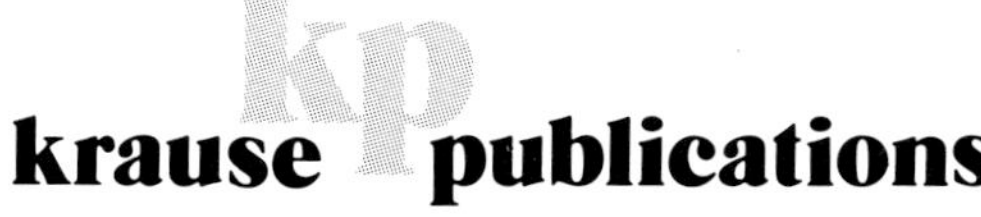

krause publications

IOLA, WISCONSIN 54990

PREFACE

For many years collectors have felt the need for a catalog of Early American tokens — those money substitutes and allied items issued from America's Colonial beginnings to the dawn of the Hard Times era (circa 1833).

Thanks to research accomplished in the 19th century, two important categories of United States tokens have received minutely detailed attention — the Hard Times tokens (1833-1844) and Civil War tokens (1861-1865).

The tokens of the Merchant era (1845-1860) are much more popular since the early 1982 publication of my illustrated catalog of these items. These pieces had received sporadic attention from writers such as Bushnell, Adams, Miller and the Fulds. The post-Civil War tokens (1866-1900) have received scant attention, though authors such as Adams, Dr. Wright, Malcolm Storer and the Fulds have helped break the ice, and my 1983 catalog of the 1866-1889 pieces is helping. But generally, the tokens before 1833 have been ignored, except for those considered Colonials which Crosby, Newman, Vlack, Yeoman and others have detailed. It is to address this oversight that the reference in your hands has been written.

Almost all private tokens issued in this country through 1832 are scarce. Uniformly, none are common. Every later era in America's token pantheon has groups of very common, available pieces; but not this Early period.

So, perhaps, it is understandable that no previous author ever "put it all together" — selling the book after it's produced is a prerequisite to keep publishers from suffering financial anguish.

A new age of appreciation for the lowly American token has dawned, though. The popularity enjoyed by my 1980 (first edition) *Hard Times Tokens* catalog proved to me — and the publishers — that the time to take the publication risk had arrived for the first edition of this work to appear in January, 1981.

Now this second, enlarged (about 100 per cent more material) and updated edition has been made necessary by new discoveries, price changes, deeper research into issuers and more photographs of specimens. Also, copies of the first edition have become difficult to locate as dealer stocks are exhausted, and new collectors enter the field every day.

For many years I had this *Early American Tokens* book in mind. That both editions are not everything I might wish is due only to human frailty. I can only trust this book might be more than its readers expected.

Russell Rulau
Iola, Wisconsin
December, 1983

About This Second Edition

My special consultants on this second edition, especially Dave Schenkman, Steve Tanenbaum and Byron Johnson, provided good quantities of original research material from city directories, census records, business registers, etc. to make the background of the issuers much more complete.

I spent many satisfying hours poring through original city directories and other business records of New York City, Philadelphia and other cities from 1797 to 1860 in the splendid genealogical library of the Mormon Church in Salt Lake City.

The Mormon facility must be considered the greatest storehouse of genealogical and related data in North America, with more than 60 million family names on record.

New discoveries and better photographs were reported to me by users of the first edition almost from its first public appearance. To them we owe a debt of gratitude, since the catalog is now much larger and more complete than the earlier version. George Fuld, Rich Hartzog, Garry Charman, Gregory Brunk, Frank Kovacs and others deserve special credit.

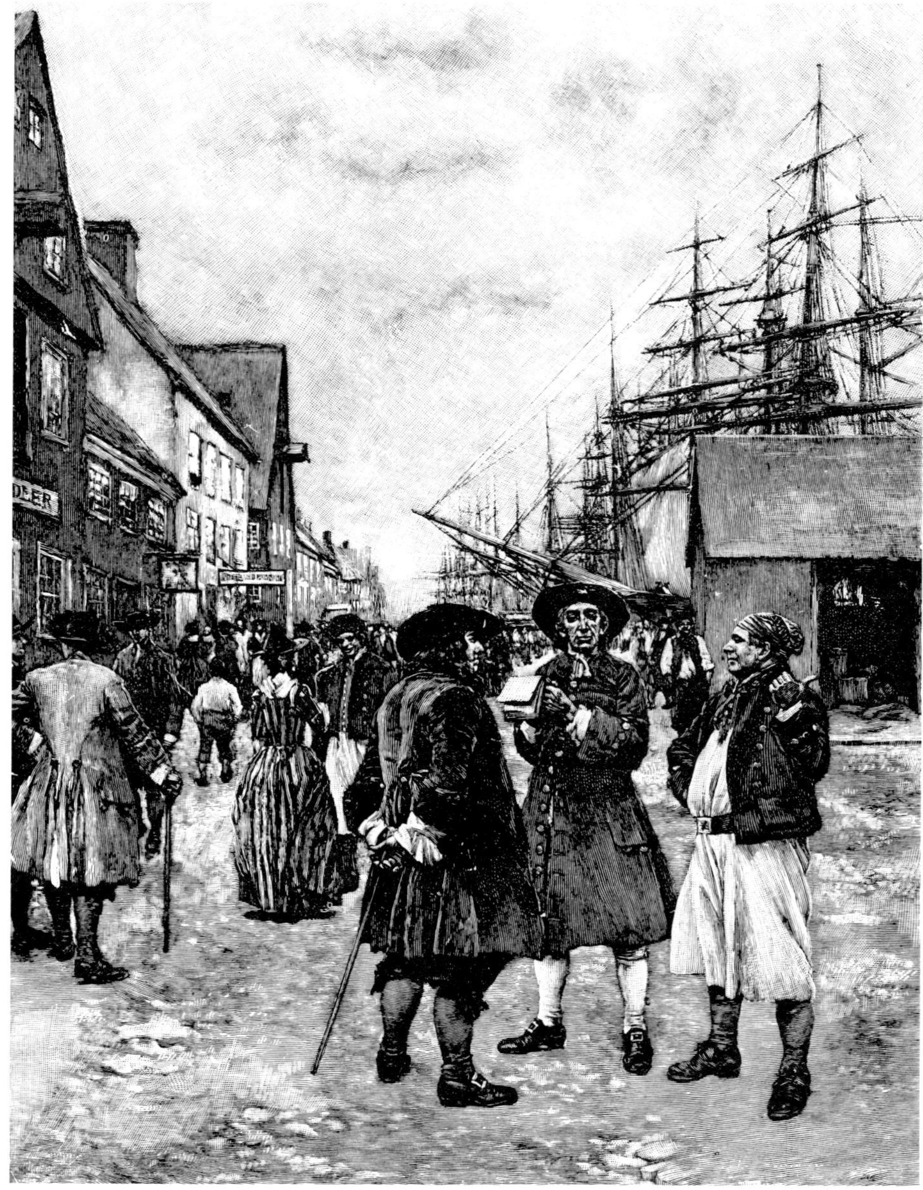

Along the waterfront in Colonial New York City, from a sketch by Tinkey. It was in such surroundings that the firms of William and John Mott — and Talbot, Allum & Lee — issued their trade tokens.

INTRODUCTION

There wasn't much private money in America in the 18th Century. The British government provided scanty coinage, but the young colonies' needs were not yet sharpened. Imports of certain British and Irish pieces provided enough change to mollify tradesmen, and several colonies (Massachusetts, Virginia, Maryland) had their own semiofficial coins to help out.

This catalog will treat with the private tokens and merchant cards — omitting some private speculations such as the Nova Eboracs, Bar cent, etc. All known tradesmen tokens of the Colonial era are included, as well as a number of private medallic issues.

Our first token was probably the Gloucester, Virginia brass shilling of 1714 issued by Rigault & Dawson, while the first private issue to achieve fairly good acceptance was the 1737 Higley copper threepence. Both issues may be found in this compilation.

In 1763 the Charles Town Social Club issued its members' medal, and in 1783 John Chalmers struck his silver coinage in Maryland.

The first true trade token — and the model for thousands of such issues since — was the 1789 Mott cent of New York. The next year, 1790, witnessed the appearance of Standish Barry's threepence and the Albany Church penny. About 1793, Ricketts Circus issued its token, and in 1794-1795 Talbot, Allum & Lee issued large numbers of private copper cents.

Then 1796 and the British settlement in Kentucky and 1797

and the French settlement at Castorland and the Theatre at New York — brought forth numismatic emissions. In 1799 the New York Associate Church issued its Communion token, and the 18th Century drew to a close.

These 18th Century tokens are not as easy to define as later American tokens. There was no national coinage until 1793, so the need for small change was great. Even after the introduction of the U.S. copper cent and half cent, and the cent's multiples, the national coinage was slow to enter trade channels. Foreign silver and gold coinage — and many British coppers — helped fill the need.

Thus the Mott, and especially the Talbot, Allum & Lee pieces, found ready acceptance as small change in New York.

The distinction between *coin* and *token* in the public mind before 1800 was blurred. The disc was *useful* — or not.

As a rule, we have omitted generalized, non-local token types from this work, such as some of the George Washington pieces, Bar cent, Kettle and Success counters. Some of the Washington pieces are included in a special Non-Local section at the back of the catalog, and we've also included the political medalets (though the larger politicals are not cataloged here).

TYPES OF PRIVATE TOKENS INCLUDED

We have included all known currency tokens, advertising tokens, admission checks, turnpike tokens, membership medalets, campaign tokens (of less than 30mm diameter), and countermarked coins (of provable or likely early vintage).

TOKENS AFTER 1800

The first decade of the 19th Century was almost devoid of token issues. In the 1806-1807 period Lancaster County, Pa., may have introduced some of its tollgate tokens for turnpikes, though some authorities feel these turnpike pieces belong to the century's second (or some later) decade. A few counterstamped coins started appearing in this decade.

About 1812-1816 Lancaster County's tollgate tokens were in full flower; the Park Theater pieces are dated 1817; Washington Market Chowder Club medalets are dated 1818, and more counterstamped pieces appeared. As can be seen, the second decade was also a time of few tokens.

The trade token as we have come to know it began developing in America in the 1820s. The later Mott tokens in New York, the Thomson tokens in Buffalo, those of John Low and Horace Porter of Boston are attributed to the third decade, as are the issues of Richard Trested in New York and the North West Company in Oregon.

The year-date 1823 appears on New York tokens of C. & I. D. Wolfe, W. H. Schoonmaker and Tredwell, Kissam & Co. In 1829 Wolfe, Spies & Clark probably began its attractive token issues depicting Washington, Jackson and George IV.

In 1825 Randel (Delaware) and several New York issuers — Rathbone & Fitch, Peale's Museum and Green & Wetmore — brought out tokens. The second half of the decade witnessed Edgar in New Orleans, Low and Porter in Boston, Wright & Bale and Doremus, Suydam & Nixon in New York begin token issues.

In 1829-1831 the character of the tokens began to resemble the cent-imitation types of the coming Hard Times era. The tokens of Buchan, Farnsworth Phipps, I. Gilbert, etc., fit this pattern.

TOKEN MAKERS

British token makers — Wyon, Skidmore, Kempson, Boulton, Jacobs — are responsible for some of the late 18th Century store cards, such as the Theatre at New York; Talbot, Allum & Lee; Mott's; and P. P. P. Myddelton. B. Jacobs signed the New York Theatre penny, which was struck by E. Skidmore; interestingly, the one Theatre muling was apparently struck by Peter Kempson. Jacobs and Skidmore were in London, Kempson in Birmingham.

Thomas Wyon reputedly engraved, and Peter Kempson struck, the Talbot, Allum & Lee tokens, and Kempson struck the TA&L mulings in Birmingham, England. Conrad Kuchler designed the Myddelton tokens, which were struck in Birmingham by Boulton & Watt. John Walker & Co. of Birmingham is reported to have struck the North West Company tokens much later (in 1820), and the same Birmingham maker may be responsible for the 1832 products of Kirkman, Green & Wetmore and others. Bushby of London reportedly manufactured the Phoenix buttons of Oregon in the 1810-20 period.

The new U.S. Mint at Philadelphia prepared the Ricketts Circus pieces about 1793 and the Peale's Museum pieces much later, perhaps as late as 1830.

Richard Trested, an English immigrant, began in the diesinking business at 70 William St., New York, about 1821. His signed works, such as the Castle Garden card and his own series of store cards, are rare, but it is now suspected that he may be responsible for some of the more available tokens of that era.

The New York Grand Canal opened in 1823, part of the later (1826) Erie Canal. Eighty-one miles in length and later called the Champlain Canal, it connected the Hudson River and Lake Champlain waterways from Whitehall to Waterford, N.Y. Its token provided the first instance in the United States of a single die being used for a number of different merchants' tokens — later this practice was to become commonplace and these became known in the trade as "stock dies." It is believed Thomas Kettle of Birmingham, England cut the series of cards celebrating the New York Grand Canal's opening for C. & I. D. Wolfe; Wolfe, Spies & Clark; and Tredwell, Kissam & Co.; these depicted an American eagle and the legend NEW YORK GRAND CANAL OPENED 1823.

Robert Lovett Sr., founder of a dynasty of American engravers and diesinkers, was in business as early as 1816-1822 in Philadelphia and then 1824-1825 at 249 Broadway, New York.

James Bale, Trested's apprentice, formed a partnership with Charles Cushing Wright in May, 1829, and bought out Trested's business from his widow when that worthy succumbed prematurely to complications arising from a cut finger. Though this partnership lasted only until about October, 1833, it was responsible for a number of attractive tokens — Henderson & Lossing; Joseph & L. Brewster; Farnsworth, Phipps & Co.; I. Gilbert, and others.

The metal firm of Pelletreau, Bennett & Cooke at 170 Broadway, New York, struck the Erie Canal medal in 1826. This had been designed by Charles Cushing Wright. Maltby Pelletreau was the senior partner in the firm. This firm may have struck tokens, though none has been identified.

(Earlier this firm was Clark, Pelletreau & Upson, jewelers, at 88 Broadway, in 1821-1822.)

Robert Scot, chief engraver of the U.S. Mint from 1793 to 1823, may have cut the dies for the Ricketts Circus tokens.

The new reference, *Exonumia Symbolism & Classification* by L. B. Fauver (Menlo Park, Calif., 1982), presents die-state and die-link evidence to show that a number of early American store cards were struck by Thomas Kettle of Birmingham, England, son of the counter-maker Henry Kettle.

Fauver's studies are convincing, and we are therefore echoing his conclusion that all the following store cards and politicals are Kettle products. In the First edition we indicated that some of these pieces may have been struck by Trested. We surmised in error, and are pleased to correct this in our Second edition.

KETTLE STRIKES

Jackson political medalets of the 1824 campaign, DeWitt AJACK 1824-1 and 2, could not have been struck before 1827, Fauver concludes. He intimates they may also have been restruck for the 1832 reelection campaign. (The other 1824 medalets, AJACK 1824-3, 4, 5 and 6, are not Kettle pieces and are still assigned to the 1824, not the 1828, campaign.)

Horace Porter & Co., Boston (Mass 84), in brass and silvered brass.

A. W. Hardie, New York (NY 295).

W. H. Schoonmaker, New York (NY 782 to 785).

Tredwell, Kissam & Co., New York (NY 920 and 921).

C. & I. D. Wolfe, New York (NY 957).

Wolfe, Clark & Spies, New York (NY 958).

Wolfe, Spies & Clark, New York, (NY 959 to 963).

THE KETTLE FIRM

Henry Kettle (firm organized late 1780's)
     KETTLE   1793-1804
     H K   1798
    engraver Benjamin Patrick BP   1803

Kettle & Sons (Thomas and William)
     K & S   1805-1812
    Thomas Kettle   KETTLE   1812-1837
    Kettle firm   H   1838-1840
     do   (None)   1838-1859

NOTE: The signature K & S from 1817 on belongs to another diesinking firm.

NUMBERING SYSTEMS

A special numbering system has been devised for this volume so that each token entry and variety may have its own identification. Users of the First Edition have asked that every piece be numbered.

To keep collectors and dealers from having to renumber their collection records or business inventories, the new Rulau-E (for Early) numbers are exactly the same as previously assigned Adams-Miller numbers (see Bibliography).

Some pseudo-Miller numbers were assigned in the First Edition of this reference, and these, too, have been retained.

All other pieces are assigned state numbers beginning with the numeral 1, where such numbers were not already in use in this book. A few days' familiarization with the numbering system should fix it in the user's mind.

DATING THE TOKENS

A number of Early American tokens bear dates, and others can be dated by their design, style or historical association.

Still more can be dated — within a reasonable span of years — by diesinker links or by city directory evidence.

A good number of the tokens in this book are included because indirect evidence — just an educated guess — indicates they might properly belong here. Such tokens are "dated" in the catalog with a question mark framed by parentheses — (?). As we learn more about them, some of these pieces may prove to be from a later era and will be added to one of the reference books on more recent tokens.

Likewise, some pieces which I have not included herein may properly be of early vintage, and future editions of this catalog will include them.

Two of my other token catalogs (*Hard Times Tokens* and *U.S. Merchant Tokens 1845-1860*), also will require adjustments as all pre-Civil War issues are eventually attributed by date.

One must begin somewhere, and we feel that an error of inclusion in preferable to one of exclusion, since knowledgeable users of this reference will be exposed to the potential errata. This Second Edition has assigned dates of issue to many tokens marked (?) in the First Edition.

Some of America's finest numismatists have assisted in selecting tokens for inclusion, but the final decision in each case has been our own. If a mistake has been made, we accept full responsibility.

For reasons we have never fully fathomed, some old-time token collectors seem to resist "dating" the classics of the American token pantheon. Perhaps they fear stripping away the aura of mystery from these rarities. But others have done much pioneering in this direction, and now we're determined to finish the task.

Comments, criticisms and suggestions about dating may be sent to me at 700 East State St., Iola, Wis. 54990.

VALUATIONS

A panel of professional numismatists and veteran collectors has assigned valuations in three grades for the tokens in this catalog. Auction records also have been considered, especially those in 1979-1983 (including the famed Garrett sales).

Quite a few Early American tokens are difficult to price, sinply because they seldom change hands.

METHOD OF PRESENTATION

The catalog number at the beginning of each line entry is the Rulau-E number of the piece. (See remarks on Numbering System).

If a date appears on the token, it is listed next on the line in the clear — e.g. 1817. If a date is given within parentheses — e.g. (1823-24) — it indicates the undated piece is attributed to such date(s) by reason of deduction or evidence.

The metallic content and diameter in millimeters are given next. Metals are rendered as they are normally understood in numismatics. White Metal is a tin or lead-based alloy sometimes referred to in old catalogs as Tin. German Silver is a nickel-copper-zinc alloy resembling silver in its physical properties.

When the denominations CENT, HALFPENNY, etc. appear in the clear, these appear on the token. When such a denomination, or other characteristic (e.g. ADMISSION) appear within parentheses, this status is inferred. A Denomination column is used only on those token listings where this seems appropriate.

In the description of each piece which follows the line listing, we have tried to give full inscriptions, with the slash (/) used to separate lines of text. Other catalog listings (e.g. Wright, DeWitt, Atwood, Baker, RB • Red Book, etc.) are also given.

Consult the Bibliography for explanations of catalog references.

We have used extensive footnotes to enhance the catalog entries. Such footnotes harken back to the 19th century practice of numismatic writers such as C. Wyllys Betts, Sylvester S. Crosby and Lyman H. Low, which fell into disfavor for many years. Their use has been revived at times by writers such as Robert P. King and Nathan Eglit, and we favor them. Users of our token catalogs tell us they welcome the extensive footnotes.

In a few cases, extra text has been included, and we've used bylines to indicate authorship on these, where needed. All entries have been edited by this author — some quite extensively — to present a consistent viewpoint throughout the volume. If, in the editing, we have weakened rather than strengthened, we apologize to the original authors.

The historical background of Dr. Higley, Charles Willson Peale, North West Company, Castorland. etc., is so interwoven with Early American tokens that the inclusion of the extra text seems justified.

SPECIE AND 'PIECES OF EIGHT'

The Spanish dollar, or piece of eight, was used extensively as currency in the United States before the Revolution and for long afterward. An interesting account of how pieces of eight were used as money, and cut into "bits" for fractional use, appeared in the 1964 book, *History of Southwestern Ohio, The Miami Valleys*, by Dr. W.E. Smith:

"After 1787, specie was brought to the Miami country by immigrants and soldiers. The first troops at Fort Washington (now Cincinnati) were paid in Spanish silver dollars, familiarly known as 'pieces of eight.' They were worth about four shillings.

"Specie was so scarce in Cincinnati that these Spanish dollars were cut into halves, quarters and eights, or 'bits' for making change. These 'bits' were known locally as 'shark skins.'

"Two bits equaled a quarter, one bit half as much, and half a bit, 6¼ cents. In a day of severely restricted supply of money, a rabbit skin passed current at 6¼ cents, raccoon (skin) at 12½, fox at 25, and deer at 50.

"After a time the soldiers were paid in $3 bills printed by the local government especially for soldiers, whose monthly stipend was three dollars. Because of their shape they were called 'oblongs.'

"Portuguese 'joes' (gold coins), reals and Mexican dollars were also used during the early years.

"Although church members preferred American money or negotiable bank notes for themselves, they put 'cut money' in the hat passed at church. An entry in the treasurer's book of the Hopewell Church near Morning Sun, Preble county (June, 1817) reads: 'To sale of cut money to John Brown, $3.40.'

"For the convenience of their readers, daily newspapers later published the exchange values of foreign coins. The *Liberty Hall and Cincinnati Gazette* for May 8, 1834 quoted the exchange values of the Spanish doubloon, English guinea and sovereign, and French napoleon and louis d'or (all gold coins). The first regular banks in Ohio were founded in 1808-1809 in Marietta, Chillicothe and Steubenville."

CIRCULAR

TO THE DISTRICT ATTORNEYS AND MARSHALS OF THE UNITED STATES.

Treasury Department,
March 25, 1829.

SIR,—By a communication just received from the Bank of the United States, it appears that counterfeit dollars are extensively circulated in some of the western states. This is corroborated by information derived from other authentic sources: and there is reason to suppose that these spurious coins will gradually be introduced into other parts of the Union. Two of these dollars, which were received at Nashville, and which are supposed to have been fabricated in Arkansaw, have been examined at the Mint. An extract from the Report of the Director of that establishment is annexed. From this it will be seen, that those counterfeits are so well made, that they can be detected only by a strict scrutiny. This circumstance renders it more imperatively the duty of the proper officers of the Government to exert themselves to discover, and punish, those who are criminally engaged in making or circulating them. And, in apprising you of this fraud, I have also to state, that the President expects that all proper diligence will be used by you in finding out and bringing to justice the perpetrators.

You are requested to report to this Deparment, from time to time, any steps that you may take, or any discovries that may be made, in relation to this subject.

I am, sir, very respectfully,

Your obedient servant,

Extract of a Report from the Director of the Mint, dated 16th March, 1829.

"One specimen, purporting to be a Mexican dollar of 1826, weighed 406 grains, being 10 grains lighter than our dollar. On assaying, it is found to contain at the rate of 4 ozs. 8 dwts. only of fine silver, in 12 ounces. The intrinsic value corresponding to which, is 47 4-10ths cents per ounce. The value of this piece is consequently 40 cents.

The other specimen, purporting to be a Ferdinand dollar of 1816, weighed 388 grains, being 28 grains lighter than our dollar. On assaying this, it is found to contain at the rate of 3 ozs. 13 dwts. of fine silver only in 12 ounces. The intrinsic value corresponding to which is, 39 3-10ths cents, per ounce. The value of this piece, consequently 31¾ cents.

The manner in which these counterfeits are executed, renders them extremely mischievous in our currency. By a chemical process, the external pellicle is made to assume the appearance of good silver; or rather to be really good—better, it may be than standard, so that even an experienced eye could not detect the fraud by inspecting the external surface merely."

CONTRIBUTORS

Many of those named below provided direct assistance on this project, which began in earnest in 1979 and took almost two years to complete. Others provided indirect assistance through their previous publications.

Pricing input is due almost entirely to these collectors and dealers, without whose co-operation such evaluations would have had less meaning.

Warren Baker
Q. David Bowers
Kenneth E. Bressett
Gregory Brunk
Carl W. A. Carlson
Garry Charman
John Cheramy
Clyde D. Cooper
Grover C. Criswell
James J. Curto
William S. Dewey
Daniel Douglas
L. B. Fauver
John Ford Jr.
Sarah E. Freeman
George J. Fuld
Harvey Gamer
Cindy Grellman
Kenneth Hallenbeck
Rich Hartzog
Alfred D. Hoch
Byron Johnson
Robert E. Julian

Charles E. Kirtley
Paul Koppenhaver
Frank L. Kovacs
Frank W. Kroha
H. Joseph Levine
Donald R. Lewis
Robert J. Lindesmith
David P. McBride
Donald M. Miller
Eric P. Newman
Donald Partrick
P. Frank Purvey
Robert M. Ramsay
Fred Reed
Harley W. Rhodehamel
Richard Rossa
David E. Schenkman
Joseph Schmidt
Nick P. Schrier
Robert Schuman
Neil Shafer
Hank Spangenberger
Stanley L. Steinberg

Elizabeth W. Steinle
Donald Stewart
Ben Z. Swanson
Steve Tanenbaum
Don Taxay
Anthony Terranova

Robert A. Vlack
R. B. White
Stewart Witham
Alan York
Michael B. Zeddies

And gratitude to those who preceded us . . . .

Edgar H. Adams
Roland Atwood
W. S. Baker
C. Wyllys Betts
P. Napoleon Breton
Charles I. Bushnell
Monica Bussell
Raymond Byrne
Sylvester S. Crosby
R. Dalton
J. Doyle DeWitt
Frank G. Duffield
William F. Dunham
Leonard Forrer

Maurice M. Gould
Samuel H. Hamer
Richard D. Kenney
Theo. E. Leon
Joseph N. T. Levick
Lyman H. Low
William T. R. Marvin
C. Mathis
Waldo C. Moore
Wayte Raymond
Alfred Sandham
Horatio R. Storer
Malcolm Storer
Benjamin P. Wright

BIBLIOGRAPHY

Adams, Edgar H., "United States Store Cards." New York, 1912.

do, "J.M.L. & W.H. Scovill," in *The Numismatist* for July, 1912.

do, "Richard Trested, Die Sinker," in *The Numismatist* for Aug., 1913.

American Vecturist Association, "Atwood's Catalogue of United States and Canadian Transportation Tokens." 3rd edition, Boston, 1970.

Baker, W.S., "Medallic Portraits of Washington." Philadelphia, 1885. (Revised edition, Iola, Wis., 1965)

Betts, C. Wyllys, "American Colonial History Illustrated by Contemporary Medals." New York, 1894.

Breton, P.N., "Illustrated History of the Coins and Tokens relating to Canada." Montreal, 1894.

Dalton, R. & Hamer, S.H., "The Provincial Token-Coinage of the 18th Century." Bristol, England, 1910. (Second printing, Lawrence, Mass., 1977)

DeWitt, J. Doyle, "A Century of Campaign Buttons 1789-1889." Hartford, Conn., 1959.

Duffield, Frank G., "The Peale Museum Tokens," in *The Numismatist* for Feb., 1912.

do, "The Cards of J. Randel Jr.," in *The Numismatist* for Oct., 1915.

Duffield, Frank, "A Trial List of Countermarked Modern Coins of the World," in *The Numismatist* for 1919-1921.

do, "Baltimore Tokens," in *The Numismatist* for Dec. 1904.

Eastwood, Sidney K., "New Orleans Store Cards in the Antebellum Days," in *Token and Medal Society Journal* for Oct. 1966.

Fauver, L.B., "Exonumia Symbolism & Classification." Menlo Park, Calif., 1982.

Freeman, Sarah E., "Medals Relating to Medicine and Allied Sciences in the Numismatic Collection of the John Hopkins University." Baltimore, 1964.

Fuld, Melvin & George, "The Talbot, Allum and Lee Cents," in *Numismatic Scrapbook Magazine* for Sept. 1956.

Gould, Maurice M., "Merchant Counterstamps on American Silver Coins." Wayland, Mass., 1962.

Gould, Maurice M., "Merchant Counterstamps on American Silver Coins." Wayland, Mass., 1962.

Gluckman, A., "Identifying Old U.S. Muskets, Rifles and Carbines." Harrisburg, Pa., 1965.

Hallenbeck, Kenneth L., "Hallmarks on U.S. Large Cents," in *TAMS Journal* for June 1964.

Kauffman, H.J., "American Copper & Brass." New York, 1968. (Contains documented lists of coppersmiths and brass founders.)

Kenney, Richard D., "Early American Medalists and Die-Sinkers prior to the Civil War." New York, 1954.

Kovel, R.M. & T.H., "A Directory of American Silver, Pewter and Silver Plate." New York, 1961.

Leon, Theo. E., "The Castorland Token," in *The Numismatist* for April, 1919.

McElroy, A., "A. M'Elroy's Philadelphia Directory for 1837." Philadelphia, 1837.

"The Philadelphia Directory for 1797."

"The Philadelphia Directory for 1828."

Miller, Donald M., "A Catalogue of U.S. Store Cards or Merchants Tokens." Indiana, Pa., 1962.

Raymond, Wayte, "The Early Medals of Washington 1776-1834." New York, 1941.

do, "The Standard Catalogue of United States Coins and Tokens." New York, 1942.

Rulau, Russell, "Hard Times Tokens." Iola, Wis., 1980.

Rulau, Russell & Fuld, George, "American Game Counters." Iola, Wis., 1972.

Sandham, Alfred, "Coins, Tokens and Medals of the Dominion of Canada." Montreal, 1869.

Schenkman, David E., "A Survey of American Trade Tokens." Lawrence, Mass., 1975.

Schenkman, David & Levine, Joseph, "Exonumia Notebook," in *The Numismatist* for May, 1980.

Scott Publishing Co., "The Comprehensive Catalogue and Encyclopedia of United States Coins." Second edition, New York, 1975.

Schmidt, J., & G. Owen, "Businesses, Merchants & Products on Counterstamped Coins." Undated (1979).

Serven, J.E., "The Collecting of Guns." New York, 1964.

Smith, Dr. W.E., "History of Southwestern Ohio, The Miami Valleys," 1964.

Storer, Horatio R., "Medicina in Numis: A Descriptive List of the Coins — Medals — Jetons Relating to Medicine, Surgery and the Allied Sciences." Boston, 1931.

Storer, Malcolm, "The Rare Token of John J. Low & Co. of Boston." in *The Numismatist* for May, 1921.

Strong, Emory, "Phoenix Buttons," in *American Antiquity* for Jan., 1960.

Vlack, Robert A., "Early American Coins." Second edition, Johnson City, N.Y., 1965.

Woodward, A., "Indian Trade Goods." Oregon Archaeological Society Publication No. 2, Portland, 1965.

Wright, Benjamin P., "American Business Tokens," in *The Numismatist* for 1898 through 1901. Reprinted in book form with addenda, Boston, 1972.

Wyler, S.B., "The Book of Old Silver." New York, 1937.

Yeoman, Richard S., "A Guide Book of United States Coins." 34th edition, Racine, Wis., 1981.

Anon., "Ricketts Circus," in *The Numismatist* for Oct., 1912.

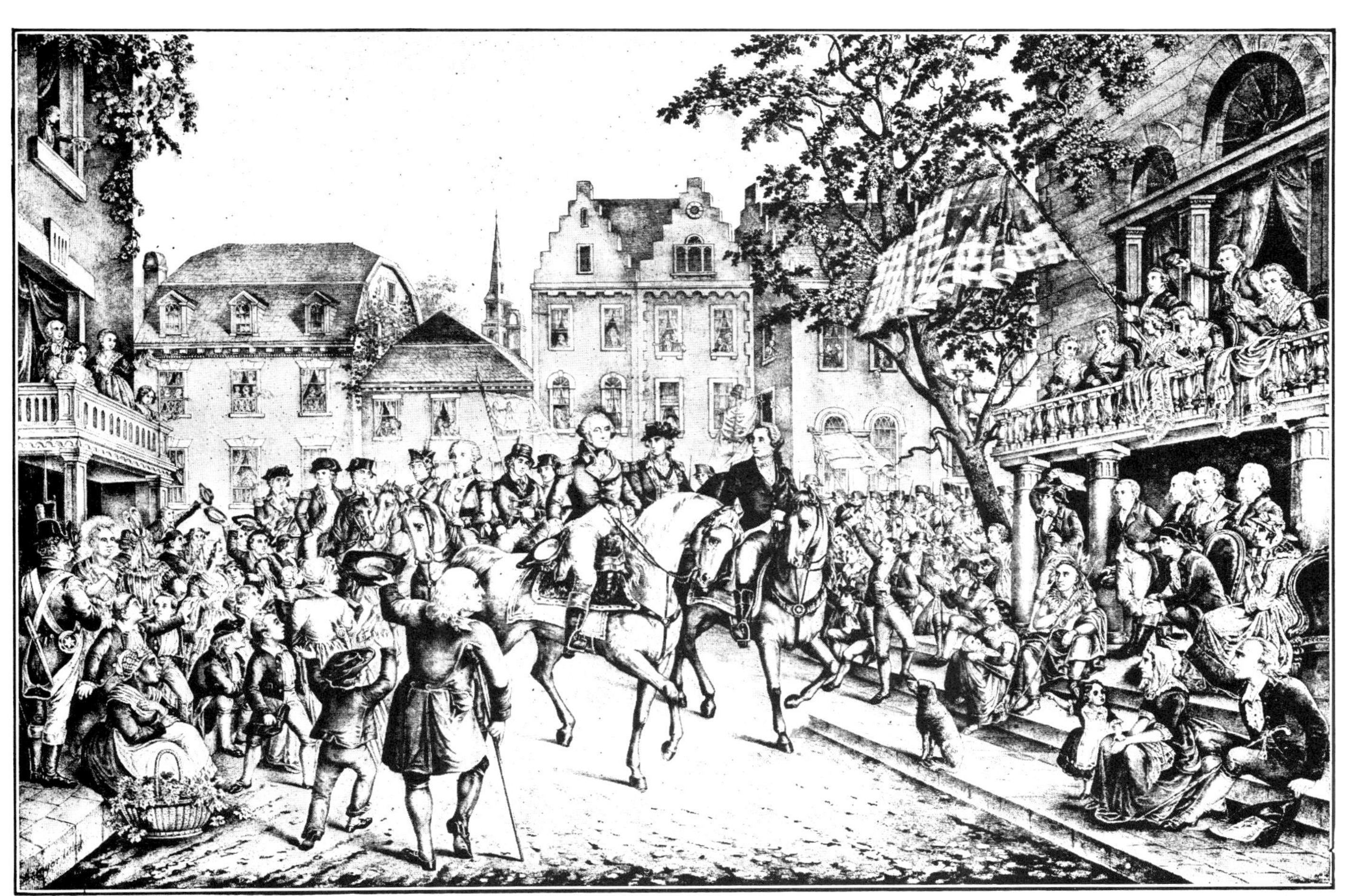

Evacuation Day (November 26, 1783), the day the British troops evacuated New York City after seven years of occupation. The British had captured the city Sept. 15, 1776. In this contemporary engraving, George Washington rides in at the head of his troops. The Treaty of Paris had been signed almost three months before Evacuation Day — on Sept. 3.

CONNECTICUT

HIGLEY Coppers
Granby, Conn.

(Enlargements of all Higley issues may be found at the end of the Higley entries)
'The Value of Three Pence'

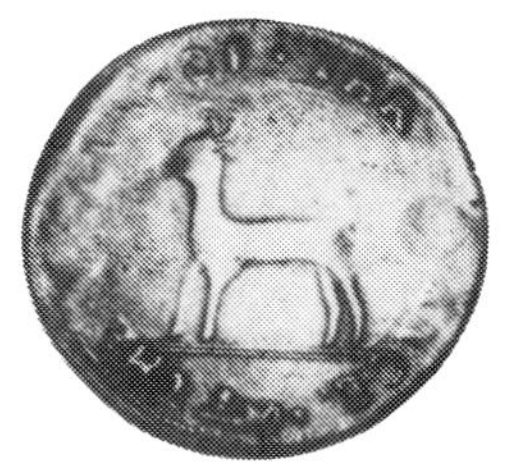 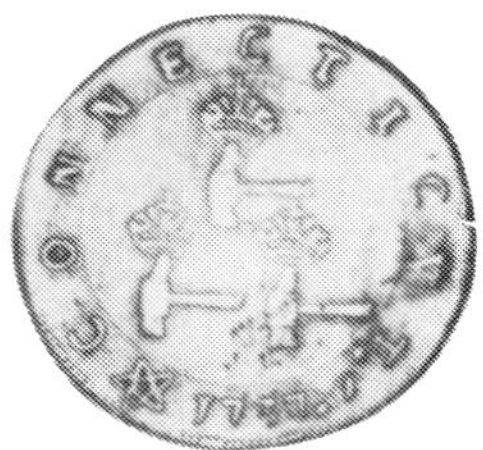

Rulau-E	Date	Metal	Size	G	VG	F
Conn 1	1737	Copper	29mm	6000.	10,000.	—

Deer standing to left, within circle. Around circle: (Hand) THE. VALVE. OF. THREE. PENCE. Rv: Three crowned hammers within circle. Around: *CONNECTICVT. 1737. Plain edge. (RB)

| Conn 2 | 1737 | Copper | 29mm | 7000. | 12,000. | — |

Obverse similar to last. Rv: Similar, but legend around circle reads: I. AM. GOOD. COPPER. 1737. Plain edge. (RB)

'Value Me As You Please'

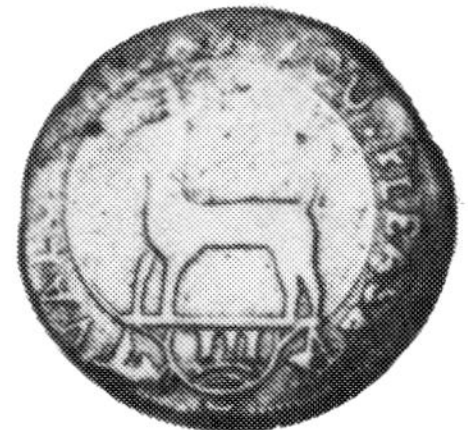 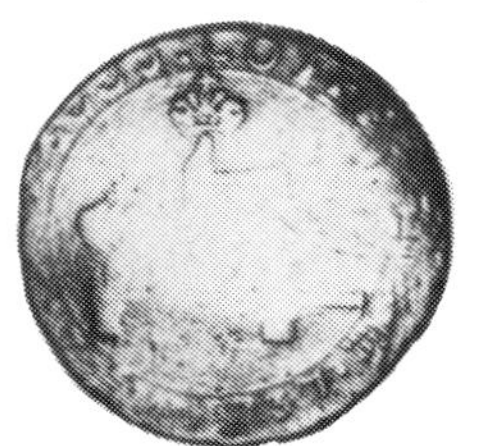

| Conn 3 | 1737 | Copper | 29mm | 6000. | 10,000. | — |

Deer standing to left, within circle. The Roman numeral III appears below the ground line. Around circle: (Hand) VALUE. ME. AS. YOU. PLEASE*. Rv: Similar to reverse of last (three crowned hammers, I. AM. GOOD. COPPER. 1737. Plain edge. (RB)

| Conn 4 | 1737 | Copper | 29mm | | | Ex. Rare |

As last, but VALVE instead of VALUE. Plain edge. (RB)

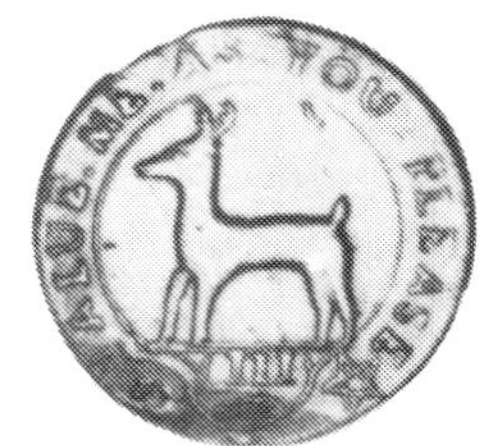 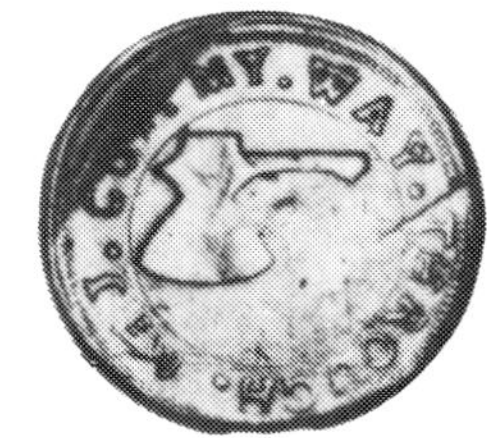

Rulau-E	Date	Metal	Size	G	VG	F
Conn 5	(1737)	Copper	29mm	7000.	12,000.	—

Obverse similar to last. Rv: Broad axe in center, (Hand) J. CUT. MY. WAY. THROUGH. around. Plain edge. (RB)

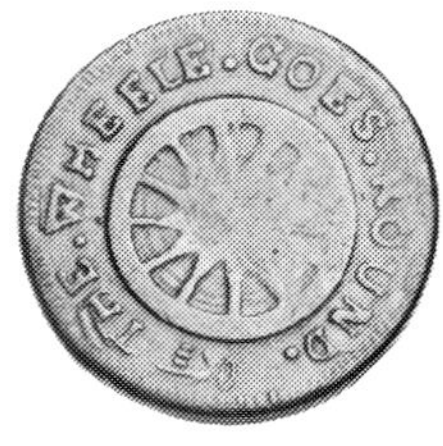 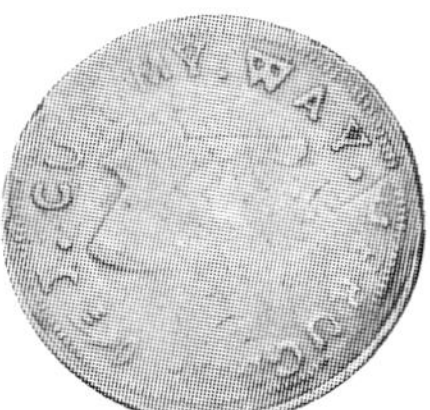

| Conn 6 | (1737) | Copper | 29mm | — | — | 75,000. |

Spoked wheel in center, (Hand) THE. WHEELE. GOES. ROUND. around. Rv: As last (Broad axe, J. CUT. MY. WAY. THROUGH.). Plain edge. Unique. (RB)

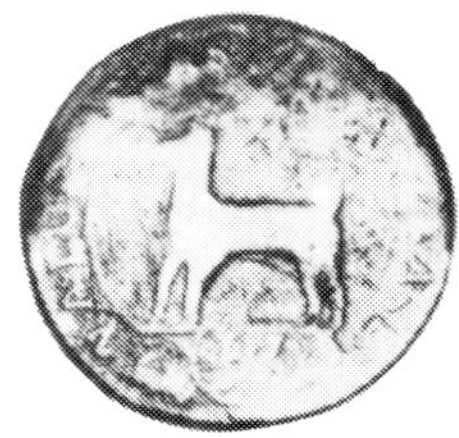 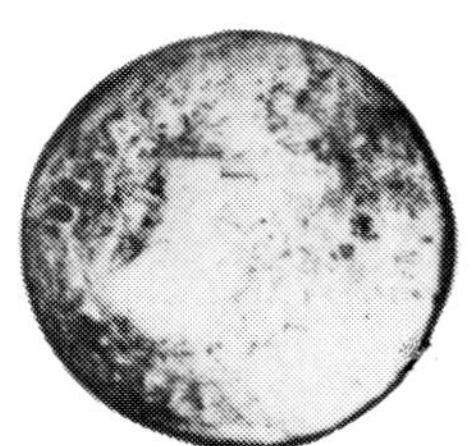

| Conn 7 | 1739 | Copper | 29mm | 8500. | 18,000. | — |

Obverse similar to first 'Value Me As You Please' issue (Deer, III, etc.). Rv: As last, but 1739 instead of no date. Plain edge. (RB)

By Q. David Bowers

Among the most interesting of all early American issues are the copper tokens struck circa 1737-1739 by Dr. Samuel Higley, of Granby, Connecticut. Higley, a medical doctor with a degree from Yale College, also practiced blacksmithing and made many experiments in metallurgy. In 1727 he devised a practical method of producing steel.

In 1728 Higley purchased property on a hill near Granby which furnished the site for many copper mines, the most famous being the extensive mine corridors and shafts which were later used as the Newgate Prison. Mines on the hill were worked extensively during the early and middle 18th century. In October 1773 the Connecticut General Assembly passed an act which pertained to the various subterranean caverns and external buildings of the copper mines in Simsbury and converted them for use as a public jail and workhouse.

Phelps, in his *History of the Copper Mines in Newgate Prison at Granby, Connecticut,* notes that:

"The prisoners were to be employed in mining. The crimes, by which the acts subjected offenders to confinement and labor in the prison, were burglary, horse stealing, and counterfeiting the public bills or coins, or making instruments and dies therefore."

By the time Newgate Prison was abandoned in 1827, the buildings had been destroyed by fire three times. The cruel, dark, damp conditions precipitated in numerous revolts and violent incidents. Escapes were frequent.

Following his 1728 purchase, Dr. Samuel Higley operated a small but thriving mining business which extracted exceptionally rich copper. Much if not most of the metal was exported to England. Sometime around the year 1737 Higley produced a copper token. The obverse depicted a standing deer with the legend THE VALUE OF THREE-PENCE. The reverse showed three crowned hammers with the surrounding legend, CONNECTICUT, and the date 1737.

Legend tells us that drinks in the local tavern sold at the time for threepence each, and Higley was in the habit of paying his bar bill with his own coinage. There was a cry against this for the Higley copper threepence was of a diameter no larger than the contemporary British halfpennies which circulated in the area; coins which had a value of just 1/6th of that stated on the Higley coin.

Accordingly, Higley redesigned his coinage so that the obverse legend was changed to read VALUE ME AS YOU PLEASE. The pieces still bore an indication of value, the Roman numeral III below the standing deer. Two new reverses were designed, one of which pictured three hammers with the inscription I AM GOOD COPPER. The other reverse, picturing a broad axe, had the legend I CUT MY WAY THROUGH. The third obverse design, of which only a single specimen is known, depicted a wagon wheel with the legend THE WHEELE GOES ROUND.

While on a voyage to England in May 1737, on a ship loaded with copper from his own mine, Samuel Higley died. His oldest son, John, together with Rev. Timothy Wood-bridge and William Cradock probably engraved and struck the issues of 1739.

Apparently the original Higley coinage was small, and circulation was effected mainly in Granby and its environs. Sylvestor S. Crosby relates that a goldsmith, who served his apprenticeship around 1810, said that Higley pieces were hard to find at the time and were in demand for use as an alloy for gold. The goldsmith related that his master delayed completing a string of gold beads for he was unable to find a copper Higley threepence with which to alloy the metal.

Today Higley issues of all types are exceedingly rare, and often a span of years will occur between offerings. Nearly all pieces show very extensive evidence of circulation, with most grading in the range of Good or Very Good.

Enlargements of
Higley Threepence Tokens
To Show Detail

(all illustrations of Garrett Collection specimens)

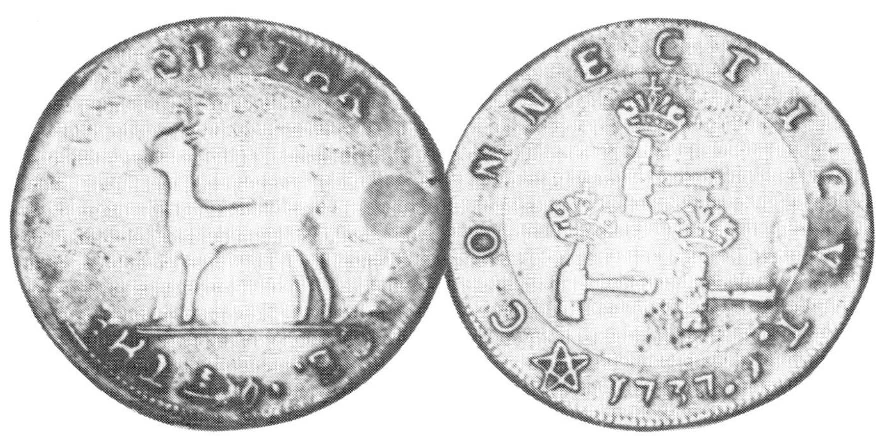

1737 "THE VALVE OF THREEPENCE"

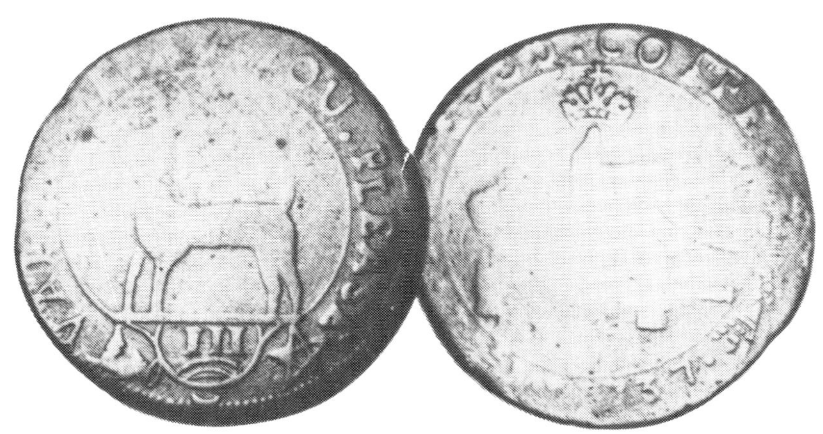

1737 "I AM GOOD COPPER"

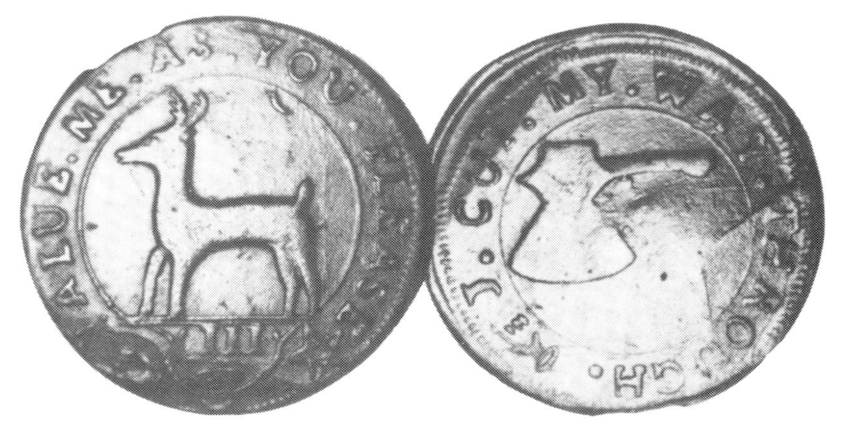

1737 "J CUT MY WAY THROUGH"

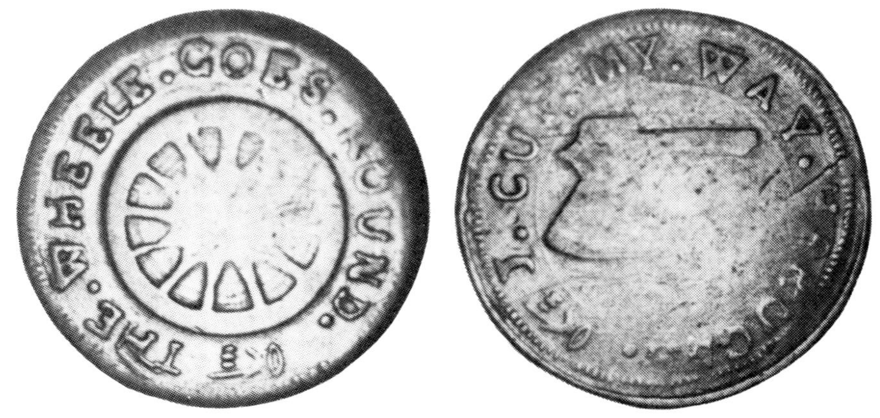

"THE WHEELE GOES ROUND"

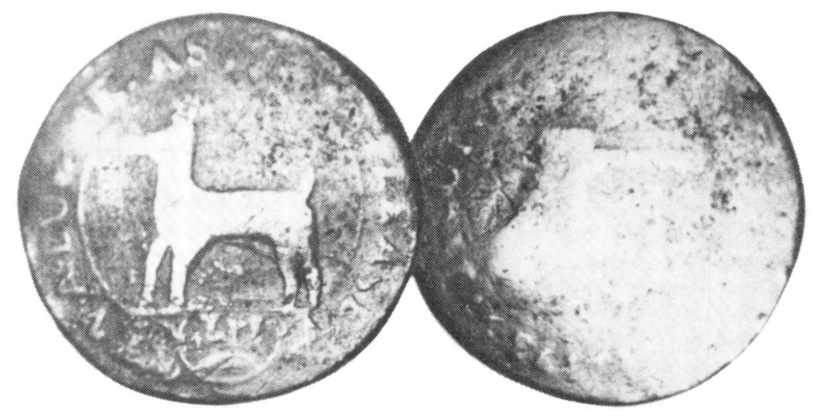

1739 HIGLEY THREEPENCE

A. B.
(A. Beach ?)
Hartford, Conn.

Rulau-E	Date	Metal	Size	VG	F	EF
Conn 9	(1823-30)	Copper	29mm	—	25.00	—

A . B in relief within toothed, recessed rectangle ctsp on U.S. 1803 Large cent. There is also an incuse C C on the face side. (Rulau coll.)

Rulau-E	Date	Metal	Size	VG	F	EF
Conn 10	(1828-30)	Copper	29mm	—	25.00	—

Similar ctsp (A . B) on U.S. 1828 Large cent. (Donald Partrick coll.)

It is believed the A . B in toothed rectangle mark is that of the issuing merchant, while the C C may be frivolous. Possibly A. Beach, a silversmith active in and after 1823 in Hartford, Conn. Another possibility is Asa Blanchard, circa 1808-38, in Lexington, Ky.

There is also the possibility this is the mark of silversmith Abel Buel (1742-1825) of New Haven, Conn., diesinker of the 1785-88 Connecticut cents (AUCTORI CONNEC pieces). Buel used a mark like this: A B within sawtooth-edge rectangle, the upper and lower edges being straight. But we discount the Buel connection as the marks do not match exactly, and the second piece would have been punched in after his death.

A. BRADLEY
New Haven, Conn.

Rulau-E	Date	Metal	Size	VG	F	EF
Conn 11	(1820-24)	Copper	29mm	—	25.00	—

A. BRADLEY in relief within rectangular depression ctsp twice on U.S. Large cent. (Stanley Steinberg 1982 sale number 94, lot 129)

Abner Bradley was a silversmith in New Haven. Born in 1753, he died in 1824. His hallmark could have been used by a successor firm until about 1835.

C. HEQUEMBOURG JR.
New Haven, Conn.

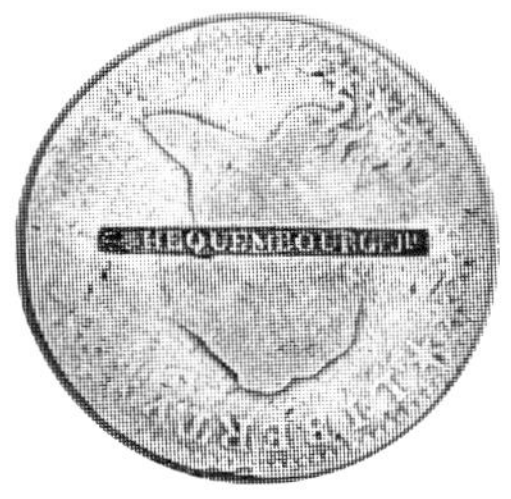
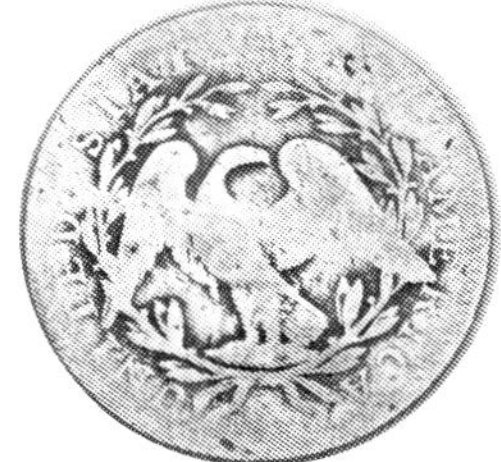

Rulau-E	Date	Metal	Size	VG	F	EF
Conn 12	(1797-1810)	Silver	32.5mm	—	185.00	—

C. HEQUEMBOURG, JR in relief within rectangular depression ctsp on U.S. 1795 Flowing Hair half dollar. (Ex-Gamer, Bowers-Ruddy)

Charles Hequembourg Jr. (born 1760, died 1851) was a silversmith in New Haven, Conn., about 1804. His teaspoon shank hallmark, which appears on the 1795 coin, is illustrated on page 295 of *The Book of Old Silver, English, American, Foreign*, by Seymour B. Wyler (1937; reprinted 1979). The hallmark is also listed in *Price Guide to Silver and their Marks* by Luckey (1978).

Hequembourg worked in New York City 1827-29 and in Buffalo, N.Y. 1835-42.

WATERBURY HOUSE
New Haven, Conn.

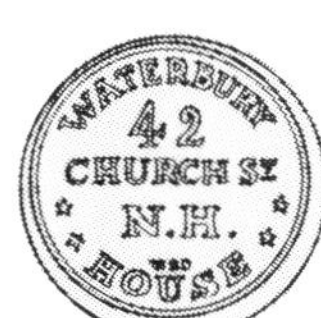

Rulau-E	Date	Metal	Size	Denomination	G	F	VF
Conn 27	(?)	Brass	20mm	4 (Cents)	—	—	1500.

WATERBURY / 42 / CHURCH ST / N.H. / **HOUSE**, tiny WBD in field. Rv: Large 4 at center, two small dogs running left below; ornamental border.

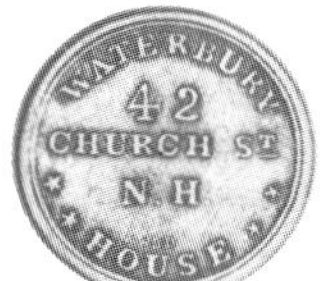
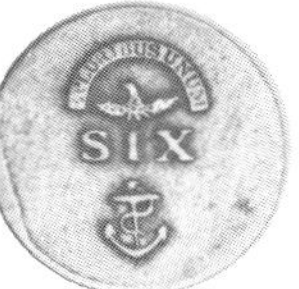

Rulau-E	Date	Metal	Size	Denomination	G	F	VF
Conn 27A	(?)	Brass	20mm	6 (Cents)	—	—	2500.

Obv. similar to 27. Rv: SIX at center; above is eagle with scroll above, the scroll lettered E PLURIBUS UNUM; below is a fouled anchor. Unique.

There is much controversy over dating the Waterbury House cards, though authorities from Raymond to Vlack feel they are very early. Conn 27A was unknown until 1981 when it was discovered by Charles E. Kirtley, Brasstown, N.C.

Joseph Barnett called this a Civil War token issuer. Fuld thinks it is from the 1850-60 period.

Dating, even attributing, these pieces has caused much furor but little enlightenment. Unless proven otherwise, we accept that 'N.H.' stands for New Haven, though other meanings could be ascribed to it. We have been unable to trace the diesinker 'WBD'. Directory verification of a Waterbury House in New Haven (or elsewhere) and identification of the diesinker will be needed before certainty can be achieved. Steve Tanenbaum, White Plains, N.Y., who owns both pieces, feels they are Early American and after examining them, we agree . . . for now.

ROATH
Norwich, Conn.

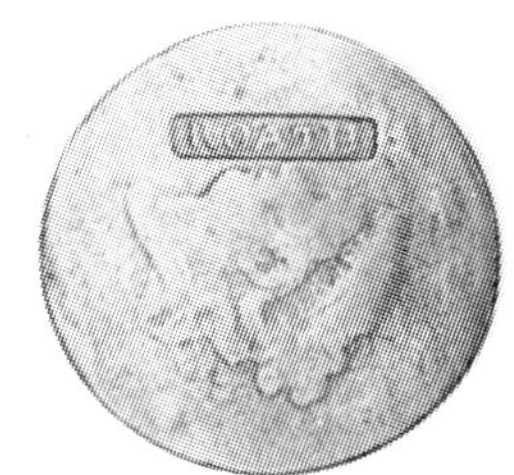

Rulau-E	Date	Metal	Size	VG	F	EF
Conn 18	(ca 1826)	Copper	29mm	—	50.00	—

ROATH in relief within rect. depression ctsp on U.S. 1816-1828 type Large cent, date worn off. (Hartzog coll.)

Roswell Walston Roath, born in 1805, was active as a silversmith in Norwich, Conn., about 1826. Much later he moved to Denver in Colorado Territory.

J.M.L. & W.H. SCOVILL
Waterbury, Conn.

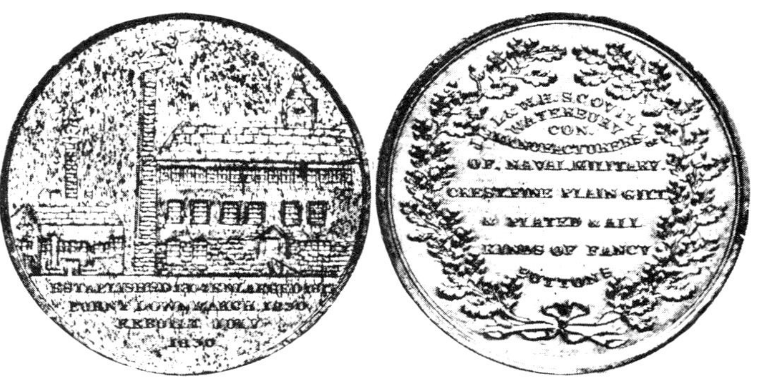

Rulau-E	Date	Metal	Size	VG	F	EF
Conn 33	1830	White Metal	37mm	—	—	1000.

View of factory buildings, ESTABLISHED 1802 ENLARGED 1813 / BURNT DOWN MARCH 1830 / REBUILT JULY / 1830. Rv: Nine lines of text within oak wreath. Medallic.

James Mitchell Lamson Scovill and William Henry Scovill established their brass works in 1802. The Scovill Manufacturing Company is still in business in 1980, though it sold off its brass mills several years ago and is now a diversified manufacturer of home products. This firm issued a number of store cards in the Hard Times Era and in the 1845-1860 period, and it was a major manufacturer of Civil War tokens and later of coins for foreign governments (such as Haiti) and planchets for the U.S. Mint.

DELAWARE

J. RANDEL JR.
New Castle County, Del. and
Cecil County, Md.

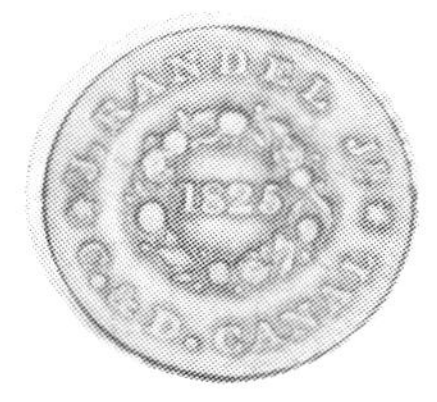 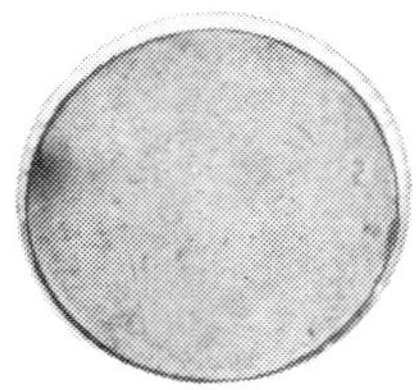

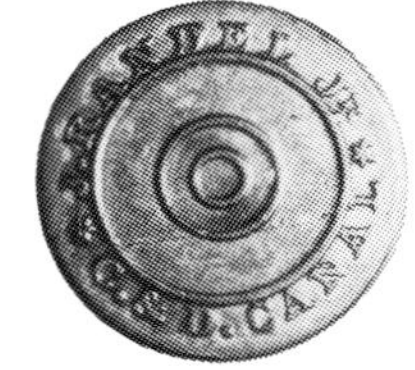

Rulau-E	Date	Metal	Size		VG	F	VF
Del 1	1825	Copper	24mm		25.00	40.00	65.00

1825 within central wreath, J. RANDEL JR. / C. & D. CANAL. Rv: Blank. (Wright 870)

Del 2	(1825)	Copper	24mm	—	750.00	—

Three concentric circles form target center, J. RANDEL JR. / C. & D. CANAL. Rv: Blank.

John Randel Jr. was the chief engineer for the 13 5/8-mile long Chesapeake and Delaware Canal from 1823 through 1825. In the fall of 1825 the company replaced him with Benjamin Wright, who completed the canal, which had begun in 1802, on Oct. 17, 1829. The canal connected the head of Chesapeake Bay with the Delaware River estuary. Randel sued the company for breach of contract, ultimately (1834) receiving $226,000 through the New Castle, Del. superior court. He used his settlement, then an enormous amount, to purchase Randalia, a large tract on Bohemia Manor near the mouth of Back Creek. He also engaged in several wild schemes, which dissipated his money. He maintained a steam saw-mill on Randalia. Later he originated the elevated railway idea. The privately owned C. & D. Canal operated with locks until 1919, when the United States government bought it and converted it to its present form — a tidal, toll-free waterway 27 feet deep, capable of accommodating all but the largest vessels.

FLORIDA

JUAN ESTEVAN DE PENA
Florida

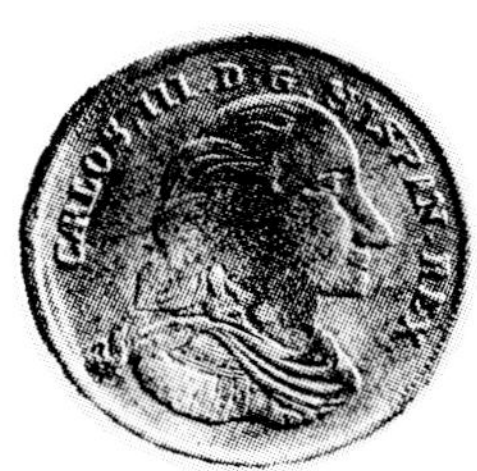 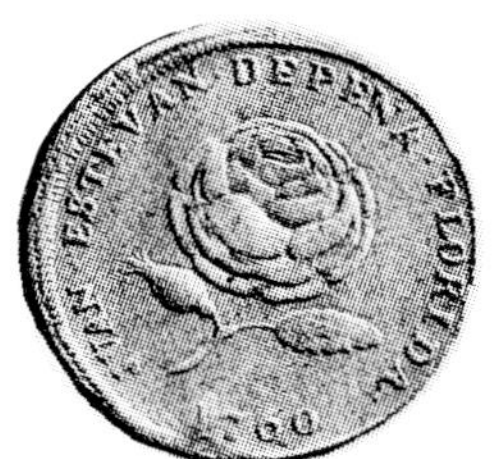

Rulau-E	Date	Metal	Size	Denomination	VG	F	EF
Fla 1	1760	Silver	31mm	(4 reales)	—	—	—

Crude, unflattering bust Carlos III of Spain in cuirass facing right, CARLOS. III. D. G HISPAN. REX around. Rv: Rose fully opened at center, with bud left and leaf right. JVAN ESTEVAN DEPENA FLOR-IDA around, 1760 below. (Herrera 56, Dickeson T.8.1, Fonrobert 1510, Ulex 275, Betts 454)

Proclamation piece of Carlos (Charles) III of Spain. Florida was under Spanish rule from 1528 to 1763. Florida was ceded to Great Britain by the Treaty of Paris, Feb. 10, 1763. It was retroceded to Spain by the Treaty of Versailles, Sept. 3, 1783. West Florida was acquired piecemeal by the United States, part in 1810 and part in 1813. The rest of Florida was purchased by the United States from Spain, Feb. 22, 1819.

The silver piece is cast, rather than struck. Some attempts have been made to show this is not an American piece, but Holland and Appleton accepted it. (See *American Journal of Numismatics*, Vol. IX, page 93.)

MAC GREGOR
Amelia Island, Florida

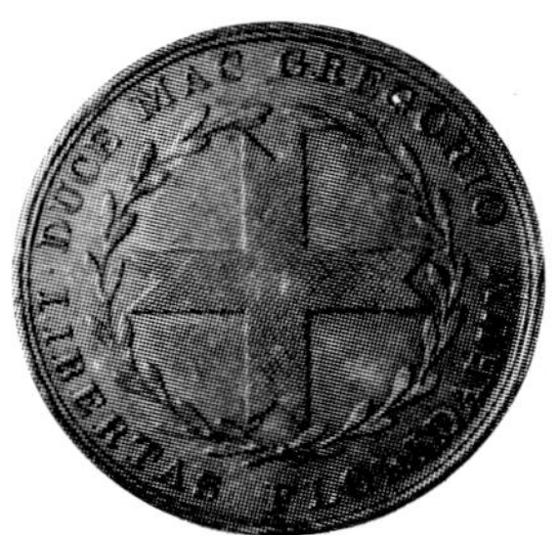 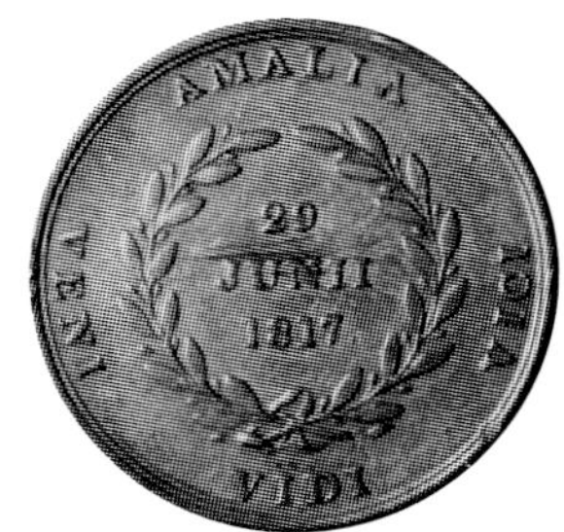

Rulau-E	Date	Metal	Size	Denomination	F	VF	Unc
Fla 10	1817	Bronze	30mm	(Medal)	—	1500.	6000.

Cross within circular palm wreath at center. Above: DUCE MAC GREGORIO. Below: LIBERTAS FLO INDAR. Rv: 20 / JUNII / 1817 within open-top palm wreath at center. Above: AMALIA. Below: VENDI VIDI VICI. Plain edge.

In the unsettled conditions following the end of the war of 1812 in 1815, one Gregor MacGregor with a force of freebooters captured Amelia Island off Florida and ran up his "Green Cross of Florida" flag. After establishing the "Duchy of Amelia," MacGregor founded an Admiralty court, a post office and a newspaper. MacGregor is the same man who established the "Cacique of Poyais" on the mosquito-infested coast of Honduras, and sold both land and bonds in England. Amelia's maritime depredations partly led to Andrew Jackson's raid in 1817-1818 into Florida.

The medal, of which only three specimens are known, was to mark the independence of Amelia. (See ANS *Numismatic Notes & Monographs 66*, 1935)

GEORGIA

I. GILBERT
Augusta, Georgia

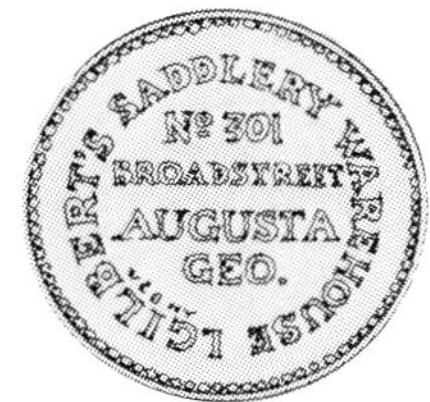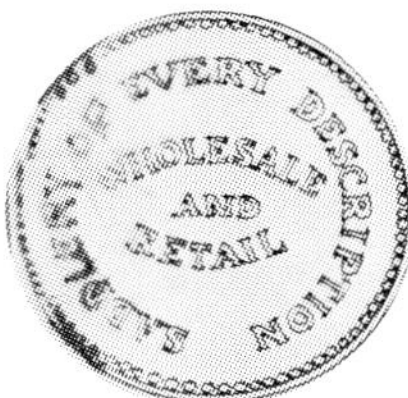

Rulau-E	Date	Metal	Size	Denomination	VG	F	VF
Ga 1	(1829-33)	Copper	28½mm	Cent	1000.	1500.	2500.

I. GILBERT'S SADDLERY WAREHOUSE / NO. 301 / BROAD STREET / AUGUSTA / GEO. / W&B NY. Rv: SADDLERY OF EVERY DESCRIPTION / WHOLESALE / AND / RETAIL. (Low 315)

Rulau-E	Date	Metal	Size	Denomination	VG	F	VF
Ga 2	(1829-33)	Brass	28½mm	Cent	1000.	1500.	2500.

As Ga 1. (Low 316)

(STEAMER) J.D.M.
(Steamer John David Mongin)
Savannah, Georgia

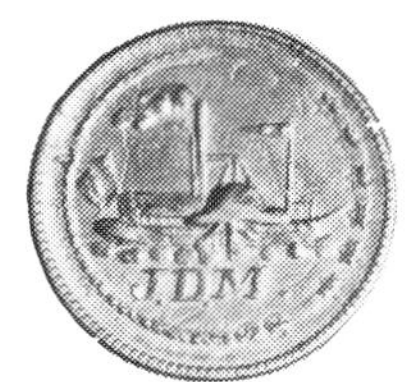

Rulau-E	Date	Metal	Size	Denomination	G	VG	VF
Ga 10	(1828-36)	Copper	24mm	(Half Cent)	—	500.	—

Paddlewheel steamer in full smoke to right, initials JDM below; all within circle composed of wreath and six stars. The design is over-struck on a U.S. Half Cent of 1828. The illustrated piece is in the David Schenkman collection. 16 pieces known. (Duffield 1438)

Rulau-E	Date	Metal	Size	Denomination	VG	F	VF
Ga 11	(1828-36)	Copper	24mm	(Half Cent)	—	500.	—

Similar, but struck on an 1811 Half Cent.

By David E. Schenkman

During the 19th century a great number of U.S. and foreign coins were counterstamped in this country by merchants and individuals, for advertising and other purposes. Most were stamped with merely a set of initials, or a name. Far more desirable from the collector's standpoint are those few coins counterstamped with a business name and address. These pieces are identifiable as legitimate "merchant counterstamps" and are sought avidly by collectors of early merchant tokens.

Rarely is a coin encountered which includes some sort of design as a part of the counterstamp. The illustrated 1828 half cent is an interesting exception: It has, in addition to the initials JDM, a paddlewheel steamboat. Even more unusual is the method of counterstamping — it was struck with a die similar in style to those used to strike coins. Thus the initials, design and surrounding circle are raised, rather than incused, on the host coin.

Frank G. Duffield, in his (1919-22) *A Trial List of Counter-marked Modern Coins of the World,* listed the JDM counter-stamp as number 1438. Although Duffield did not comment on the piece, it has been attributed by others to Baltimore, no doubt because several examples have been found here over the years.

The Duffield specimen was counterstamped on an 1828 half cent. Kenneth Hallenbeck, in his 1967 *The Numismatist* article entitled "Counterstamped U.S. Half Cents," lists a specimen stamped on an 1811 half cent. In my collection are two examples — one on an 1828 half cent and one with no date visible.

Among my reference books on ships is one titled *Merchant Steam Vessels of the United States 1790-1868.* Compiled by William M. Lytle and Forrest R. Holdcamper from various government records, it lists every steam vessel registered or licensed in this country up to 1868. Only two steamers with the initials JDM are recorded in this work. One, the *Julius D. Morton,* was a sidewheel steamer of 472 tons. Built in 1848 at Monroe, Michigan, its home port was Detroit. The ship was destroyed by fire in 1863.

The other steamer listed is the *John David Mongin,* a side-wheeler of 169 tons. It was built in 1828 in New York City and operated out of Savannah, Georgia. This vessel was abandoned or dismantled in 1836.

Based on the date in the Lytle-Holdcamper list, it is logical to attribute the JDM counterstamp to the steamer *John David Mongin,* and to include it with the early merchant tokens of Savannah. The period during which this vessel operated ties in with the dates on the 1811 and 1828 coins; the other JDM steamer is from a much later period.

Why were the coins counterstamped? Since all 16 specimens reported were stamped on half cents, they probably had a specific use rather than advertising. Perhaps they were given to customers at the company's ticket office when fares were purchased, and collected when the vessel was boarded.

B. LORD
Athens, Ga.

Rulau-E	Date	Metal	Size	VG	F	EF
Ga 30	(1830-33)	Copper	29mm	—	100.	—

B. LORD in relief within toothed rect. depression ctsp. on U.S. 1804 Large cent. (Donald G. Partrick collection)

Benjamin Lord (born 1770, died 1843) was a silversmith of some renown, who was the principal of the firm of B.B. Lord & Co. (with Ebenezer Lord and Joel White) of Athens, Georgia, in the 1830-39 period. The mark is his hallmark, according to *A Directory of American Silver, Pewter and Silver Plate* by Ralph and Terry Kovel.

Lord began his silversmith trade in Pittsfield, N.H. in 1796. The next year he moved to Rutland, Vt., where he formed the firm of Lord & Goddard with Nicholas Goddard (1797-1807). He next appears in the directories in Athens, Ga., in the B.B. Lord & Co. silverware and jewelry manufacturing firm.

KENTUCKY

P.P.P. MYDDELTON
Kentucky

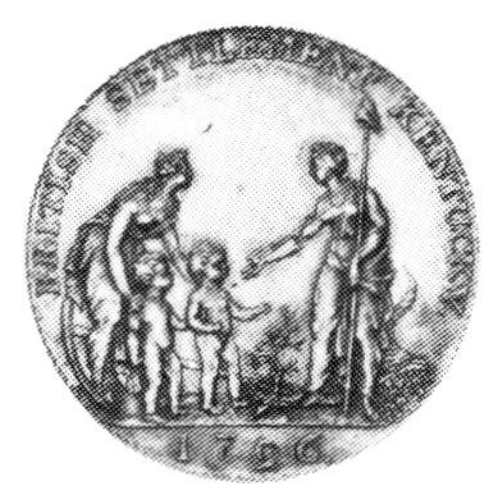

Rulau-E	Date	Metal	Size	Denomination	EF	Proof
Ky 1	1796	Copper	30mm	(Halfpenny)	—	5500.

Female and two nude boys being welcomed by Liberty, BRITISH SETTLEMENT KENTUCKY 1796. Rv: Seated Britannia with British shield and downcast head, PAYABLE BY P.P.P. MYDDELTON. (RB) (4 to 6 known)

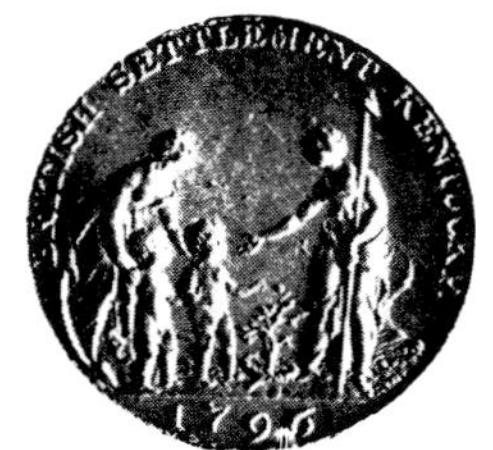

Rulau-E	Date	Metal	Size	Denomination	EF	Proof
Ky 2	1796	Silver	30mm	(Halfpenny)	—	5000.

As last. (RB) (20 known)

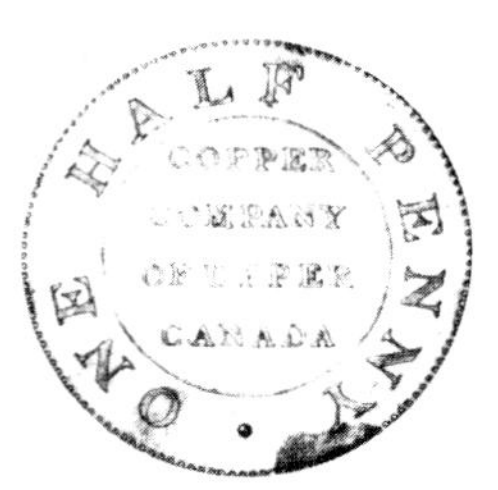

Rulau-E	Date	Metal	Size	Denomination	EF	Proof
Ky 4	1796 (1806-10)	Copper	30mm	Half Penny	—	2000.

Muling of Myddelton reverse with Copper Company of Upper Canada token reverse. (Struck circa 1806-1810) (RB)

Philip Parry Price Myddelton, who owned a tract of land in Kentucy, enticed hundreds of Englishmen to emigrate and reside on his property in 1795-1796. Anticipating the need for small change, he had halfpence made by Boulton & Watt of Birmingham after designs by Conrad Kuchler. He was arrested in August, 1796, by British authorities, halting the settlement and the coinage. About 1806-1810 Boulton & Watt muled the Myddelton and Upper Canada dies to create presentation pieces, which had no connection with the Myddelton Kentucky tract.

H.E. THOMAS & CO.
Louisville, Ky.

Rulau-E	Date	Metal	Size	Denomination	VG	F	EF
Ky 33	(1832)	White Metal	28mm	(1 Cent)	—	—	1000.

Hardware implements. H.E. THOMAS & CO. HARDWARE STORE. Reeded edge.

The hardware implements design side is a copy of Breton 561, the T.S. Brown cards of Montreal, Quebec, which was struck in Birmingham, England, in 1832. The evidence given in Sandham to the conclusive dating of the Brown card leads to the supposition that Thomas may have had the same die struck for himself on a trial basis in white metal. The Thomas piece could be later, in the Hard Times period of course, but for now we're assigning it here. The hardware implements die used on the T.S. Brown and H.E. Thomas & Co. cards was also used on a white metal piece of Green & Wetmore of New York (Low 298, Adams N.Y. 290).

LOUISIANA

W. EDGAR JUNR.
New Orleans, La.

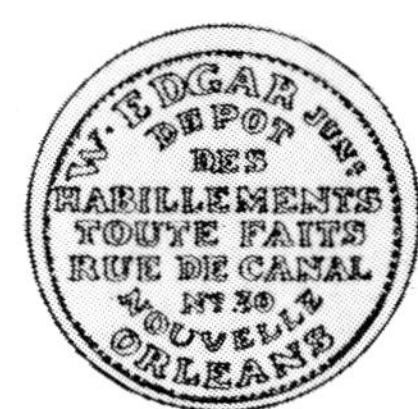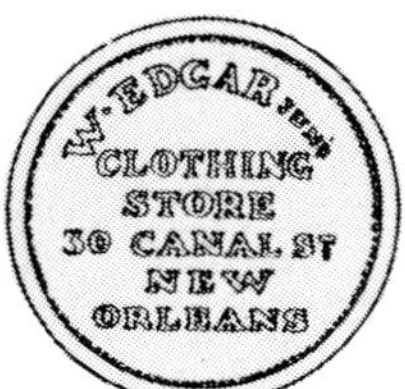

Rulau-E	Date	Metal	Size	VG	F	EF
La 8	(1825-34)	Brass	26mm	200.00	500.00	1250.

W. EDGAR JUNR. / DEPOT / DES / HABILLEMENTS / TOUTE FAITS / RUE DE CANAL / NO. 30 / NOUVELLE / ORLEANS. RV: W. EDGAR JUNR. / CLOTHING / STORE / 30 CANAL ST. / NEW / ORLEANS.

The clothing store of William Edgar Jr. was located at 16 Levee Street, corner Custom House Street, in 1824. In 1825 the business moved to 30 Canal Street where it continued for several years. In 1835, Edgar & Smith's clothing store at 4 Chartres Street was probably a successor to this business. (See Sidney K. Eastwood's ''New Orleans Store Cards in the Antebellum Days'' in *TAMS Journal* for October, 1966.)

MARYLAND

ANNAPOLIS TUESDAY CLUB
Annapolis, Md.

Rulau-E	Date	Metal	Size		F	VF	Unc
Md 5	1746	Copper	44mm		—	—	Rare

CONCORDIA RES PARVAE CRESCUNT * (by harmony small things increase) / THE / TUESDAY CLUB / IN / ANNAPOLIS (script) (heart enclosing two clasped hands) MARYLAND (script) / MAY 14, 1746. Rv: Liberty as a nude boy with pole and Liberty cap, seated on grass at right, beside altar inscribed LIBERTAS / ET / NATALE / SOLUM (Liberty and native land). Around: CAROLUS COLE ARMIGER PRAESES * (Charles Cole, Esquire, president). Plain edge. Medallic. (Betts 383)

The Tuesday Club was founded between 1740 and 1745, and remained in existence until about 1780. An account of the club may be found in *Scribner's Monthly* for Jan. 1879. The dies reportedly were cut by John Kirk of London.

I. CHALMERS
Annapolis, MD.

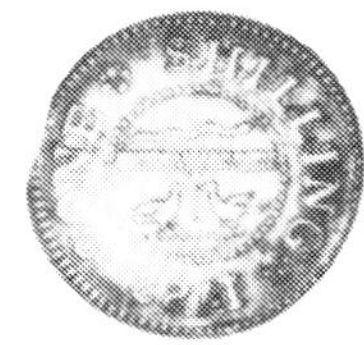 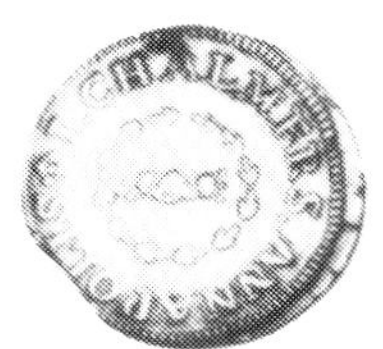

Rulau-E	Date	Metal	Size	Denomination	VG	F	VF
Md 1C	1783	Silver	21mm	1 Shilling	500.00	750.00	1200.

Two birds holding long worm. Rv: Two clasped hands within wreath. (RB)

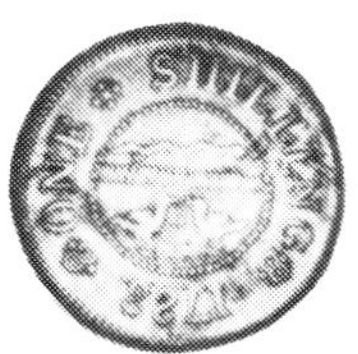 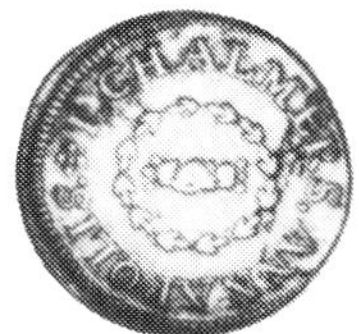

					VG	F	VF
Md 1B	1783	Silver	21mm	1 Shilling	475.00	700.00	1100.

Similar, but shorter worm. (RB)

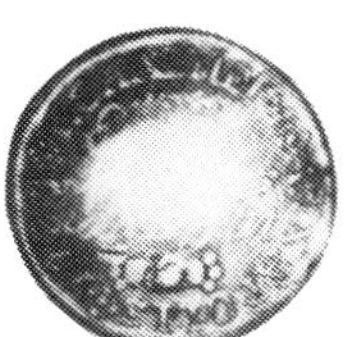 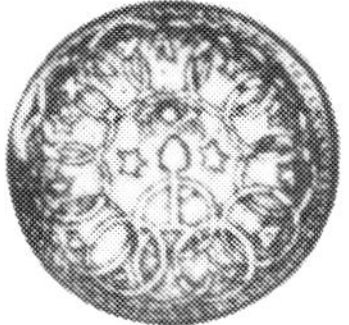

Rulau	Date	Metal	Size	Denomination	VG	F	VF
Md 1D	1783	Silver	21mm	1 Shilling	Ex. Rare	—	75,000.

Similar obverse. Rv Wreath of interlocked rings and stars. (RB) (Garrett lot 1313)

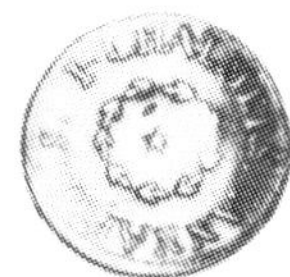 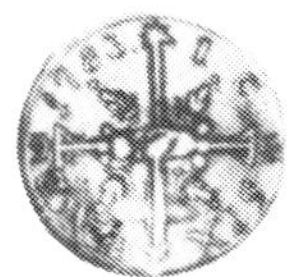

Rulau	Date	Metal	Size	Denomination	VG	F	VF
Md 1E	1783	Silver	18mm	6 Pence	875.00	1200.	2100.

Star within wreath. Rv Cross with two clasped hands. Small date. (RB)

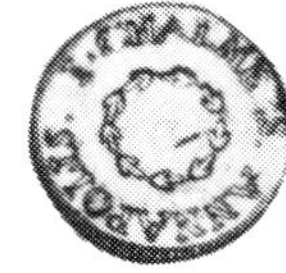 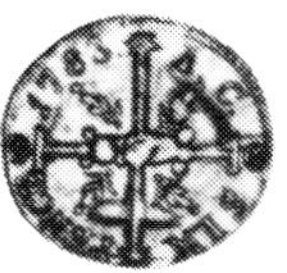

Rulau	Date	Metal	Size	Denomination	VG	F	VF
Md 1F	1783	Silver	18mm	6 Pence	700.00	1200.	2100.

Similar, large date. (RB)

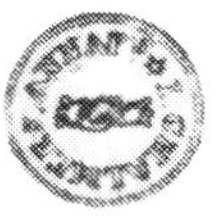

					VG	F	VF
Md 1G	1783	Silver	13mm	3 Pence	550.00	1000.	1500.

Clasped hands. Rv Wreath encircles small branch. (RB)

Goldsmith and silversmith John Chalmers struck a series of silver tokens at Annapolis in 1783. This shortage of change and the refusal of the people to use underweight cut Spanish coins, or ''bits,'' prompted the issuance of these pieces, according to a contemporary account of a German traveler. Dr. John D. Schopf. Chalmers was born 1750, eldest son of silversmith and tavernkeeper James Chalmers of Annapolis. He took over his father's business in 1781. The silver tokens were struck at his shop at the corner of Cornhill and Fleet Streets. At that time it was customary to cut a Spanish silver dollar into halves, quarters or eighths, the eighth being a ''bit.'' Unscrupulous persons would cut five ''quarters'' or 10 ''eighths'' from a dollar, increasing their return. Schopf reported that Chalmers redeemed the fractions, exchanging his own coins for them and charging a commission for the service. His coinage was apparently extensive, the shilling occurring most frequently today.

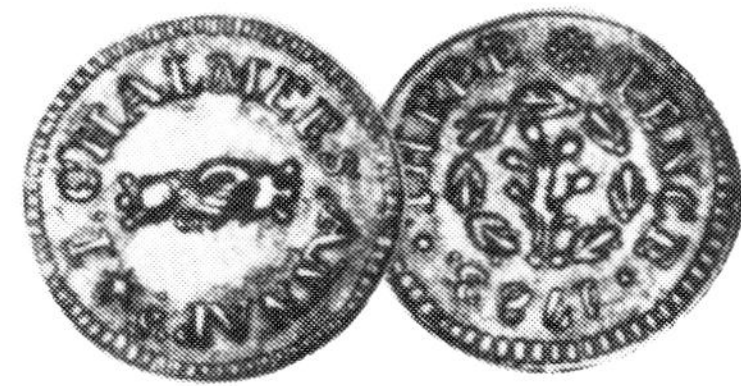

Enlargement of Threepence

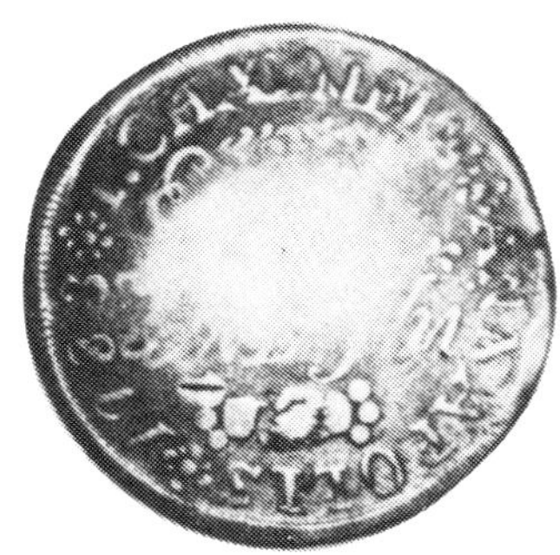 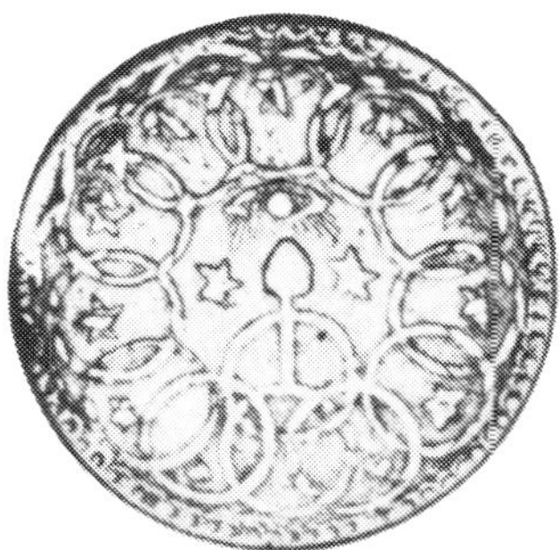

Enlargement of Third Type
Shilling (Interlocked Rings)

STANDISH BARRY
Baltimore Md.

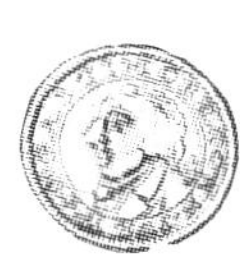 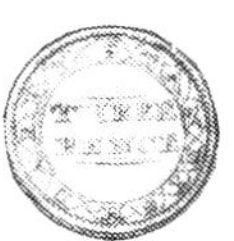

Rulau-E	Date	Metal	Size	Denomination	VG	F	VF
Md 11A	(17) 90	Silver	14mm	3 Pence	1400.	2200.	3250.

Man's head left, BALTIMORE TOWN, JULY 4, 90. Rv: THREE PENCE. (RB)

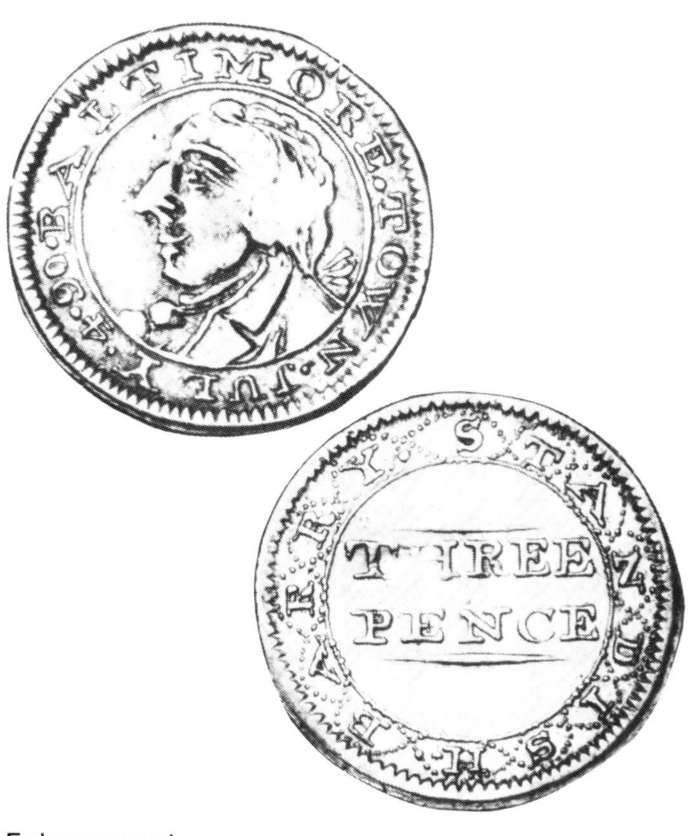

Enlargement

Silversmith Standish Barry, then 27, circulated a silver token in 1790 which may depict George Washington or Barry himself. He was also a watch and clockmaker and an engraver. The tokens were an advertising venture at a time small change was scarce. The reverse die supposedly broke after only about 12 pieces were made, but more pieces are known. Edges were crudely reeded.

(BALTIMORE TOKEN)
Baltimore, Md.

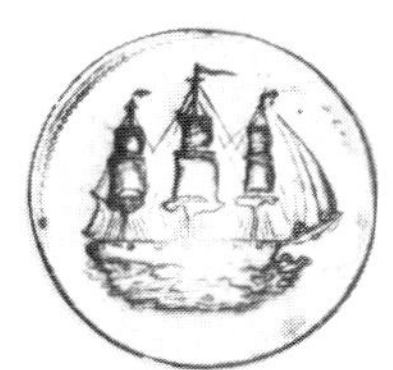 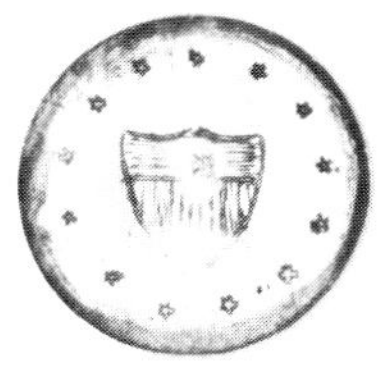

Rulau-E	Date	Metal	Size	VG	F	EF
Md 7	(1830-36)	Brass	23mm	60.00	150.00	200.00
		Three-masted sailing ship right. Rv: U.S. shield surrounded by 13 stars. Thick planchet.				
Md 7A	(1830-36)	Brass	23mm	60.00	150.00	200.00
		Same as 7, counterstamped H.M.				
Md 7B	(1830-36)	Brass	23mm	60.00	150.00	200.00
		Same as 7, counterstamped A. FIELD				
Md 8	(1830-36)	Brass	23mm	60.00	150.00	200.00
		Similar to 7, but smaller stars. Thin planchet.				
Md 8A	(1830-36)	Brass	23mm	60.00	150.00	200.00
		As 8, ctsp 5				
Md 8B	(1830-36)	Brass	23mm	60.00	150.00	200.00
		As 8, ctsp J.W.				
Md 8C	(1830-36)	Brass	23mm	60.00	150.00	200.00
		As 8, ctsp S.				
Md 8D	(1830-36)	Brass	23mm	60.00	150.00	200.00
		As 8, ctsp C.S.				

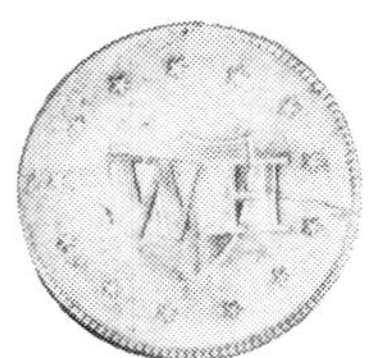

Rulau-E	Date	Metal	Size	VG	F	EF
Md 8E	(1830-36)	Brass	23mm	60.00	150.00	200.00
		As 8, ctsp W.H.				

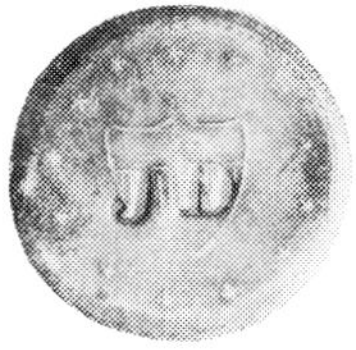

Md 8F	(1830-36)	Brass	23mm	60.00	150.00	200.00
		As 8, ctsp J.D.				

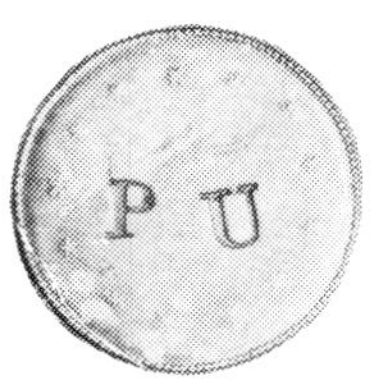

Md 8G	(1830-36)	Brass	23mm	60.00	150.00	200.00
		As 8, ctsp P.U.				
Md 8H	(1830-36)	Brass	23mm	60.00	150.00	200.00
		As 8, ctsp B.H.				
Md 8J	(1830-36)		23mm	60.00	150.00	200.00
		As 8, ctsp 10 / ICE.				

The diesinker for the Baltimore Tokens is not known, but the ship die was also used for the James Cole cards following. This relationship of die work was explored by Frank Duffield, without clear conclusions, in *The Numismatist* for Dec. 1904. The counterstamps show this mute token device was adapted as a trade check by a number of firms in the area. Some day a scholar might trace some of these counterstamps, or the token itself.

There are two distinct reverse dies on these pieces, with differently shaped shields.

JAMES COLE
Baltimore, Md.

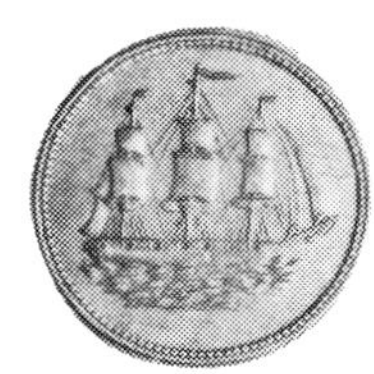 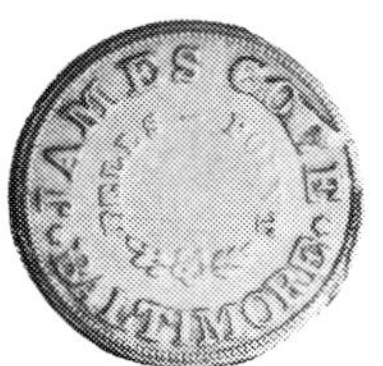

Rulau-E	Date	Metal	Size	VG	F	EF
Md 38	(1833-36)	Brass	23mm	100.00	150.00	300.00
		Three-masted sailing ship right. Rv: JAMES COLE/FELLS. POINT/(wreath)/*BALTIMORE*.				
Md 37	(1833-36)	Copper	23mm	100.00	150.00	300.00
		Same as 38.				
Md 38 ctsp. F.W.				—	—	300.00
Md 38 ctsp ICE				—	—	300.00

James Cole was born at St. Inigoes, Md., Aug. 22, 1802, son of Robert and Ann Fenwick Cole. He located in Fell's Point, Baltimore, in 1825. A mariner, he entered politics and in 1833 was rewarded by being named harbor master. He was harbor master 1833-1839 and state Wharfinger 1839-1845. He also operated a grocery on South Wolfe Street, Fell's Point, 1835-1836 while harbor master, and the tokens may date from this latter period. Cole kept a hotel in Fell's Point 1847-1849, and again a grocery on Wolfe Street 1849-1851. He was a ship's captain and pilot 1851-1860, then a farmer in Anne Arundel County 1860-1866, then a Baltimore restaurateur (721 So. Broadway) 1866-1869. Retiring at age 67, he farmed until his death in 1882. "Fell's Point" was settled by William Fell, a ship carpenter, who came from England in 1730. It was annexed to Baltimore in 1773. In our 1980 *Hard Times Tokens* book we assigned the Cole cards to the Hard Times period, but repeat them here because it is not logical to separate the die-linked Baltimore and Cole tokens.

MASSACHUSETTS

BALDWIN & JONES
Boston, Mass.

Rulau-E	Date	Metal	Size		VG	F	EF
Mass 4	(1813-19)	Copper	29mm		—	65.00	—

BALDWIN & JONES in relief in scroll-shaped depression ctsp on U.S. 1808 Large Cent.

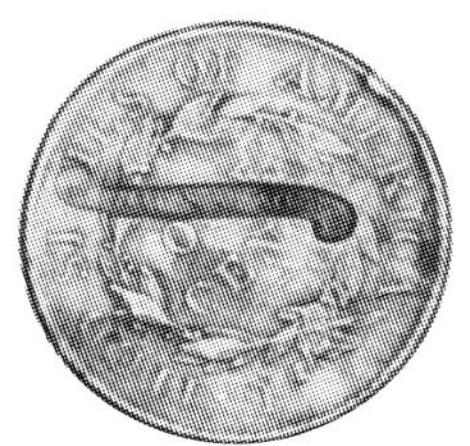 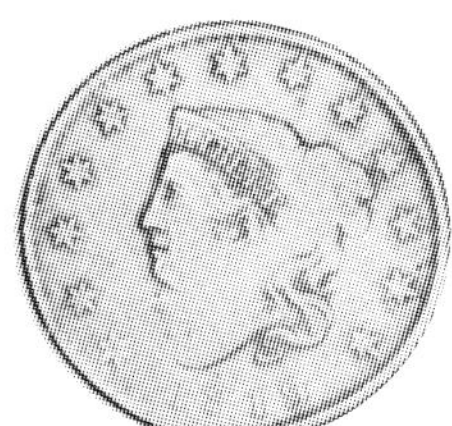

| Mass 5 | (1819) | Copper | 29mm | | — | 65.00 | — |

Similar ctsp on U.S. 1819 Large Cent.

Jabez L. Baldwin (1777-1819) and John B. Jones (1782-1854) were partners in the silversmith's trade circa 1813-1819. After Baldwin's death in 1819, Jones continued under the same name for a time; by 1838 this was known as John B. Jones & Co., and in 1839 Jones, Ball & Low. (See token of John J. Low & Co.)

FARNSWORTH, PHIPPS & CO.
Boston, Mass.

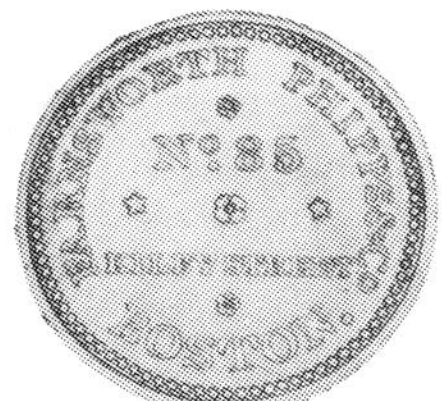 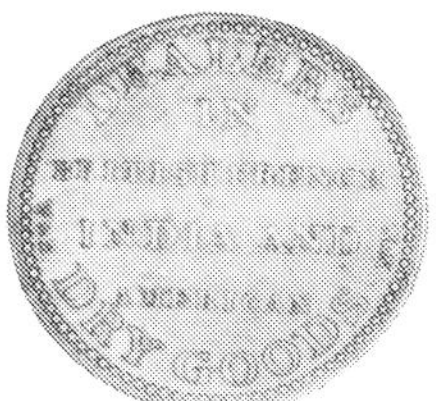

Rulau-E	Date	Metal	Size	Denomination	VG	F	Unc
Mass 38	(1829-33)	Copper	28½mm	Cent	12.50	30.00	300.00

FARNSWORTH PHIPPS & CO. / NO 85 / KILBY STREET / BOSTON. Rv: DEALERS / IN / BRITISH FRENCH / INDIA AND / AMERICAN / DRY GOODS. Tiny W. & B. — N.Y. flanks DRY GOODS. (Wright 356; Low 314)

This token spans the Early American and Hard Time eras. Cut by Wright & Bale of New York, who were in partnership May 1829 to October 1833.

HOWARD & DAVIS
Boston, Mass.

Rulau-E	Date	Metal	Size		VG	F	EF
Mass 7	(?)	Silver	27mm		—	100.00	—

HOWARD & DAVIS / BOSTON L.Y. ctsp on U.S. 1819 Bust quarter.

JOHN J. LOW & CO.
Boston, Mass.

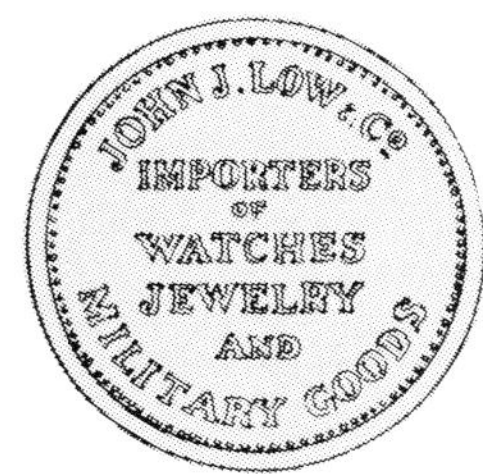 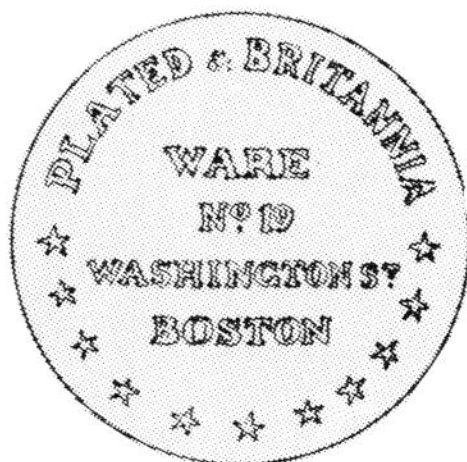

Rulau-E	Date	Metal	Size		VG	F	EF
Mass 48	(1828-1835)	Brass	32mm				Unique

JOHN J. LOW & CO. / IMPORTERS / OF / WATCHES / JEWELRY AND / MILITARY GOODS. Rv: PLATED & BRITANNIA / WARE / NO. 19 / WASHINGTON ST / BOSTON / (eleven stars). (Wright 628)

Rulau-E	Date	Metal	Size		VG	F	EF
Mass 48A	(1828-35)	WM	32mm		—	—	Unique

As 48.

John J. Low & Co. was founded in 1828 and changed its name to Jones, Ball & Low in 1839. Later this firm became known as Shreve, Crump & Low, still in business in 1921. The only known specimen was in the W. Eliot Woodward and B.P. Wright collections, eventually passing in 1921 to the Massachusetts Historical Society. In the May, 1921, *The Numismatist*, MHS curator Malcolm Storer published the token with a photograph. It apparently has a gilt surface.

O + H
(Otis Howe)
Boston, Mass.

Rulau-E	Date	Metal	Size		VG	F	EF
Mass 15	(1792-1803)	Copper	29mm		—	50.00	—

O + H in large divided toothed rectangular cartouche ctsp on England Halfpenny token of the "Britannia Rules the Waves" type. (Donald Partrick Coll.)

| Mass 17 | (1803) | Copper | 29mm | | — | 50.00 | — |

O.HOWE ctsp on U.S. 1803 Large Cent.

Otis Howe was a Boston silversmith active in the 1788-1803 period. Mass 15 may be misattributed. O + H seems to imply a partnership.

PEIRCE
Boston, Mass.

Rulau-E	Date	Metal	Size		VG	F	EF
Mass 19	(1810)	Copper	29mm		—	35.00	—

PEIRCE in rectangle ctsp on U.S. 1802 Large Cent.

John Peirce (or Peirse) was a silversmith in Boston about 1810. He may have changed his name to Pierce later, and been succeeded about 1824 by O. Pierce.

HORACE PORTER & CO.
Boston Mass.

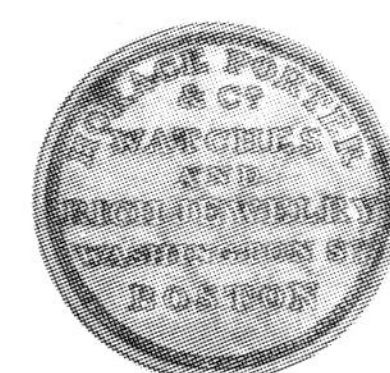 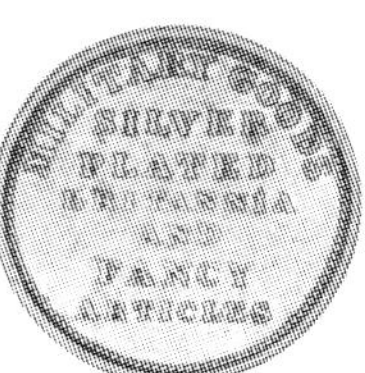

Rulau-E	Date	Metal	Size		VG	F	EF
Mass 84	(1826-33)	S/Brass	24mm		50.00	100.00	160.00

HORACE PORTER / & CO. / WATCHES / AND / RICH JEWELRY / WASHINGTON ST. / BOSTON. Rv: MILITARY GOODS / SILVER / PLATED / BRITANNIA / AND / FANCY / ARTICLES.

| Mass 84A | (1826-33) | Copper | 24mm | | — | — | — |

As 84. (Wright 1578). This piece may not exist.

Horace Porter is listed in the Boston directories at Washington Street from 1826 through 1833.

RUETER & ALLEY
RUETER & CO.
Boston, Mass.

Mass 85, 85A and 86, under these titles, have proven to be post-Civil War in vintage, probably 1870's. Neither name appears in any Boston directory or census record 1820-1863. The 1888 directory lists: Rueter & Co., Highland Spring Brewery, Heath corner Terrace.

L. WALKER
Boston, Mass.

Rulau-E	Date	Metal	Size		VG	F	EF
Mass 20	(ca 1825)	Silver	27mm (25 Cents)		—	125.00	—

L. WALKER ctsp on reverse of Spanish-American 1756-LME-JM 2-reales. (Stanley Steinberg 1982 sale)

L. Walker was a Boston silversmith of about 1825, located in the Joys Building. Attribution doubtful.

A. & G. WELLES and G. LIBBY
Boston, Mass.

Mass 22   (1830)   Copper   29mm   Ex. Rare
A & G WELLES in relief ctsp within rectangular depression, and G LIBBY 1796 ctsp incuse, all on a U.S. 1802 Large cent. (Duffield 1585; Hallenbeck 23.505)

The A. & G. Welles stamp was a silversmith's mark applied about 1830. The G. Libby stamp is possibly frivolous or personal, recording some event.

Andrew and George Welles began in business about 1804 as jewelers and silversmiths. George died about 1827, but Andrew lived to 1860. They were involved in several partnerships (e.g. Welles & Gelston and Welles & Co. with Hugh Gelston).

PORCELLIAN CLUB
Cambridge, Mass.

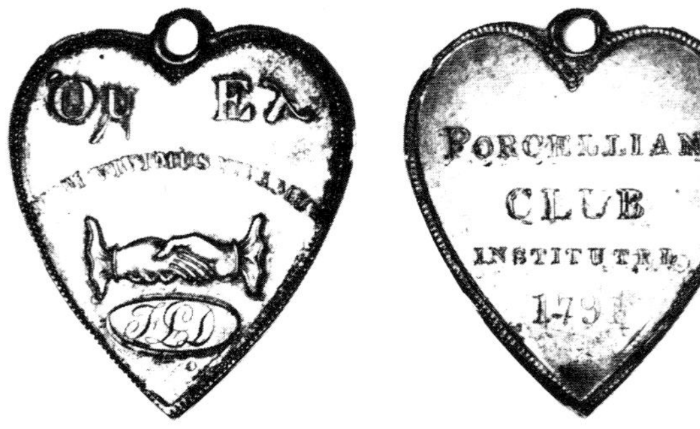

Rulau-E	Date	Metal	Size		F	VF	Unc
Mass 25	(ca 1831)	Silver	**		—	100.00	—

** Heart-shaped flan, 35 by 43mm.
O U E / DIEM (?) VIVIMUS VIVAMUS (?) / (clasped hands) / Script FLD engraved within oval. Rv: PORCELLIAN / CLUB / INSTITUTED / 1791. Plain edge. (Storer 35)

The member whose initials are engraved was Francis Low Dutton, who received a B.A. degree in 1831.
    The Porcellian group was "one of the swellest clubs in existence" according to W.D. Orcutt in "Clubs and Club Life at Harvard" *(New England Magazine, 1892).*
    Harvard University, founded 1636, is the oldest institution of higher learning in the U.S. Harvard's Law School was founded in 1817 and its Divinity School in 1819. In 1823 the state of Massachusetts ceased its financial support of the university.

A. WATERS
Millbury, Mass.

Rulau-E	Date	Metal	Size		VG	F	EF
Mass 45	1825	Copper	29mm		—	50.00	—

C.B. / A. WATERS / U S / MILLBURY/ 1825 ctsp on U.S. 1796 Large cent. (Brunk report)

NEW HAMPSHIRE

C. WARNER
Portsmouth, N.H.

Rulau-E	Date	Metal	Size		VG	F	EF
NH 3	(1824)	Copper	29mm		—	50.00	—

C. Warner ctsp on U.S. 1818 Large cent.

Caleb Warner (1784-1861) was a silversmith in Portsmouth circa 1824. Later he moved to Salem, Mass.
    A very similar hallmark, C. WARNER (all capital letters) belongs to silversmith Cuthbert Warner (1760-1838) of Baltimore, Md. There was also another Cuthbert Warner active as a silversmith in Philadelphia 1837-1850.

NEW JERSEY

JOHN STEVENS
Hoboken, N.J.

Rulau-E	Date	Metal	Size		VG	F	EF
NJ 1	1829	Brass	29mm		—	—Unique?

PAY / THE BEARER ON / DEMAND / ONE DOLLAR / AND CHARGE THE SAME / TO / JOHN STEVENS / HOBOKEN JUNE 20 1829 / TO JOHN V. BOSKERCK / FERRY MASTER / W & B. Rv: A wreath. ONE / DOLLAR / PAYABLE IN / SPECIE / WRIGHT & BALE. Plain edge.

The only known specimen of this token is in the collection of the American Numismatic Society. It was first reported to a wide audience by Edgar Adams in *The Numismatist* in 1912, and was catalogued by Damia Francis in "New Jersey Tokens" in the *TAMS Journal* for Aug. 1969.

It is the earliest known $1 denomination trade token used in America, though the 1845 $1 token of Johnson, Himrod & Co. of Erie, Pa. is the first of dollar size (38mm). Struck by Wright & Bale, New York City.

Descriptions of this Hoboken token are sometimes confused with the Hoboken Ferry car check of New York City (Atwood NY 630R), a 27mm brass token used much later in the 19th century.

E. & I. BRAGAW
Newark, N.J. & Mobile, Ala.

Rulau-E	Date	Metal	Size	VG	F	EF
NJ 28	(1829-33)	Copper	28mm	400.00	1000.	3000.
		W&B NY. Rarity 7. HAT MFGS. (Low 302)				
NJ 29	(1829-33)	Brass	28mm	400.00	1000.	3000.
		As 28. Rarity 7. (Low 303)				
NJ 30	(1829-33)	WM	28mm	400.00	1000.	3000.
		As 28. Rarity 7. (Low 304)				

NEW YORK

CHURCH PENNY
(Albany Church)
Albany, N.Y.

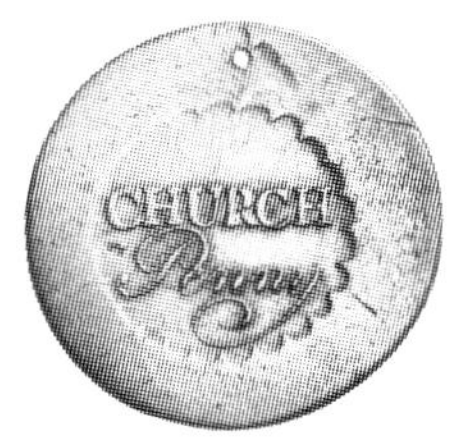

Rulau-E	Date	Metal	Size	Denomination	G	VG	F
NY 1	(1790)	Copper	28mm	1 Penny	800.00	1100.	1750.

CHURCH / PENNY within scalloped recession. Rv: Blank. (RB) (Only 4 known)

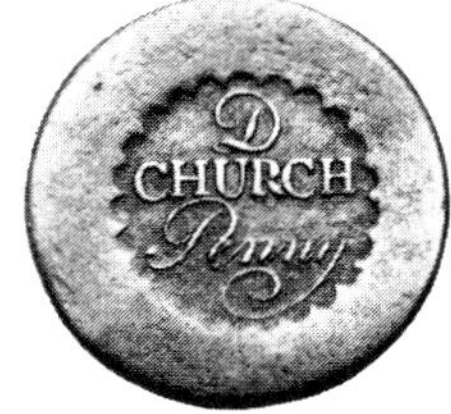

NY 1A	(1790)	Copper	28mm	1 Penny	750.00	1000.	1500.

Similar, large D added above CHURCH. (RB)

The First Presbyterian Church of Albany authorized an issue of 1,000 uniface copper pennies on Jan. 4, 1790. These passed at 12 to the shilling and were used to stop contributions of worn and counterfeit coppers. The specimens known are of two types, but struck from the same die, which was later altered. They have the word CHURCH in capital letters and the word PENNY in script below, all within a circular panel of 24 scallops, and are struck on one side of the planchet only. The letter D in script appears on many of the specimens, while on others it is omitted. The significance of the D has been thought to be the initial of a town, or Latin for denarium, but, more likely, it may have stood for the Dutch Church of Albany which was close by. Since the method of exchange proved satisfactory for the Presbyterian Church, the die may have been borrowed, reengraved with a D for the Dutch Church, and used as such. One strong factor in support of this is that in both 1790 and 1793, the Dutch Reformed Church of Schenectady issued paper money for exactly the same purpose as the tokens. Though two different Dutch Churches were involved, the trend of the practice was evident. Three of these metal tokens were stolen from the Howard Kurth collection in upstate New York in 1978.

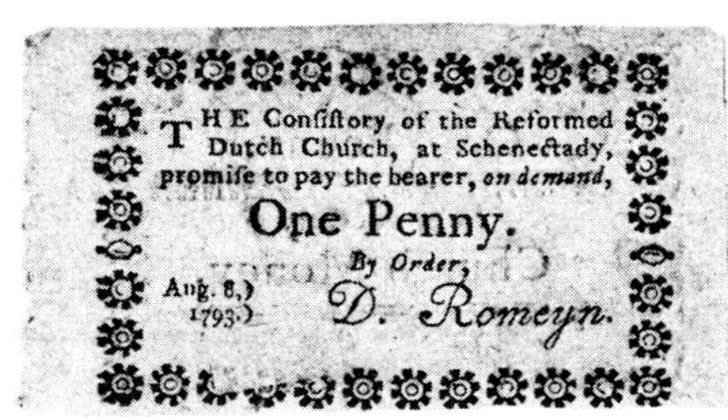

T. C.
(Thomas Carson)
Albany, N.Y.

Rulau-E	Date	Metal	Size	VG	F	EF
NY 3	(1815)	Silver	40mm		— 350.00	—

T . C in relief within rectangular depression, ctsp twice on obverse of U.S. 1802 Bust dollar. Similar ctsp, once, on reverse of coin. (Roy Van Ormer coll.)

The hallmark is an exact match with that of silversmith Thomas Carson of Albany, active circa 1815. The estimate of value is based upon owner's cost basis.

E. NEWBURY
Brooklyn, N.Y.

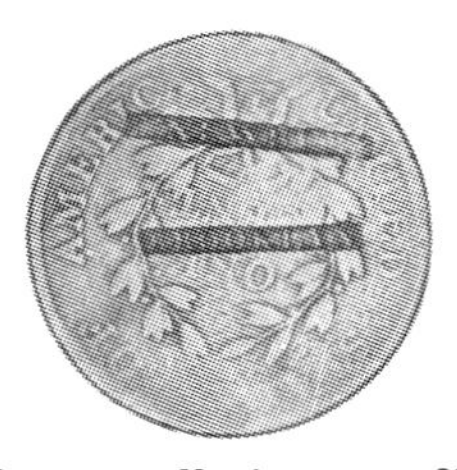
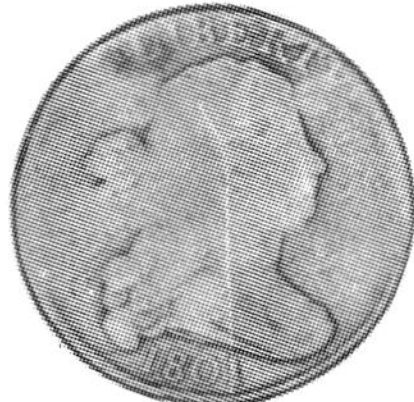

Rulau-E	Date	Metal	Size	VG	F	EF
NY 6	(?)	Copper	29mm		— 65.00	—

E. NEWBURY / BROOKLYN ctsp in relief in two separate rectangular depressions, on U.S. 1801 Large cent reverse. (Tanenbaum coll.)

Ralph M. and Terry H. Kovel's *A Directory of American Silver, Pewter, and Silver Plate*, (1961), listed an Edwin C. Newberry of Brooklyn, N.Y., silversmith circa 1828. This could be the same person despite the name spelling difference. The punches used appear to be those of a manufacturing jeweler or silversmith, similar to those found on the shank of silver teaspoons or on other silver tableware.

W.A. THOMSON
Buffalo, N.Y.

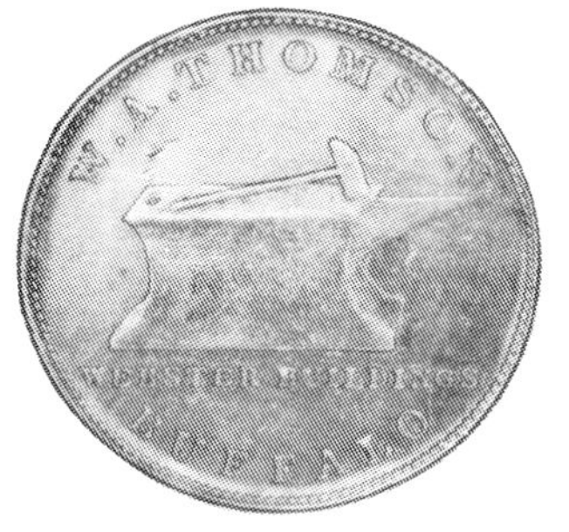
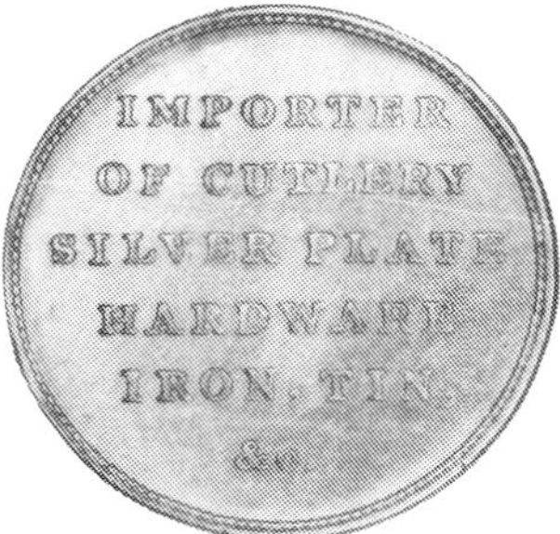

Rulau-E	Date	Metal	Size		VG	F	EF	Unc
NY 25	(1820's)	Copper	38mm		10.00	22.50	75.00	250.00

Anvil and hammer in center, NO. 9 on side of anvil. W.A. THOMSON above, WEBSTER BUILDINGS/BUFFALO below. Reeded edge.

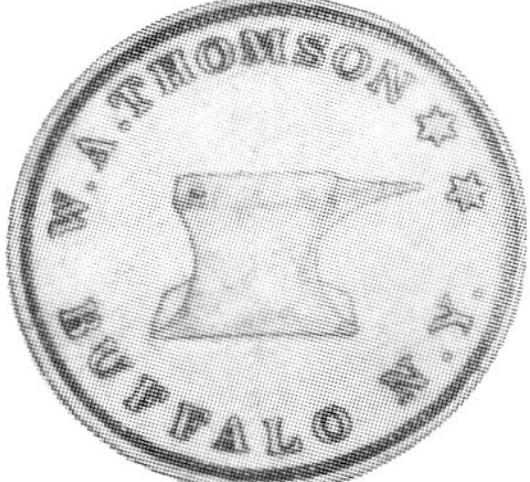
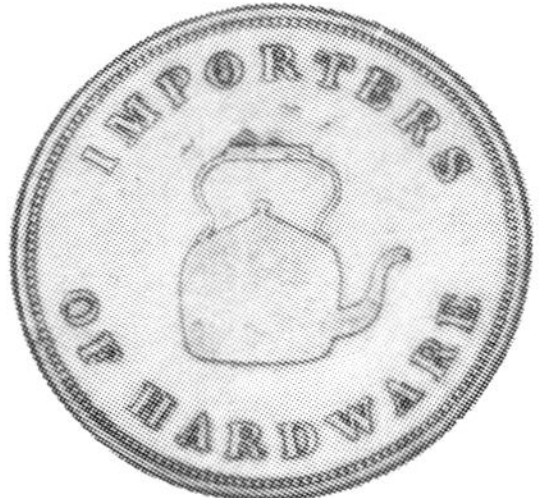

NY 26	(1820's)	Copper	33mm		10.00	20.00	40.00	225.00

Anvil in center, W.A. THOMSON ** above, BUFFALO N.Y. below. Rv: Teakettle in center, IMPORTERS above, OF HARDWARE below. Reeded edge. (Wright 1142)

Dating the Thomson pieces has proven an elusive task, though we accept the Fulds' conclusion (in "Token Collectors Page" in *The Numismatist)* that these pieces emanate from the 1820s. We have seen several specimens of NY 25 with laminated flans, the striking having been done over the lamination. The reeding is vertical on both pieces.

Thomas L. Elder in "A Plea for American Token Collecting" (1915) said that the two Thomson & Co. tokens were issued "between the years 1840 and 1845." We do not know the source of his claim, and it differs by 20 years from the claim of the Fulds much later that these pieces were issues in the 1820's.

Should Elder's statement prove correct, the Thomson cards would have to be added to my book on *Hard Times Tokens*.

FRANCO-AMERICANA COLONIA
Castorland, N.Y.

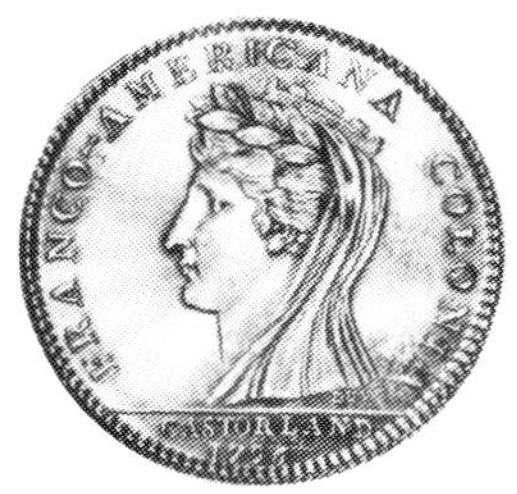
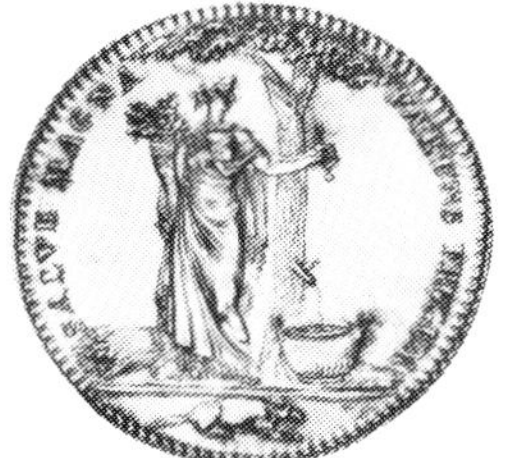

Rulau-E	Date	Metal	Size	Denomination	VF	Unc	Proof
NY 30	1796	Silver	32mm	(50 Cents)	—	4250.	—

Crowned, veiled female head left, FRANCO-AMERICANA COLONIA (French-American colony) around, CASTORLAND / 1796 in exergue. Small DUV. under head. Rv: Standing female Sybele tapping maple tree, beaver below; SALVE MAGNA PARENS FRUGUM around. Thick planchet. Reeded edge. Original. (RB)

NY 31	1796	Copper	32mm	(50 Cents)	—	3200.	—

Same as last. Reeded edge.

NY 33	1796	Silver	33mm		—	—	200.00

Restrike on thin planchet. Reeded edge.

Rulau-E	Date	Metal	Size	Denomination	VF	Unc	Proof
NY 34	1796	Silver	33mm		—	—	35.00

Later restrike. ARGENT on plain edge.

NY 35	1796	Copper	33mm		—	—	130.00

Restrike on thin planchet. Reeded edge.

NY 36	1796	Copper	33mm		—	—	25.00

Later restrike. CUIVRE on plain edge.

Rulau-E	Date	Metal	Size	Denomination	EF	BU	Matte Unc
NY 38	1796	Silver	33mm	—	—	25.00	25.00

Modern restrike from newer dates. ARGENT on reeded edge.

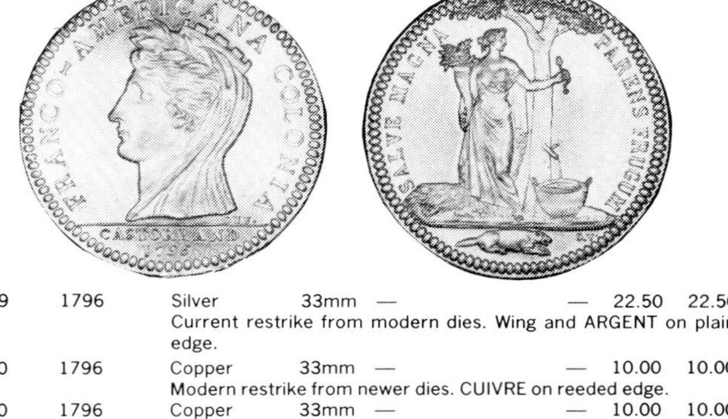

NY 39	1796	Silver	33mm	—	—	22.50	22.50

Current restrike from modern dies. Wing and ARGENT on plain edge.

NY 40	1796	Copper	33mm	—	—	10.00	10.00

Modern restrike from newer dies. CUIVRE on reeded edge.

NY 50	1796	Copper	33mm	—	—	10.00	10.00

Current restrike from modern dies. CUIVRE on plain edge.

NY 51	1796	Bronze	33mm	—	—	10.00	10.00

Current restrike from modern dies. Wing and BR on plain edge.

NY 52	1796	Gold	33mm	—	—	—	—

Current restrike from modern dies. Wing and OR on plain edge.

In August, 1792, French settlers under Pierre Chassanis of Paris organized as the Castorland Company, settled at Castorville (at the head of navigation of the Beaver River) and also at what now is Carthage, N.Y., both in Lewis and Jefferson Counties of the state. Chassanis bought the tracts from William Constable, and organized his company under agent Rudolph Tellier in 1791.

The original silver medallions, or honorariums for officers, were of the size and weight of the United States half dollar and specimens are known to have circulated as such. The reeded edge also indicates their circulation potential, as it was pointless to mill a medal's edge. They were designed by DuVivier. Restrikes off original dies, and the restrikes off replica dies have been made at the Paris Mint for nearly 200 years; they are still available today in bronze, silver and gold, with brilliant or matte finish. The author purchased some at the mint in September, 1979. The pieces are very attractive and quite collectible; their inclusion in the Red Book gives them a status few modern copies enjoy.

The following article gives many more details about Castorland:

By Theo. E. Leon

The office of Land Commissioners was created in 1786, and they were clothed with discretionary powers in selling the unappropriated lands of the state of New York. On June 22, 1791, Alexander Macomb of the city of New York, acting as agent of a company said to consist of himself, Daniel McCormick and Wm. Constable, all of New York, applied for the purchase of a tract of land since known as Macomb's Purchase. The whole of Macomb's contract was estimated to contain 3,670,715 acres. The proposed price was eight pence per acre.

Soon after perfecting his title to a portion of his tract, Macomb employed Wm. Constable as his agent to sell lands in Europe; and on June 6, 1792, he released, and October 3, 1792, conveyed to him tracts 4, 5 and 6, containing 551,600 acres, for £50,000.

The first direct measure taken for actual settlement of the section of New York state embraced in Jefferson County was in 1792. On Aug. 31, Constable, then in Europe, executed a deed to Pierre Chassanis of Paris for 630,000 acres south of Great Lot no. 4, which now constitutes part of Jefferson and Lewis counties. Chassanis acted as "the agent for the associated purchasers of land in Montgomery County," and the lands were to be held in trust for the use of Constable and disposed of by sections of 100 acres each at the rate of eight livres tournois (equal to $1.50) per acre; in which conveyance it is declared that Chassanis should account for the proceeds of the sales to Constable, according to the terms of the agreement between them, excepting one-tenth thereof.

A deed for 625,000 acres having been made from Constable to Chassanis and delivered as an escrow to Rene Lambot, to take effect on the payment of 52,000 pounds, it was agreed that the price for this land should be one shilling per acre.

This company contemplated certain plans whose execution the stormy period of the French Revolution very probably prevented, as the agreement of Constable and Chassanis of August 30, 1792, was canceled and the tract reconveyed March 25, 1793, in consequence of the amount falling short upon survey, far beyond the expectations of all parties. On April 12, 1793, Constable conveyed 210,000 acres, by deed, for £25,000 to Chassanis, since known as the Chassanis tract, Castorland, or the French Company land.

On April 11, 1797, Chassanis appointed Rudolph Tellier, "member of the sovereign counsel of Berne," to direct and administer the properties and affairs concerning Castorland.

At a very early period a settlement was begun by Tellier and others near the High Falls, east of Black River, and several families were settled. Several extensive sales were made to Frenchmen of the better class, who had held property and titles in France before the Revolution. Among these was Henri Boutin, who purchased about 1,000 acres of Rudolph Tellier, agent of the French Company, on the east side of Black River, and in or about 1798 made an extensive clearing on the site of Carthage village, the immediate locality then and for several years afterward being known as the "Long Falls," in allusion to the succession of rapids or falls in the river.

The natural water power thus afforded attracted Boutin to the place. He and his company of men erected a few buildings for dwelling purposes, and soon thereafter Boutin set out to return to France to settle his business affairs, having determined to make Long Falls his permanent place of abode; but by accident the pioneer was drowned (probably in Black River). His company of workmen soon abandoned the improvement, and the lands passed to Vincent LeRay by purchase from James LeRay as administrator of the Boutin estate.

Soon after the advent of Boutin, Jean Baptiste Bossout came to the place. Bossout is generally known as Battise. He was a native of Troyes, France, and came to America with Baron von Steuben. Like Boutin, he was induced to come to Castorland through the agency of the French Company. After the improvement had been abandoned by the employees of Boutin, Bossout alone remained. All recollections of Jean Bossout denote that he was a worthy resident and enterprising pioneer.

The occasional travelers of this region sought to cross Black River, hence Bossout constructed a rude ferry, charging for its use a moderate toll, and also built on the east bank of the river a small public house. It has been said that he opened the first store on the village site, but this has not been proved.

To these two worthy French pioneers is due the first improvements of the lands purchased from the French Company Land or Castorland.

S. ASHTON
New York, N.Y.

Rulau-E	Date	Metal	Size	Denomination	F	VF	Unc
NY 44	(?)	Brass	(?)mm	3 Pence	—	—	—
		S. ASHTON AMERICAN INN, CANAL ST. Rv: 3 D.					

There are growing indications this is an English token. John Ford believes it is English.

JOHN BARKER
New York, N.Y.

Rulau-E	Date	Metal	Size		VG	F	EF
NY 57	(1829-33)	Brass	—mm		500.00	1000.	2500.

A Washington head is right within olive wreath, AMERICAN REPOSITORY OF FINE ARTS around. Reverse: JOHN BARKER / 16 MAIDEN LANE / DEALER IN / MUSIC PRINTS / & / FANCY /STATIONARY. Only nine pieces are known. (Baker 511; Low 338)

Cut by Wright & Bale, which dates it to the 1829-1833 period.
Barker, stationer, is listed at 16 Maiden Lane 1829-30 in the directories.

BENEDICT
New York, N.Y.

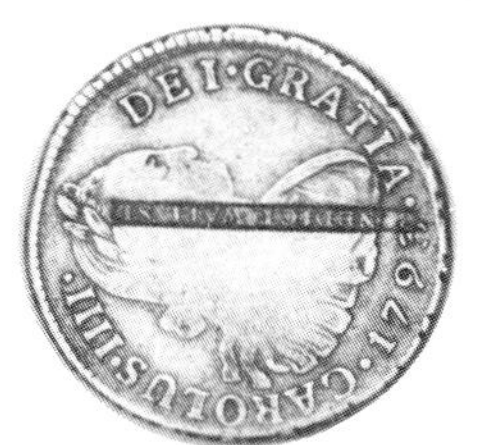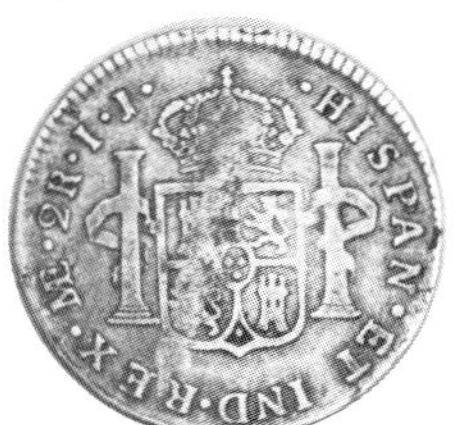

Rulau-E	Date	Metal	Size		VG	F	EF
NY 60	(1820-45)	Silver	27mm			—	300.00

BENEDICT WALL ST. in relief within rectangular depression ctsp on Spanish-American 1793-LME-IJ 2-reales. (Tanenbaum coll.)

This is most likely the hallmark of silversmith Samuel W. Benedict of 5 Wall Street, New York, active in the 1820's to the 1840's.

A. C. BENEDICT (et al)
New York, N.Y.

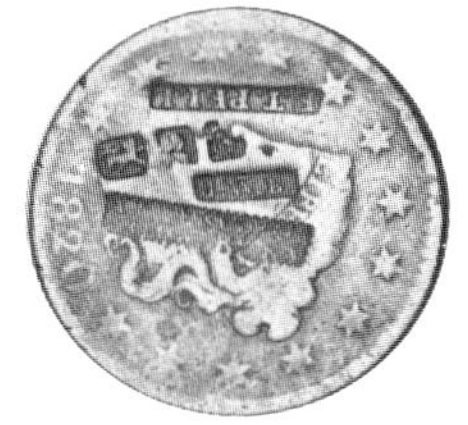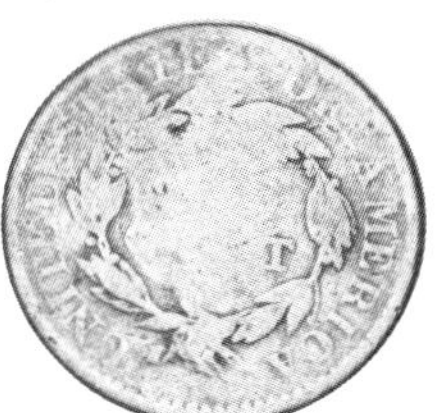

Rulau-E	Date	Metal	Size		VG	F	EF
NY 63	(1827-30)	Copper	29mm			—	200.00 —

Four separate relief counterstamps applied to a U.S. 1820 Large cent, viz: E. T. PELL in rectangular depression; (Lion) (Sheaves ?) G in three square depressions, on line horizontally; J. W. B. in rectangular depression; A. C. BENEDICT / 28 BOWERY N.Y. in large toothed rectangular depression. (Tanenbaum coll.)

Emmett T. Pell was a New York silversmith 1824-41.
The lion-sheaves-G mark resembles the 1890-91 plate mark of Chester, England, but we believe it stands for a still-to-be-identified New York maker, possibly who emigrated from England. (It could be Benjamin Gurnee, N.Y., 1824-40).
Joseph W. Boyd was a N.Y. silversmith circa 1820.
Andrew C. Benedict was a N.Y. silversmith at 28 Bowery, 1827-40.
This token may have been a test piece used successively by several silversmiths to test their punches. It is tempting to believe all the hallmarks were applied at about the same time, but there could be other explanations. We assigned an 1827-30 date to the piece as this range accommodates the known overlap of the silversmiths.

G. BOYCE

Gerardus Boyce, silversmith, was in business from about 1814. He was at 101 Spring St. 1829-1833 and at 110 Greene 1834-1841. His one reported counterstamp is on an 1831 Large cent; the mark is his hallmark.

His name is also given as Geradus, Gheradus and Jared. His counterstamped coin appears in "Hard Times Tokens."

E. BRASHER
New York, N.Y.

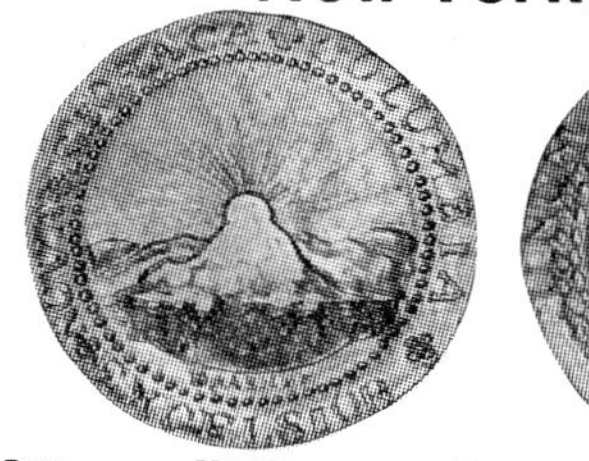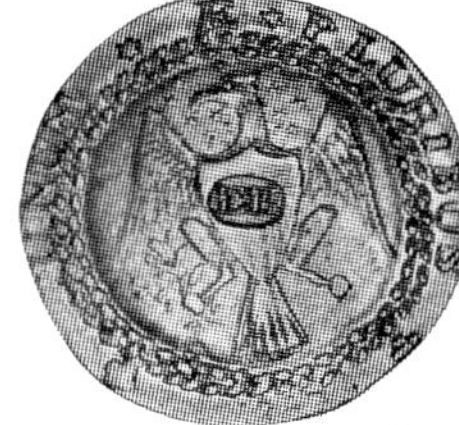

Rulau-E	Date	Metal	Size		VG	F	VF
NY 82A	1787	Gold	30mm			—	625,000.

Sunrise over mountains at center, small BRASHER beneath. Around: + NOVA + EBORACA + COLUMBIA + EXCELSIOR. Rv: Scrawny eagle with drooping wings, U.S. shield on its breast. Above: UNUM * E * PLURIBUS. Below: + 1787 +. Brasher's hallmark, EB within an oval, is punched on the eagle's breast. Unique. Weight: 411.5 grains.

The Garrett specimen, the only known "punch on breast" variety, realized $625,000 in the 1981 Garrett IV sale by Bowers & Ruddy Galleries.

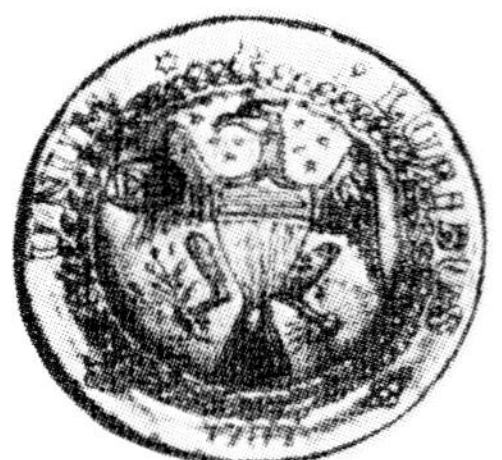

Rulau-E	Date	Metal	Size		VG	F	VF
NY 82B	1787	Gold	31mm		430,000.		725,000.

Similar to NY 82A, but EB punch on eagle's wing. 5 or 6 specimens known. Weight: 407.9 grains for the Ellsworth-Garrett specimen.

Two specimens were sold in 1979, one realizing $430,000 and the other (the Garrett specimen) $725,000. The Yale specimen was offered recently for $600,000.

The Nova Eborac tokens of New York were apparently made by the maker of the Brasher pieces, according to punch linkage study by Anthony Terranova.

Rulau-E	Date	Metal	Size	VG	F	VF
NY 82C	1742 (1787)	Gold	30mm	—	—	—

Imitation of 8-Escudos of Philip V of Spain of the Lima, Peru, Mint, with small BRASHER under water lines beneath the pillars. EB-in-oval punch is at center of the cross. Weight: 407.3 grains for the Newcomer-Garrett specimen.

'EB' PUNCH ON COINS

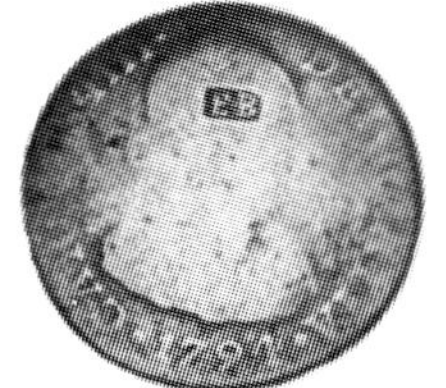 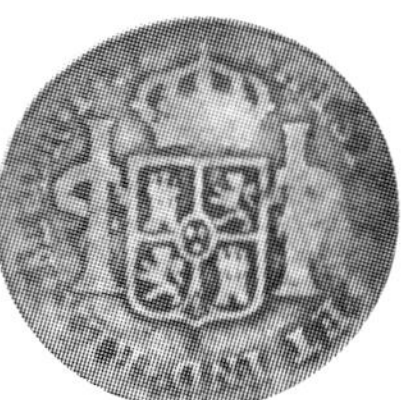

Rulau-E	Date	Metal	Size	VG	F	EF
NY 82E	(1787)	Silver	27mm	—	—	—

EB punch on Spanish American 1794-LME-IJ 2-reales. (Mayfield coll. in 1928, examined and reportedly okayed by Burdette G. Johnson and Howland Wood and Farran Zerbe; sold 1932 to Wayte Raymond for about $300; in Merkin auction of Nov. 1968, lot 521; offered Oct. 1981 by Don Medcalf for $3500.)

NY 82F	(1787)	Silver	27mm	—	—	—

EB punch on U.S. 1811 Quarter dollar. Weight 95 grains. Authenticity questionable; Brasher died in 1810.

NY 82G	(1787)	Gold	16mm	—	—	—

EB punch on England 1718 1/4-Guinea. Weight 31.5 grains.

NY 82H	(1787)	Gold	25mm	—	—	—

EB punch on England 1734 Guinea. Weight: 126 grains.

NY 82J	(1787)	Gold	25mm	—	—	—

EB punch on England 1749 Guinea. Weight: 125.5 grains.

NY 82K	(1787)	Gold	25mm	—	—	—

EB punch on England 1775-1778 George III Guinea. Weight: 123 grains.

NY 82L	(1787)	Gold	—mm	—	—	—

EB punch on France louis d'or (Lot 282 in Kagin's 1983 ANA sale)

NY 82M	(1787)	Gold	32mm	—	—	—

EB punch on Portugal 1755 4-Escudos. Weight: 216 grains.

Ephraim Brasher (1744-1810), was a New York goldsmith. In 1790 the firm became E. Brasher & Co. His marks include E.B in oval, E.B. in square, and BRASHER in rectangular depression. All marks are in relief.

Another Brasher, Amable Brasher, was a New York silversmith circa 1790-1840. His mark was A. BRASHER in relief in rect. depression. A son (?) took the name Amable Brasier and became a silversmith in Philadelphia 1794-1828, using the mark A BRASIER in rectangle.

DAVID C. BUCHAN
New York, N.Y.

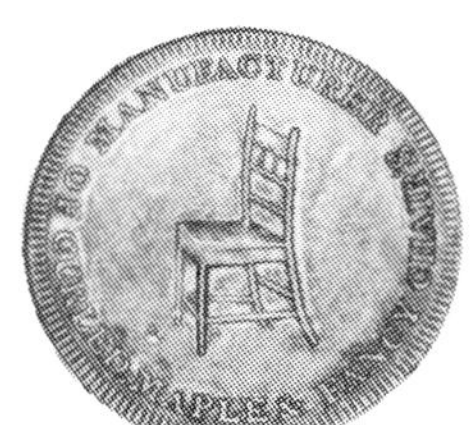 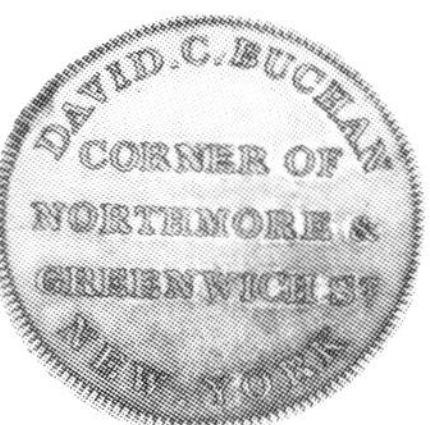

Rulau-E	Date	Metal	Size		F	VF	Unc
NY 137	(1828-31)	Brass	27mm		150.00	300.00	800.00

Chair at center, MANUFACTURERS OF CURLED MAPLE & FANCY CHAIRS. Rv: DAVID C. BUCHAN / CORNER OF / NORTHMORE & / GREENWICH ST. / NEW YORK. (Wright 119; Low 224)

| NY 138 | (1828-31) | Sil Br | 27mm | | 250.00 | 500.00 | 1000. |

As 137. (Low 225)

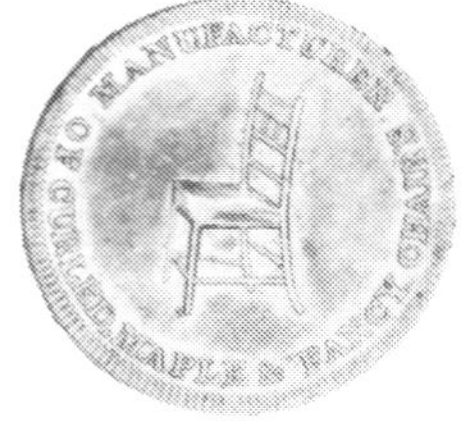 

NY 139	(1828-31)	Brass	27mm		200.00	400.00	800.00

As 137, but NORTHMOORE instead of NORTHMORE. (Low 226)

| NY 139A | (1828-31) | Sil Br | 27mm | | — | Rare | |

As 139. (In ANS collection)

David C. Buchan, chairmaker, is listed at 80 No. Moore St., corner Greenwich, 1825-1827. He then is listed at 364 Greenwich, corner No. Moore, 1828-1841. Both addresses seem to be the same site!

North Moore St. led from Chapel to the North River; it was the fourth street above Duane.

J. CHINERY
New York, N.Y.

Rulau-E	Date	Metal	Size	VG	F	EF
NY 141	(1829-30)	—	—	—	45.00	80.00

J. CHINERY / DIE CUTTER / 205 SM ST. N.Y. ctsp on unspecified coins. (Brunk 89)

| NY 142 | (1829-30) | Silver | 16mm | — | 45.00 | — |

Similar ctsp on Spanish-American half-real.

James Chinery, letter and tool cutter, appears in the 1830 directory at 90 William Street. Chinery does not appear in the 1844 directory. A directory match with the address on the token is needed before further refinement of the issue date is possible.

CLINTON LUNCH
New York, N.Y.

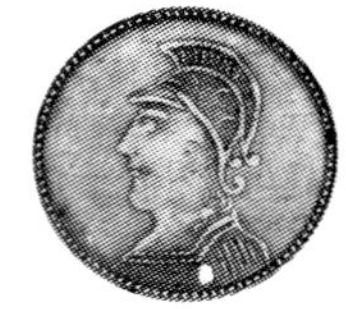 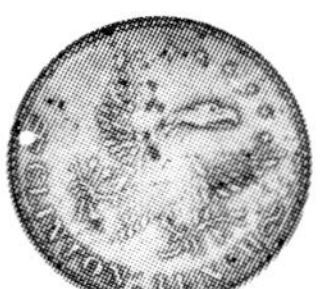

Rulau-E	Date	Metal	Size	VG	F	EF
NY 161	(?)	Brass	19.5mm	—	250.00	400.00

Bust left in crested Greek helmet and cuirass. Rv: Eagle displayed, head turned right, 7 stars above, CLINTON. LUNCH below. (Wright 197)

| NY 162 | (?) | GS | 19.5mm | | 150.00 | 425.00 | — |

As 161.

Dr. Wright described NY 161 as antique 'hand', but it is thought he meant 'head'. The Spangenberger specimen of 162 is illustrated.

In the PCAC sale of May '81, a VF NY 162 brought $425. In the PCAC sale of May '82 an AU NY 161 realized $320. George Fuld notes he once owned three specimens of NY 161 at one time.

W. COLLINS
New York, N.Y.

Rulau-E	Date	Metal	Size	VG	F	EF
NY 165	(1820's ?)	Copper	29mm	50.00	—	—

W. COLLINS / W. COLLINS / W. COLLINS ctsp on worn flat copper planchet, probably a Large cent or British halfpenny. (The top and bottom lines are incused; the central is in relief in a rectangular depression similar to early jewelers' marks.) Rv: N.YORK ctsp incuse on reverse of coin. Plain edge. (Tanenbaum collection)

Possibly related to W. & L. Collins, New York silversmiths about 1829-35. William & L. Collins, silversmiths are listed at 67 Maiden Lane in 1829-30. William Collins also kept a boarding house at 135 Cherry St. in 1830.

DOREMUS, SUYDAM & NIXON
New York, N.Y.

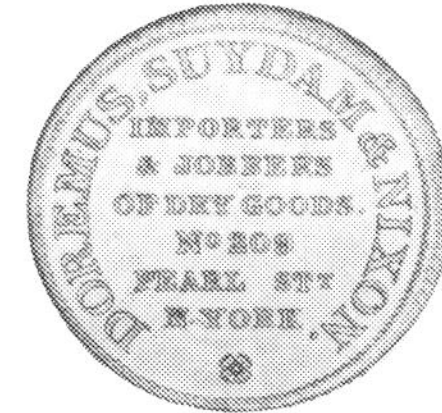 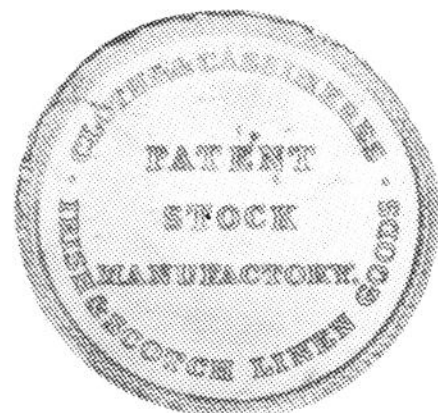

Rulau-E	Date	Metal	Size	F	VF	EF
NY 211	(1831-33)	Copper	26½mm	50.00	150.00	500.00

Inscription both sides. 209 PEARL ST., with period after NIXON. N-YORK. (Low 306)

NY 212	(1831-33)	Brass	26½mm	50.00	150.00	500.00

Same as 211. (Low 307)

NY 213	(1831-33)	Copper	26½mm	50.00	150.00	500.00

Similar to 211, but no period after NIXON. N. York (Low 308)

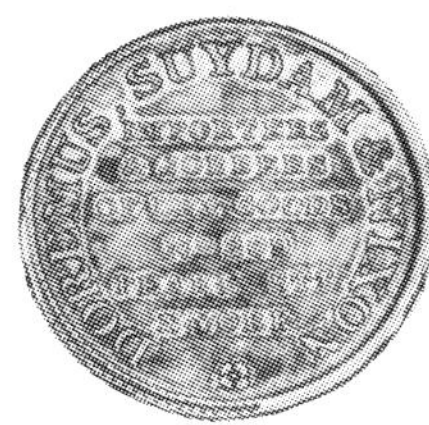 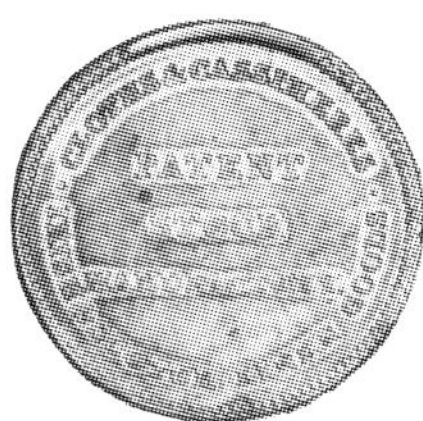

NY 214	(1831-33)	Brass	26½mm	50.00	150.00	500.00

Same as 213. (Low 309)

NY 214A	(1831-33)	Brass	26½mm	50.00	150.00	500.00

Same as 214. Reeded edge. (Low 309A)

This dry goods firm issued a number of tokens spanning the Early American and Hard Times periods. The cards listed above may have been struck for D.S. &N. by Wright & Bale. Trested's business was sold by his widow, Ann, to Wright & Bale on May 25, 1829, and W&B NY (later BALE NY and B&S NY) began to appear on tokens for D.S.&N. Some 1832-33 pieces were included as Low 310-311 under Rulau's *Hard Times Tokens*, still at the 209 Pearl Street address.

NY 215	(1832-33)	Copper	26.5mm	50.00	150.00	500.00

As 214, W.&B. N.Y. on obverse. Rv: LINENS SHEETINGS & DAM-ASKS in center. (Low 310)

NY 216	(1832-33)	Brass	26.5mm	50.00	150.00	500.00

As 215. (Low 311)

THE DOREMUS-SUYDAM DRY GOODS FIRMS

Thomas C. Doremus and James Suydam Jr. were in business as Doremus & Suydam, dry goods store, at 171 Broadway, at least from 1821 to 1826. This became Doremus, Suydam & Co. at 171 Broadway, 1826-1828.

The firm became Doremus, Suydam & Nixon, dry goods, still at 171 Broadway, 1829-1830. The new partner was John W. Nixon. This firm was at 209 Pearl St. 1832-1833; 50 and 52 William St. 1834 until December 31, 1835. According to a note in the 1835-36 directory, the firm moved on New Year's Day, 1836, to 37 and 39 Nassau St. Its address in 1840-1841 was 39 Nassau St., corner Liberty.

The firm name became Doremus & Nixon 1844-1849, still at 39 Nassau St., corner Liberty. In the 1850's the address changed to 21 Park Place. Dated tokens at the latter address are known bearing either 1853 or 1861.

Another firm which apparently did not issue any tokens was composed of Lambert and Cornelius R. Suydam, who may have been related. L. & C. Suydam, merchants, were at 212 Pearl St. 1821-1822; 71 Maiden Lane 1826-1828; 111 Pearl St. 1829-1830.

A third firm was composed of Suydam (first name not determined) and Daniel Jackson. This firm, Suydam & Jackson, Indian contractors, issued Low 1 and varieties, a pro-Andrew Jackson political token of 1832.

Suydam & Jackson, merchants, were at 140 Pearl St., 1826-1828. They became known as Suydam, Jackson & Co. at 140 Pearl St., 1829-1830, and were located at 78 Pearl St., 1832-1835.

Henry (Hy.) Suydam and William Boyd were in business as Suydam & Boyd, dry goods, at 183 or 187 Broadway (there is a discrepancy in the 1830 directory) 1829-1830; then at 187 Pearl St., corner Cedar; 1831-1834; then at 157 Peark St., 1834-1837. Store cards were issued from the latter two locations, spanning the Early American and Hard Times token periods.

The Doremus-Suydam firms were large issuers of store cards from 1831 to 1861 or later. Their dates of issuance are approximately:
Low 306-309A (NY 211-214A), 209 Pearl St., 1831-1833
Low 310-311 (NY 215-216), 209 Pearl St., 1832-1833 (W&B NY)
Low 242-243, 50 & 52 William St., 1834-1835 (BALE NY)
Low 244, 37 & 39 Nassau St., 1836
Low 245-245A, 37 & 39 Nassau St., 1836-1838
Low 245B-245C (NY 219-219A), 39 Nassau St., 1840-1844
(as a result, these latter should be moved from the MT to HTT books)
NY 222-223 (Doremus & Nixon), 39 Nassau St., 1844-1849
NY 224-224-224B, 21 Park Place, 1850-1853
NY 225-229, (mulings), 1853-1861

A.F.
New York, N.Y.

				VG	VF	Unc
NY 167	1824	Copper	23mm	—	Rare	—

A.F. in large Old English letters at center, REMEMBRANCE around, 1824 below. Rv: Open book within rays, small letters partly formed below book. The partly formed below book. The partially formed letters resemble: I L' A L'. Plain edge. (Curto collection)

This is a Communion token.

FRANCIS PATENT SCREW
New York, N.Y.

Rulau-E	Date	Metal	Size	VG	F	EF
NY 265	(1832-33)	Brass	26.5mm	500.00	1000.	3000.

FRANCIS/(rosette)/PATENT SCREW/(rosette)/N. YORK. There are small letters H (?) flanking each rosette. Rv: FRANCIS/FANCY BOAT/(star)/ESTABLISHMENT/NO. 399/& 402 WATER ST./PATENT SCREW.

Joseph Francis, boat builder, was at 402 Water St. circa 1832-1833.

A.S.C.
New York, N.Y.

				VG	VF	Unc
NY 169	1786	Lead	Square, 19 by 19mm	—	—	—

A S C incused across center. Rv: N.Y. / 1786 incused. Plain edge. (Curto coll.)

This is a Communion token, tentatively attributed to New York.

J. FISHER
New York, N.Y.

				VG	F	EF
NY 171	(1821-32)	Copper	29mm	—	50.00	

J. FISHER ctsp on U.S. 1818 Large cent.

Fisher was a silversmith located at 13 Collect 1821-1822 and 138 Mott St. 1825-1826.

J. FOSTER
New York, N.Y. and Winchester, Va.

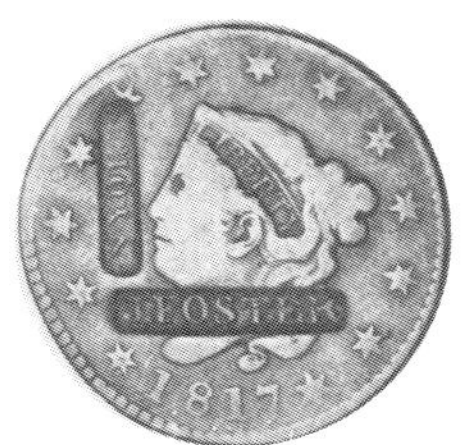 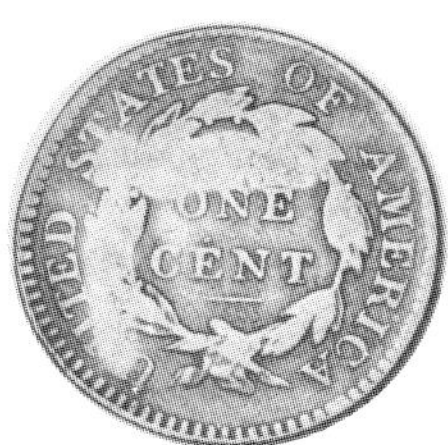

Rulau-E	Date	Metal	Size	VG	F	EF
NY 175	(1820's)	Copper	29mm	—	100.00	—

N. YORK / J. FOSTER, both in relief, within separate oval depressions at right angles to each other, ctsp on U.S. 1817 Large cent. (Tanenbaum coll.)

Silversmith John Foster was in business in New York, N.Y. 1811-17, then Winchester, Va. 1817-25, Woodstock, Va. 1825, and Martinsburg, Va. 1827-35. Most likely this stamp was applied while Foster worked in Virginia, using the old punches as a form of prestige — ''Foster of New York.''

Martinsburg has been in West Virginia since 1863.

GREEN & WETMORE
New York, N.Y.

 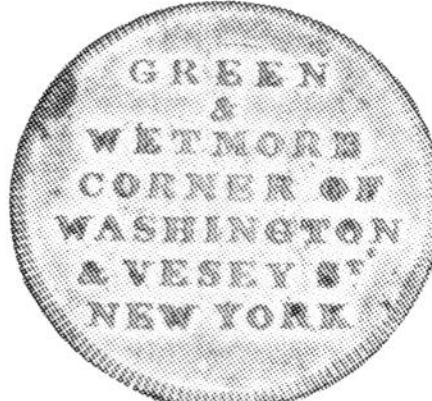

Rulau-E	Date	Metal	Size		VG	F	EF
NY 288	(1825-32)	Brass	28.5mm		35.00	100.00	250.00

Anvil, hammer and tongs at center, DEALERS IN HARDWARE, BAR-IRON / STEEL around. Rv: GREEN /// WETMORE / CORNER OF / WASHINGTON / & / VESEY ST / NEW YORK. Plain edge. (Low 295: Wright 403)

Rulau-E	Date	Metal	Size		VG	F	EF
NY 289	(1825-32)	Brass	28.5mm		35.00	100.00	250.00
NY 289A	(1825-32)	Sil Brass	28.5mm		50.00	150.00	300.00

As 288. (Low 297)

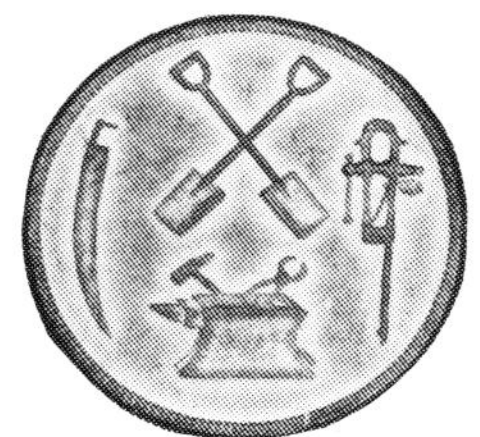 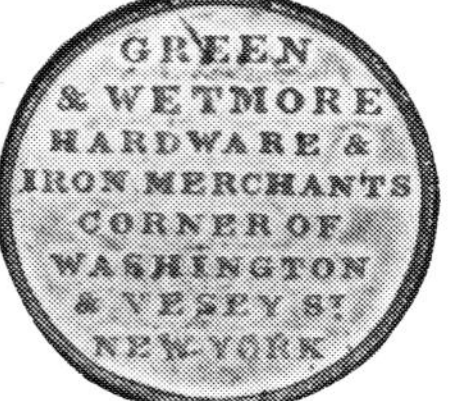

Rulau-E	Date	Metal	Size		VG	F	EF
NY 290	(1832)	WM	29mm		200.00	500.00	1500.

Hardware implements. Rv: GREEN / & WETMORE / HARDWARE & / IRON MERCHANTS / CORNER OF / WASHINGTON / & VESEY ST / NEW YORK. (Low 298)

The hardware implements design of NY 290 is a copy of Breton 561, the T.S. Brown card of Montreal, Quebec, which was struck in Birmingham, England, in 1832. The evidence given in Sandham to the conclusive dating of the Brown card leads to the supposition that Green & Wetmore (and also H.E. Thomas & Co. of Louisville, Ky.) had the same die struck for them in white metal on a trial basis. All these cards are similar to another Canadian token, the J. Shaw & Co. piece of Quebec, Breton 565, dated by Sandham as 1837.

William Green Jr., A.R. Wetmore and D.W. Wetmore founded Green & Wetmore, hardware and iron store. This was located at 194 Greenwich 1821-1822; 179 Washington, corner Vesey, 1824-1833. The firm disappeared in the 1835 and later directories.

A.W. HARDIE
New York, N.Y.

 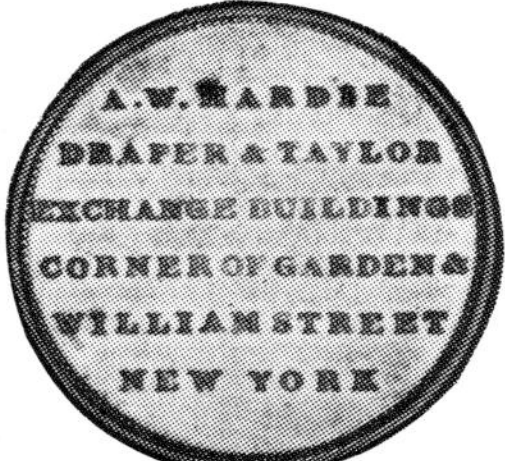

Rulau-E	Date	Metal	Size	VG	F	EF
NY 295	(1826-27)	Brass	31mm	50.00	75.00	150.00

EXCHANGE TAYLORING ESTABLISHMENT / NAKED / AND YE / CLOTHED / ME / (8-pointed rosette). Rv: A. W. HARDIE / DRAPER & TAYLOR / EXCHANGE BUILDINGS / CORNER OF GARDEN & / WILLIAM STREET / NEW YORK. Reeded edge. (Wright 424)

Rulau-E	Date	Metal	Size	VG	F	EF
NY 295A	(1826-27)	Gilt/B	31mm	50.00	75.00	150.00

As 295.

Allen W. Hardie, merchant tailor, appears at the Garden and William St. location only in the 1827 directory. This tailor moved frequently, as the following list of business addresses attests:

196 Fulton St., 1821-1825
183 Greenwich St., 1825-1826
Garden corner William, 1826-1827
173 Reed St., 1827-1828
36 Cortlandt St., 1829-1830
The tokens were struck in Birmingham, England by Thomas Kettle.

ROBERT LOVETT SR.
Philadelphia, Pa. and New York, N.Y.

This early American diesinker was active in Philadelphia 1816-1822 and in New York 1825-1860 or later. His own store card, part of the Hard Times series, appeared in 1833-1834, but he may have been responsible for several early American tokens before the HT era.

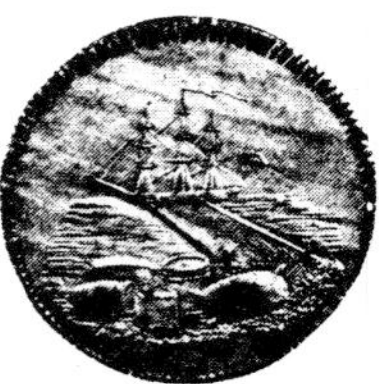 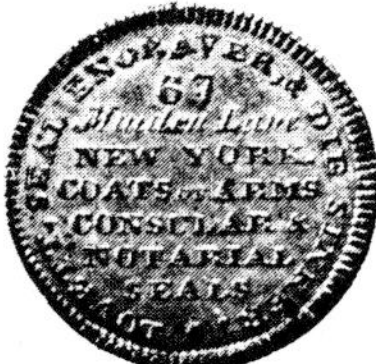

He was the father of three accomplished diesinkers — George Hampden Lovett, Robert Lovett Jr. and John D. Lovett.

This early American diesinker was active in Philadelphia 1816-1822 and in New York 1824-1860's.

Dates	Business	Residence
1816-1822	Philadelphia	
1824-1828	259 Broadway	1824-25 414 Broome St.
1829-1830	297 Broadway	1827-28 63 Church St.
1832-1835	67 Maiden Lane	1833-34 362 Hudson
1840's	183 Broadway	1840's 4 Grove St.
1848-1851	5 Dey St.	
1850's	131 Fulton St.	

F.M.
(Frederick Marquand)
New York, N.Y.

Rulau-E	Date	Metal	Size	VG	F	EF
NY 300	(1823-30)	Copper	29mm	—	40.00	—

F M in relief within rectangular depression ctsp on U.S. 1823 Large cent. (Duffield 1592)

Frederick Marquand (1799-1882) was a New York silversmith of the 1820's. The stamp is his hallmark. (See *The Book of Old Silver* by Seymour B. Wyler, New York, 1937.)

Marquand's jewelry business was located at 166 Broadway 1829-30.

H.M.
New York, N.Y.

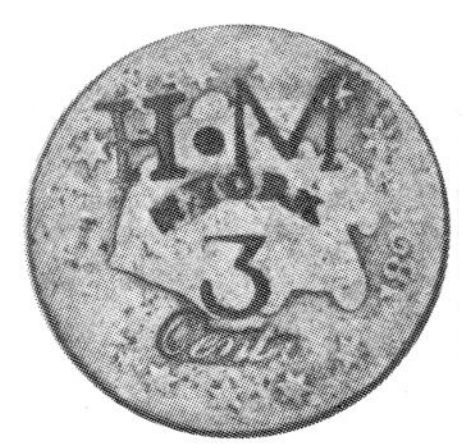 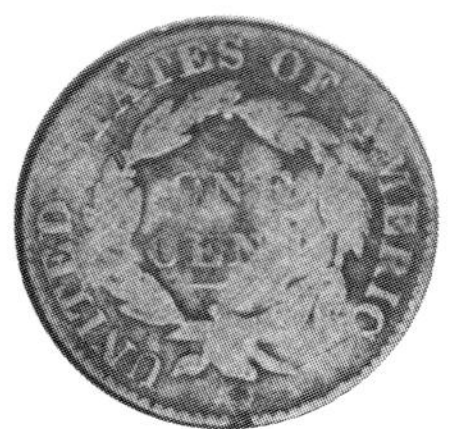

Rulau-E	Date	Metal	Size	VG	F	EF
NY 302	(1830's)	Copper	29mm	—	200.00	—

H. M. / N. YORK / 3 / Cents (relief, in oval depression) ctsp in four separate punches on U.S. 1828 Large cent. (Tanenbaum coll.)

MOTTS, IMPORTERS
New York, N.Y.

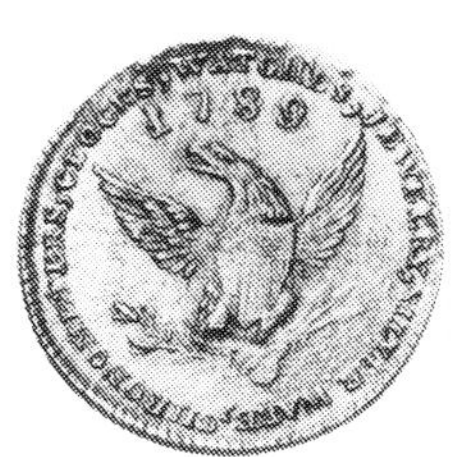 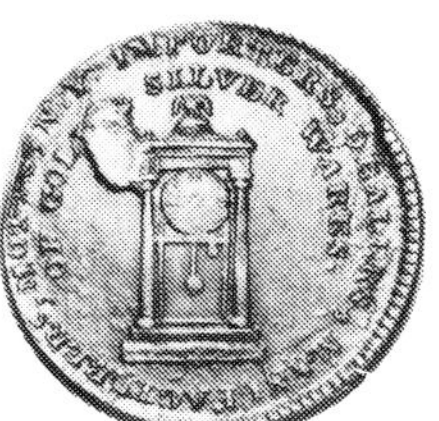

Rulau-E	Date	Metal	Size	Denomination	VG	F	EF
NY 610	1789	Copper	28mm	(Penny)	90.00	150.00	500.00

Eagle with shield on breast, 1789 above. Rv: Tall ornate clock. Thick planchet. Broken dies. (RB: Wright 728)

Rulau	Date	Metal		Size	Denomination	VG	F	EF
NY 611	1789	Copper		28mm	(Penny)	125.00	200.00	700.00
		Similar, thin planchet. Perfect dies. (RB)						
NY 612	1789	Copper		28mm	(Penny)	150.00	400.00	1200.
		Similar, edge engrailed. (RB)						
NY 613	1789	Copper		28mm		285.00	600.00	1550.
		Similar, edge lettered: PAYABLE AT LIVERPOOL, LONDON OR BRISTOL.						
NY 613A	1789	Pewter		28mm	(Penny)	—	—	Ex.Rare
		Similar.						

William and John Mott were importers, dealers and manufacturers of gold and silver wares, jewelry, watches and clocks, located at 240 Water Street, then a fashionable section of New York. In 1789 they ordered the first true tradesmen's tokens of America, probably from an English medallic firm which has not been traced. The thick planchet tokens normally are struck from dies heavily broken on the clock side; they usually weigh about 170 grains. The thin planchet pieces usually are struck from unbroken dies. Perfect-die thick flan and broken-die thin flan pieces do exist.

What is not so well known is that the firm survived well into the 19th century. William & John Mott, merchants, were still located at 240 Water Street 1821-1822. They next appear in the directories listed as grocers for 1827-1828, at 739 Greenwich Street. Still listed as grocers, they appear in 1829-1830 at 154 15th Street, near 7th Avenue. What happened in 40 years to turn the firm from jewelry to grocery needs further study.

A possible related firm which did not issue tokens in its own name was W.W. & R. Mott, hardware store, at 241 Pearl Street. William W. Mott was the senior partner, and this firm appears at this address 1821-1827. Then it became William W. Mott & Co., merchants, at 241 Pearl Street, 1829-1830. William W. Mott died about 1832 and was succeeded in the business by his widow, Susan F. Mott.

The firm of William H. Mott, hardware, issued tokens with the address 'Corner Old Slip & Water St.' On some of the tokens the address is given in error as 'Old Ship' rather than 'Old Slip.'
The firm has not been traced at this Old Slip and Water Street corner back to the 1822 New York city directories, however.
The firm does appear in 1829-1830 as hardware merchants at 396 Hudson. His home at that time was at 442 Greenwich Street. In 1832-1833 his business address was 109 King Street.

WM. H. MOTT
New York, N.Y.

						VG	F	EF
NY 614	(1820s)	Brass		29mm	(Cent)	35.00	50.00	150.00

Anvil, DEALERS IN HARDWARE, CUTLERY, IRON, STEEL. Rv: WM. H. MOTT / CORNER OF / OLD SLIP & / WATER ST. / NEW YORK. (Wright 729)

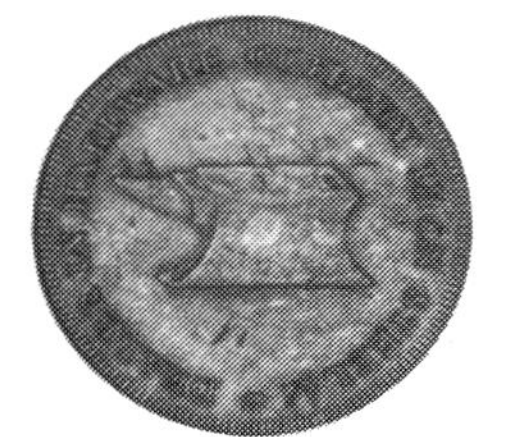
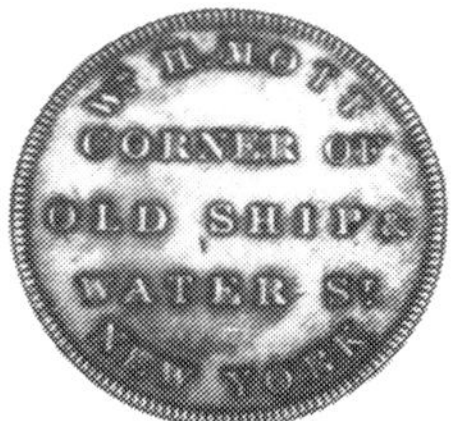

NY 615	(1820s)	Brass		29mm	(Cent)	40.00	75.00	150.00

Similar, but OLD SHIP & / WATER ST. (error)

MOTT ST. LOCKSMITHS
New York, N.Y.

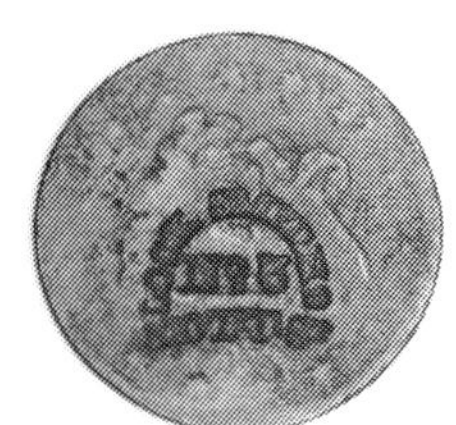
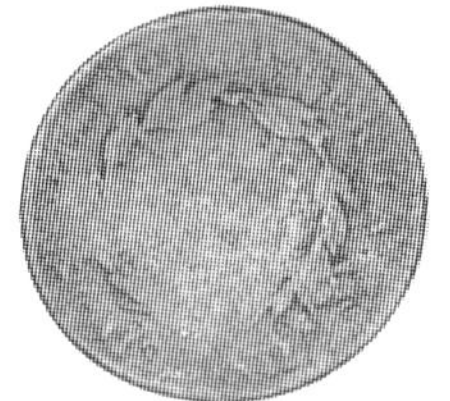

Rulau-E	Date	Metal	Size	Denomination	F	VF	EF
NY 620	(?)	Copper	29mm	(Cent)	—	85.00	—

LOCK SMITHS / NO. 3 / MOTT ST ctsp on U.S. 1820 Large cent. (Tanenbaum coll.)

NEW YORK ASSOCIATE CHURCH
New York, N.Y.

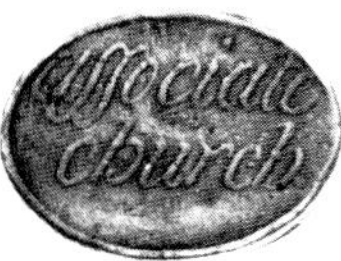
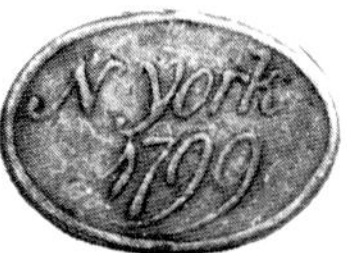

Rulau-E	Date	Metal	Size		F	VF	EF
NY 622	1799	Lead	Oval 23x17mm		300.00	750.00	Rare

(All lettering in script form.) N.YORK / 1799. Rv: ASSOCIATE / CHURCH. There is a heavy raised rim on each side. Plain edge.

The words "associate church" are all in lower case letters, with the Old English "ff" standing for "ss". Robert Vlack refers to this piece as the earliest dated American Communion token. (See Thomas Warner's 1888 "Communion Tokens" in American Journal of Numismatics.)

THE THEATRE AT NEW YORK
(Park Theater)
New York, N.Y.

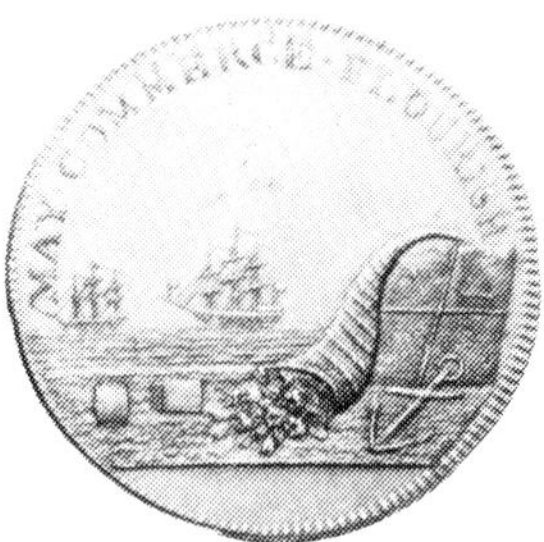

Rulau-E	Date	Metal	Size	Denomination	F	EF	Unc
NY 892	(1797)	Copper	34mm	1 Penny	—	—	5000.

View of the theater's facade, THE THEATRE AT NEW YORK above, AMERICA in exergue. JACOBS in small letters below building. Rv: MAY COMMERCE FLOURISH. Edge lettered: I PROMISE TO PAY THE BEARER ON DEMAND ONE PENNY. (RB; Wright 1130)

NY 893	(1797)	Copper	34mm	1 Penny	—	Rare	—

Similar, plain edge.

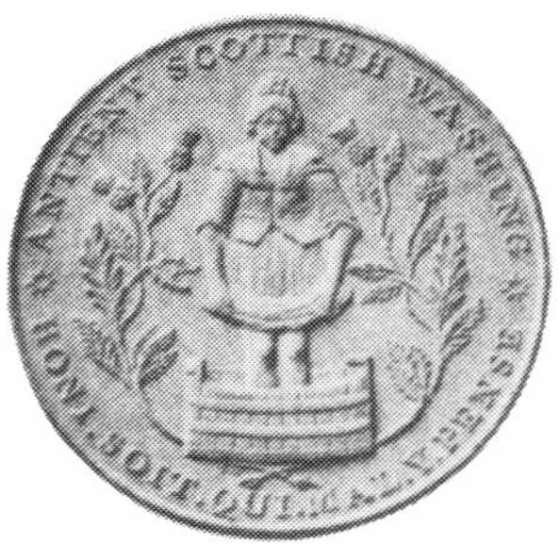

NY 894	(aft 1800)	Tin	34mm	—	—	—	Ex. Rare

Obverse as 892. Rv: Woman treading clothes with her bare feet in a tub. ANTIENT SCOTTISH WASHING — * HONI SOIT QUI MAL Y PENSE *. Plain edge. (Wright 1130A)

This penny token, designed by Jacobs and struck in England by Skidmore, was issued by the Park Theater in New York. The theater was constructed beginning June 1, 1795, and completed in 1798. The proprietors petitioned for permission to erect a portico over the sidewalk, but it was not granted. About 12 specimens of NY 892 are known, that in the Garrett collection of JHU being a proof.
The Theatre at New York/Antient (sic) Scottish Washing token is a muling made in England, utilizing the old die for the American penny. The reverse is the reverse of the Loch Leven penny. It was first published by Dr. B.P. Wright about 1900.
The Loch Leven penny was a 1797 product for Scotland, catalogued as D&H Kinross 1. The muling is not mentioned by Dalton and Hamer, however. Interestingly, the normal Loch Leven obverse (Loch Leven Castle, where Queen Mary was imprisoned in 1567), carries this signature: P.K. FECIT, indicating Peter Kempson of Birmingham made the original copper penny for Scotland.

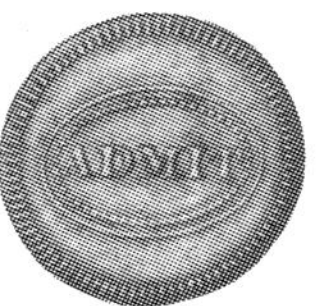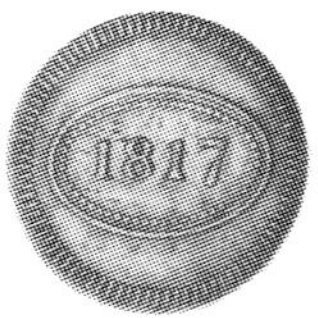

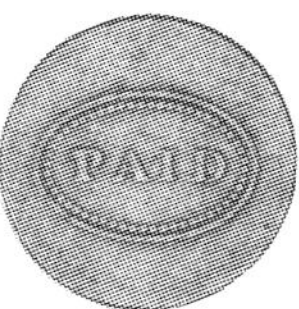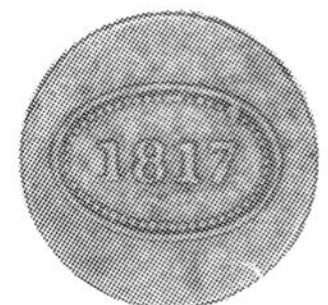

Rulau-E	Date	Metal	Size	Denomination	F	VF	Unc
NY 41	1817	Copper	19mm	1 Admission	7.50	15.00	—

Obverse: ADMIT in horizontal oval. Rv: 1817 in similar oval. Dentilated rims. (Wright 4)

Rulau-E	Date	Metal	Size	Denomination	F	VF	Unc
NY 41A	1817	Copper	19mm	1 Admission	12.00	20.00	—

Obverse: PAID in horizontal oval. Rv: 1817 in similar oval. Dentilated rims.

These two last admission checks to the old Park Theater in New York, opened in 1798. The theater was burned during construction in 1797, again May 25, 1820, and again in 1821. In February, 1824, a grand ball was given for the benefit of the Greeks, then in rebellion against Turkey, and $2,000 was realized. The theater was destroyed by fire Dec. 16, 1848.

The ADMIT and PAID checks were the subject of a special examination by George and Melvin Fuld in the April, 1961, *The Numismatist*. Lyman Low in the Betts sale catalog (1898) attributed their period of use to the 1820-1824 period. We feel the period of use should cover the 1817-1824 period.

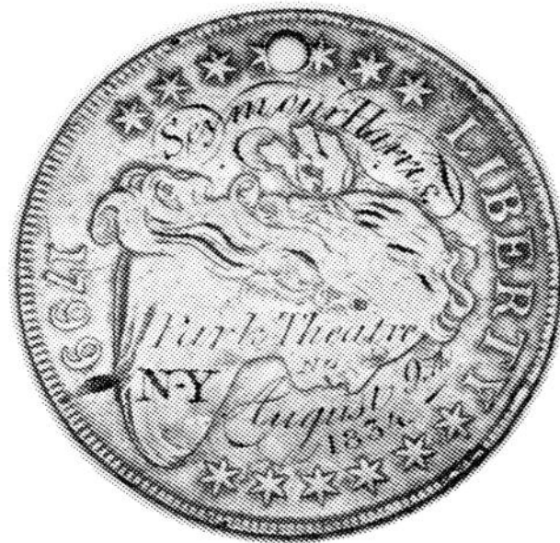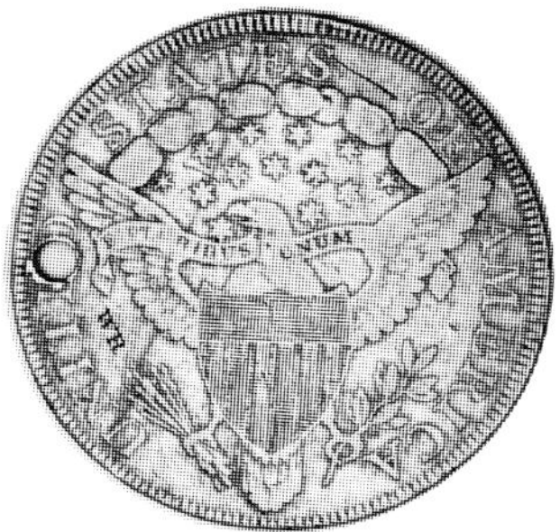

Rulau-E	Date	Metal	Size	Denomination	G	VG	F
NY 42	1834	Silver	38mm	(Memento)	—	—	400.00

SEYMOUR HARRIS / PARK THEATRE / NO. ( ) / NEW YORK, AUG. 9, 1834 engraved on a U.S. 1799 silver dollar. Rv: W.R. engraved on the dollar's reverse. Unique.

This interesting item was in the Maurice M. Gould collection. It may yet provide some clues to the Park Theatre's later existence.

PEALE'S MUSEUM
New York, N.Y.

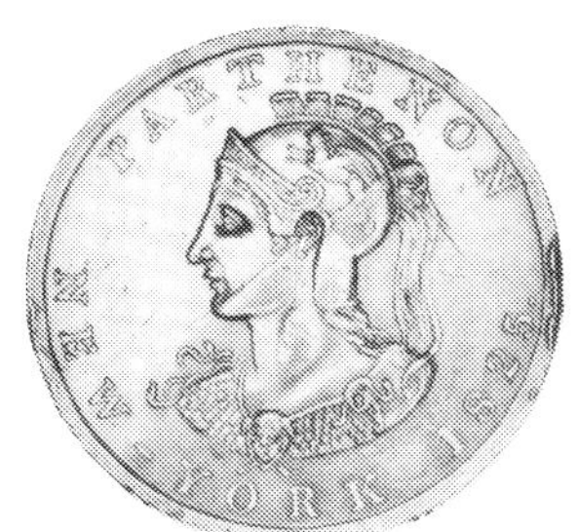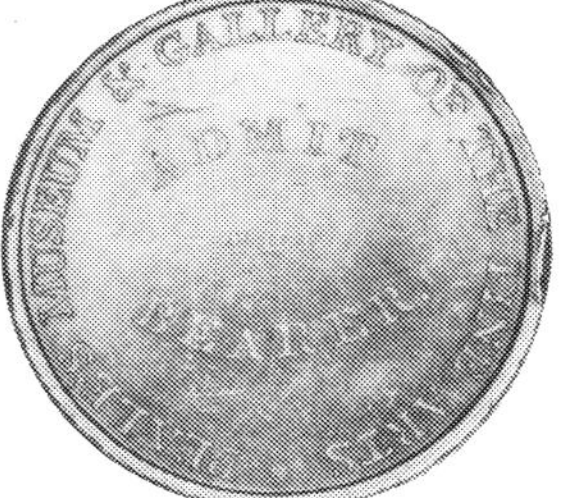

Rulau-E	Date	Metal	Size	Denomination	F	VF	Unc
NY 632	1825	Copper	34mm	1 Admission	50.00	100.00	Rare

Female bust left in Greek helmet and armor, PARTHENON / NEW YORK 1825. Rv: ADMIT / THE / BEARER in center. PEALE's MUSEUM & GALERY OF THE FINE ARTS. (Wright 5: Low 269)

Rulau-E	Date	Metal	Size	Denomination	F	VF	Unc
NY 633	1825	White Metal	34mm	1 Admission	—	—	Ex. Rare

Same as 632. (Low 270)

Rubens Peale established his museum in 1825 in the Parthenon, at 252 Broadway opposite City Hall. The Long Room contained snakes, lizards and an Egyptian mummy. Another gallery contained paintings. Lectures and special appearances were made. In 1831 the museum was renovated and enlarged. Tickets for a whole family for one year were $10; single admissions were 25 cents. The copper ADMIT THE BEARER checks may have been used for annual subscribers. These admission checks were apparently used 1825-1841. The museum was incorporated as the New York Museum in 1841, and in 1843 was sold to P.T. Barnum.

Rubens' father, Charles Wilson Peale, opened the Philadelphia Museum in 1784; he incorporated it in 1821. This museum issued two different types of ADMIT checks, which see. Rubens' brother, Franklin Peale, became chief coiner of the U.S. Mint in 1839.

PLATT & BROTHER
New York, N.Y.

Rulau-E	Date	Metal	Size	VG	F	EF
NY 640	(1831)	Copper	29mm	35.00	—	75.00

PLATT & BROTHER in relief within rectangular depression ctsp on U.S. 1831 Large cent. Another ctsp, J.B. in relief within cartouche, also appears on this piece. (Rulau Z77; Duffield 1594; Hallenbeck 16.517)

The 'J B' has not yet been traced. If it is another silversmith, there are many possibilities. It is not unusual to find coins counterstamped by two unconnected merchants.

George W. and Nathan C. Platt were silversmiths in New York City operating under the name Platt & Brother circa 1820-1831. The counterstamp is one of four registered hallmarks of the firm.

A possible successor, James Platt, may have used the hallmark until 1835 or later. In 1829-30 the firm was at 140 Chatham St.

D. PROSKEY
New York, N.Y.

Rulau-E	Date	Metal	Size	VG	F	EF
NY 641	1799 ?	Copper	29mm	—	85.00	

D. PROSKEY / * / 57 COURTLAND / ST / NEW YORK CITY ctsp on U.S. Large cent, the date of which has been reengraved to read '1799'. (Brunk report)

T. PYE
New York, N.Y.

Rulau-E	Date	Metal	Size	VG	VF	EF
NY 642	(1830)	Copper	23.5mm	—	100.00	

T. PYE / o NEW o / YORK ctsp on U.S. 1809 Half cent. (Tanenbaum coll.)

Thomas Pye, locksmith, was at 143 Leonard St. 1829-30. A successor, Thomas L. Pye, lockmaker, was at 285 Delancey in 1867-68.

JONATHAN RATHBONE &
FRANCIS B. FITCH
New York, N.Y.

Rulau-E	Date	Metal	Size	VG	F	VF
NY 654	1825	Lead	Oval 49.2x25.4mm			

View of Castle Garden, CASTLE GARDEN above. Rv: JONATHAN RATHBONE & FRANCIS B. FITCH, PROPRIETORS, 1825. Flying eagle with scroll. Below scroll is engraved: D POMEROY 890 Only 4 or 5 specimens known.

Rulau-E	Date	Metal	Size	VG	F	VF
NY 654A	1825	S/Brass	Oval, same			2 Known

As 654. (John Ford coll.)

This advertising check was cut by Richard Trested of New York.

Castle Garden was a concert hall and scene of many receptions, including one for Marquis de Lafayette on Aug. 30, 1824. Jenny Lind appeared there in 1850. A reception for Louis Kossuth was held in 1851.

The number 890 on Pomeroy's check was a stockholder or subscriber number. D. Pomeroy was a merchant located at 63 Water St. in Brooklyn. The Pomeroy specimen is in the ANS collection, New York City.

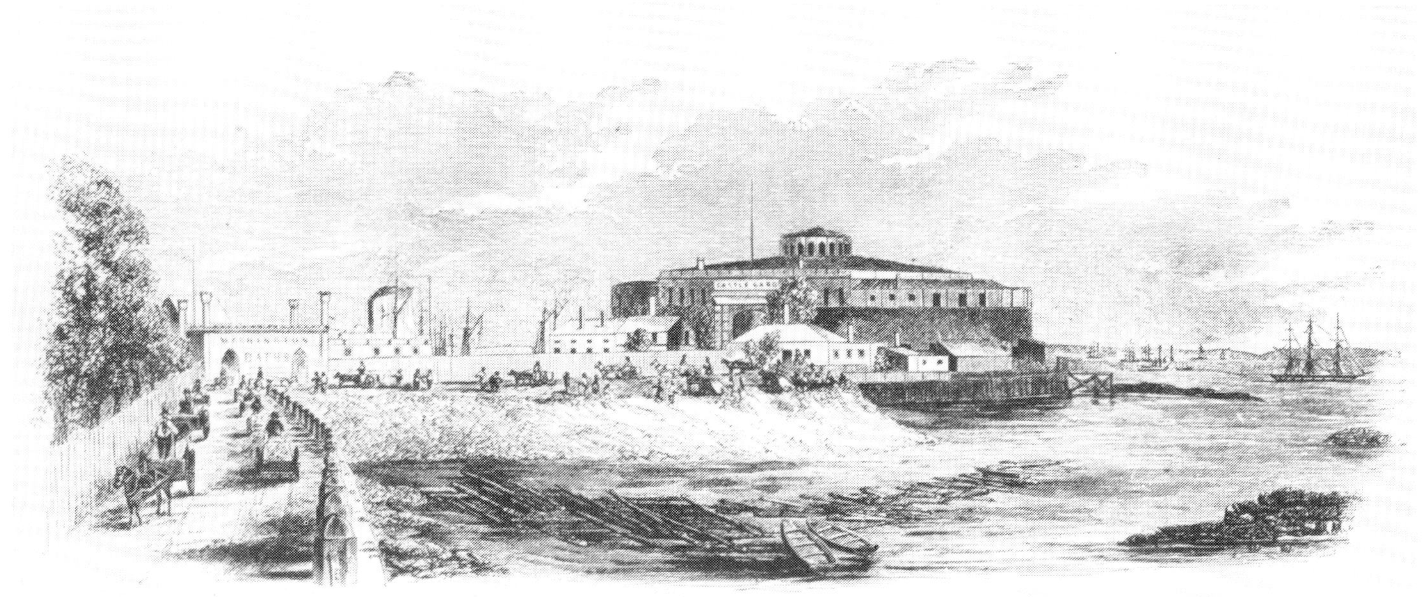

Castle Garden in the 1850's.

RATHBONE, FITCH AND POMEROY

Jonathan Rathbone is traced in the New York city directories at a number of different locations. It seems he moved constantly.
JONATHAN B. RATHBONE, MERCHANT

1821-1822	108 Broadway
1824-1825	Fort Clinton
1825-1826	50 Pearl St.
1826-1827	Castle Garden
1827-1828	29 Old Slip
1829-1830	95 Washington

Frances B. Fitch also moved around a good bit. He first appears as a teacher about 1821 and last appears as a grocer in 1830.
FRANCIS B. FITCH

1821-1822	Teacher	50 Frankfort
1826-1827		61 Canal St.
1827-1828		Whitehall
1829-1830		386 7th Ave

Daniel Pomeroy Jr. was a merchant.
DANIEL POMEROY JR., MERCHANT

1821-1826	60 Front St., Brooklyn
1826-1827	101 Water St.
1827-1830	47 Front St., Brooklyn
	(Pomeroy & Rogers, 60 Front St., 1824-1826)

S + R
(Sayre & Richards)
New York, N.Y.

Rulau-E	Date	Metal	Size	VG	F	EF
NY 660	1802-11	Copper	29mm	—	—	—

S + R in relief within toothed square depression on U.S. 1802 Large cent.

John Syre & Thomas Richards were silversmiths in New York beginning circa 1802-11. John Sayre was born 1771, died 1852. Joel Sayre was born 1778, died 1818. Thomas Richards was in business for himself 1815-34, except for short-lived partnerships in 1815 and 1825.

W.H. SCHOONMAKER
New York, N.Y.

Rulau-E	Date	Metal	Size	VG	F	VF
NY 782	(1829-30)	Brass	26mm	500.00	1000.	—

W.H. SCHOONMAKER BROADWAY N.Y. No. 181 GUNS, PISTOLS, RIFLES & C. Rv: MILITARY GOODS SILVER PLATED BRITANNIA AND FANCY ARTICLES.

Rulau-E	Date	Metal	Size	VG	F	VF
NY 782A	(1829-30)	Sil Br	26mm	500.00	1000.	—
		Same as 782. (Wright 953)				
NY 783	(1829-30)	Ger Sil	26mm	500.00	1250.	—
		Same as 782.				
NY 784	(1829-30)	Brass	26mm	600.00	1250.	—
		Obverse similar to 782. Rv: Bust of Andrew Jackson facing small central octagonal frame, PRESIDENT above. The reverse field is plain.				
NY 785	(1829-30)	Brass	26mm	500.00	1000.	—
		Obverse as 782. Rv: George IV of England head left, GEORGE IV KING OF GREAT BRITAIN.				

The Schoonmaker cards contain mulings of the dies used for the Wolfe Spies & Clark cards (which see).

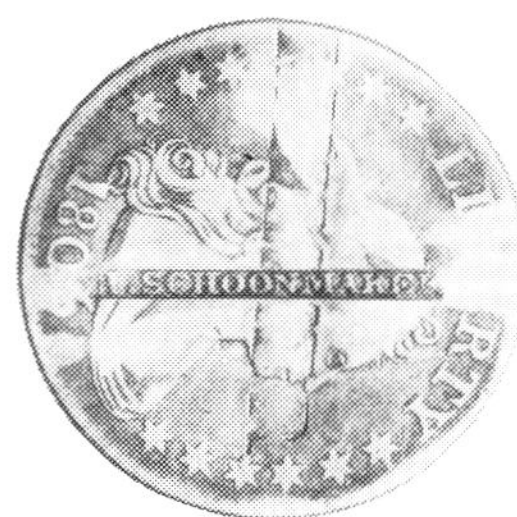

Rulau-E	Date	Metal	Size	VG	F	
NY 786	(1829-30)	Silver	27mm	—	350.00	—

W. SCHOONMAKER in relief ctsp in a rectangular depression on an 1806 quarter.

There is no evidence of connection between the Schoonmaker tokens and the above silversmith-type impression, which is published here for the first time. Yet the coincidence seems too close to ignore.

William H. Schoonmaker, military cutlery and fancy hardware, is first located in 1829 at 181 Broadway. He does not appear after 1830. Thus NY 782-785 must be assigned to the 1829-1830 period, which is consonant with the Wolfe, Spies & Clark cards.

STICKLER
New York, N.Y.

Rulau-E	Date	Metal	Size	VG	F	EF
NY 800	(1821-25)	Copper	29mm	—	35.00	—
		STICKLER ctsp on U.S. 1819 Large Cent.				
NY 801	(1821-25)	Copper	29mm	—	35.00	—
		Similar ctsp on U.S. 1825 Large Cent.				
NY 802	(1821-25)	Copper	29mm	—	35.00	—
		Similar ctsp on U.S. Large Cent, date worn off.				

John Stickler, silversmith, as located at 104 Broadway 1821-1822. His hallmark appears on 1819 and 1825-dated U.S. Large cents.

TALBOT, ALLUM & LEE
New York, N.Y.

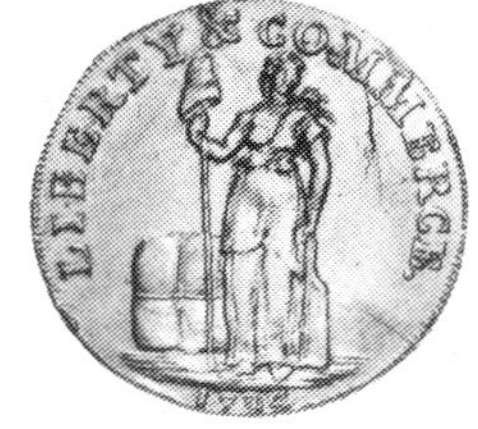 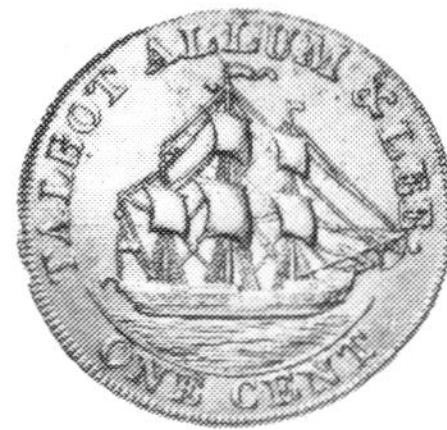

Rulau-E	Date	Metal	Size	Denomination	VG	VF	Unc
NY 877	1794	Copper	29mm	1 Cent	35.00	110.00	800.00

Commerce with Liberty cap on pole, standing. LIBERTY & COM-MERCE. above, 1794 in exergue. Rv: Sailing ship, TALBOT ALLUM & LEE / NEW YORK / ONE CENT. Edge: PAYABLE AT THE STORE OF****. Small d's in obverse and reverse legends. (RB; Fuld 1794-4)

Rulau-E	Date	Metal	Size	Denomination	VG	VF	Unc
NY 877A	1794	Silver	29mm	1 Cent	—	1000.	—

Similar to 877. (Fuld 1794-4)

| NY 877B | 1794 | Copper | —mm | 1 Cent | — | — | Rare |

Same dies as 877, but struck on a broad flan, plain edge. (Fuld 1794-4A)

| NY 878 | 1794 | Copper | 29mm | 1 Cent | — | — | 2 known |

Similar, large '&'. Plain edge. (Has been verified as genuine.)

| NY 878A | 1794 | Copper | 29mm | 1 Cent | 45.00 | 135.00 | 550.00 |

Rulau-E	Date	Metal	Size	Denomination	VG	VF	Unc
NY 879	1794	Copper	29mm	1 Cent	50.00	135.00	560.00

Similar, but '&' much smaller. Edge: PAYABLE AT THE STORE OF, but differently made. (Fuld 1794-3)

| NY 879A | 1794 | Copper | 29mm | 1 Cent | — | — | Rare |

Same dies as 879, but plain edge. (Vlack 5)

| NY 880 | 1794 | Copper | 29mm | 1 Cent | 200.00 | 625.00 | 2000. |

Similar, but NEW YORK omitted from reverse, (RB: Fuld 1794-1)

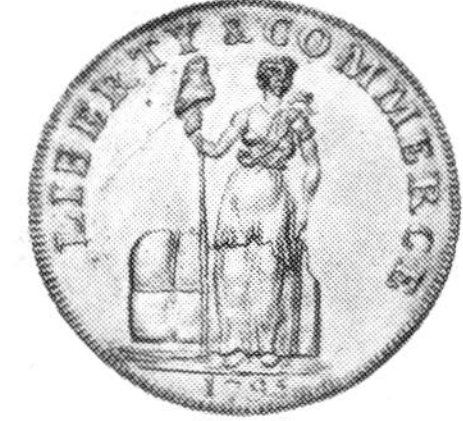 

| NY 881 | 1795 | Copper | 29mm | 1 Cent | 30.00 | 100.00 | 650.00 |

Obverse similar, but date change to 1795. Reverse similar, but ONE CENT omitted. Legend around periphery. Edge: WE PROMISE TO PAY THE BEARER ONE CENT. (RB; Fuld 1795-1; Wright 1088)

| NY 881A | 1795 | Copper | 29mm | (1 Cent) | — | — | Unique |

As 881, but edge reads: CURRENT EVERYWHERE *****. (Fuld 1795-1A)

| NY 881B | 1795 | Copper | 29mm | (1 Cent) | — | — | Unique |

As 881, but edge with twin olive leaves. (Fuld 1795-1B)

| NY 882 | 1795 | Copper | 29mm | (1 Cent) | — | — | Unique |

As 881, but plain edge. (Fuld 1795-1C)

THE T.A.&L. MULINGS

Rulau-E	Date	Metal	Size	Denomination	VF	EF	Unc
NY 883	1794	Copper	29mm	½ Penny	80.00	150.00	250.00

Obverse as NY 877 (Commerce standing with Liberty cap on pole). Rv: Nude boy standing, BIRMINGHAM HALFPENNY 1793. Edge: PAYABLE IN LONDON, balance engrailed. (Fuld Mule 1; D&H Warwick 54)

| NY 883A | 1794 | Brass | 29mm | ½ Penny | — | — | Ex. Rare |

Same as 883. (Fuld Mule 1A)

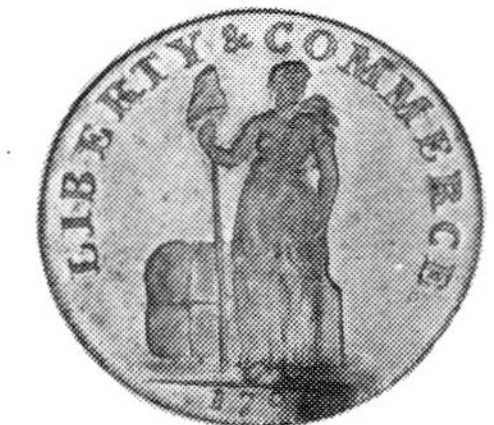 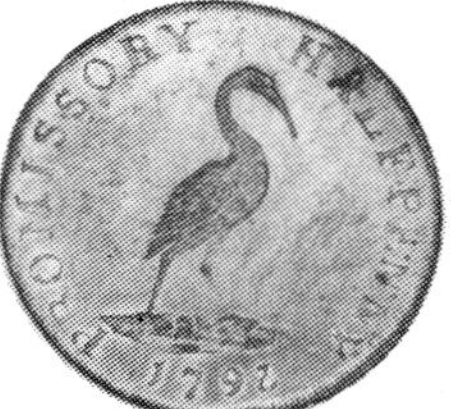

| NY 884 | 1794 | Copper | 29mm | ½ Penny | 50.00 | 80.00 | 250.00 |

Obverse as NY 877. Rv: Stork right, PROMISSORY HALFPENNY 1793. Edge: PAYABLE IN LONDON, balance engrailed. (Fuld Mule 2; D&H Hamps. 52a)

| NY 884A | 1794 | Brass | 29mm | ½ Penny | — | — | Rare |

Same dies as 884, but Brass.

| NY 885 | 1794 | Copper | 29mm | ½ Penny | 100.00 | 200.00 | 350.00 |

As 884, but edge reads: PAYABLE AT THE WAREHOUSE LIVER-POOL ***. (Fuld Mule 2A; D&H Hamps. 52)

Rulau-E	Date	Metal	Size	Denomination	VF	EF	Unc
NY 885A	1794	Copper	29mm	½ Penny	—	—	Rare

Same as 885, but Plain edge. (Fuld Mule 2B) (Donald Miller described this piece erroneously)

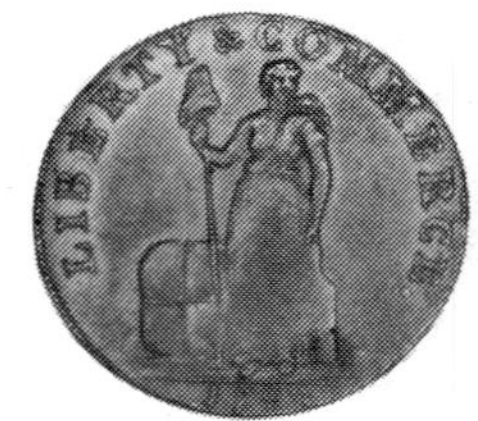 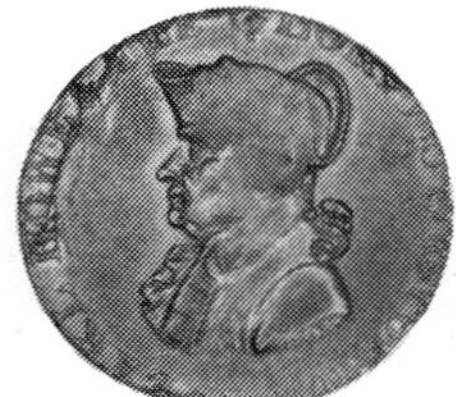

| NY 887 | 1794 | Copper | 29mm | (½ Penny) | 50.00 | 80.00 | 250.00 |

Obverse as NY 877. Rv: Uniformed bust left, EARL HOWE & THE GLORIOUS FIRST OF JUNE, point of hat to H of THE. Edge: PAY-ABLE IN LONDON, balance engrailed. (Fuld Mule 3; D&H Hamps. 25)

| NY 887A | 1794 | Copper | 29mm | (½ Penny) | — | — | Rare |

Similar to NY 877. Point of hat to E of THE. Plain edge. Broken die. (Fuld Mule 4)

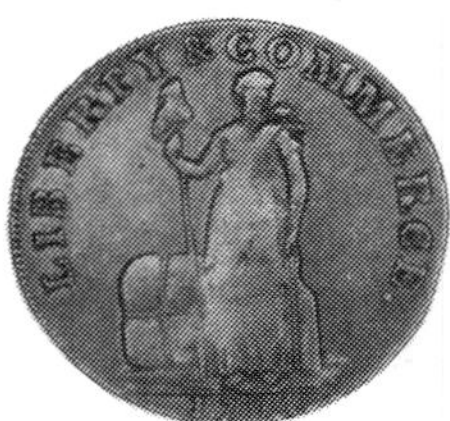 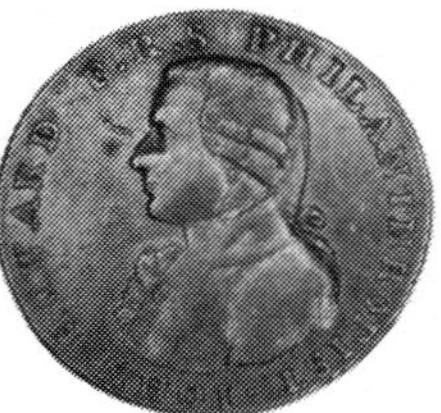

| NY 886 | 1794 | Copper | 29mm | (½ Penny) | 50.00 | 80.00 | 250.00 |

Obverse as NY 877. Rv: Bust left, IOHN HOWARD F.R.S. PHILAN-THROPIST. Edge: X — PAYABLE IN LONDON, balance engrailed. (Fuld Mule 5; D&H Hamps. 56)

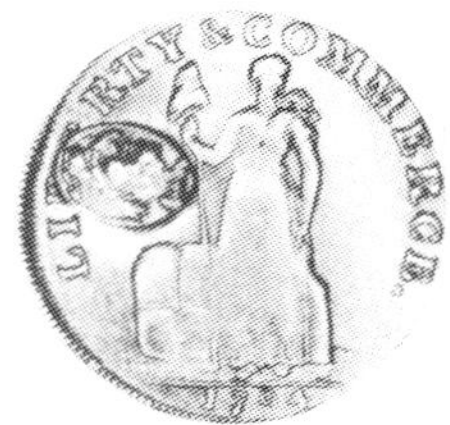 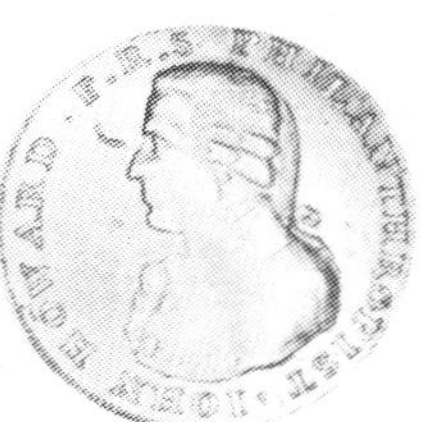

| NY 886A | 1794 | Copper | 29mm | ½ Penny | — | — | — |

Same as 886, but counterstamped with head of John the Baptist for circulation in Malta in 1814. (Vlack collection)

In 1814 the islands of Malta were recognized as a British dependency by the Congress of Vienna. With this turnover, a coinage of sorts was needed for the islands, but England had ceased its coinage operations in 1807.

As a result, some worn specimens of the early George III (1770 to 1775) halfpence were counterstamped with the head of John the Baptist, the patron saint of Malta. The counter-stamp was easily recognized and accepted by the inhabitants as having official status, thus these pieces circulated with little or no difficulty for a short period of time.

There was also a great surplus of English tokens struck during the 1787 to 1800 period, and probably because these were no longer acceptable for trade, some were apparently counterstamped along with the halfpence. Somehow, somewhere, this specimen became one of these pieces, and thus tied Malta to England to America.

| NY 888 | 1795 | Copper | 29mm | (½ Penny) | — | — | 400.00 |

Obverse as NY 881. Rv: Drum, power horn, spears and flag, BLO-FIELD CAVALRY FIFTH TROOP. Edge: Engrailed. (Fuld Mule 6; D&H Norfolk 10)

| NY 888A | 1795 | Copper | 29mm | (½ Penny) | — | — | 600.00 |

Obverse as NY 881. Rv: Cathedral, YORK 1795. Edge: FEAR GOD AND HONOUR THE KING.XX (Fuld Mule 7; D&H York 65)

| NY 888B | 1795 | Copper | 29mm | (½ Penny) | — | — | Rare |

As 888A, but plain edge. (Fuld Mule 7A; D&H York 65a)

| NY 888C | 1795 | Copper | 29 | (½ Penny) | — | — | Rare |

Same dies as 888A. Edge: PAYABLE ON DEMAND. (Vlack Mule 21)

William Talbot, William Allum and James Lee, engaged in the India trade and located at 241 Pearl Street, placed a large quantity of English-made copper cents in circulation during 1794 and 1795. These seem to have been made for T.A.&L. by Thomas Wyon, engraver, and Peter Kempson, manufacturer, in Birmingham, England. Kempson also caused to be struck, using the T.A.&L. New York cent obverse (standing Commerce with Liberty cap on pole, a bale in background, LIBERTY & COMMERCE above) a number mulings with British halfpenny token dies. Though these mules were made for English collectors of the day, they could have (and did) enter circulation to a limited degree. The mules cannot be disso-ciated from the American token series. George Fuld wrote up this series of cents and mules in the *Numismatic Scrapbook Magazine* for September, 1956.

The T.A.&L. firm had a brief, though flourishing, history. The company was founded in 1794, the year the cent pieces were introduced. One of the partners, James Lee, retired from the company in 1796. The firm then continued under the name Talbot & Allum until it was dissolved in 1798.

WM. THOMSON
New York, N.Y.

Rulau-E	Date	Metal	Size	VG	F	EF
NY 900	(1819-33)	Copper	29mm	—	35.00	—
		Script WM. THOMSON Ctsp on U.S. 1819 Large cent.				
NY 902	(1819-33)	Copper	29mm	—	35.00	—
		Similar ctsp on U.S. 1825 Large cent.				

William Thomson, silversmith, was in business in New York circa 1810-1834. His hall-mark in script appears on Large cents of 1819 and 1825.
Thomson was at 177 Broadway, 1821-1822, and at 129 William St., 1824-1833.

TREDWELL, KISSAM & CO.
New York, N.Y.

Rulau-E	Date	Metal	Size	VG	F	Unc
NY 920	1823	Brass	26mm	25.00	40.00	300.00
		Eagle, NEW YORK GRAND CANAL/ OPENED / 1823. Rv: TRED-WELL / KISSAM / & CO. / HARDWARE / CUTLERY / LOOKING / GLASSES/ N.Y. (Wright 1157)				

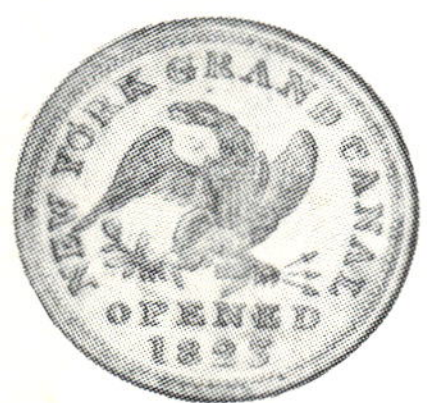
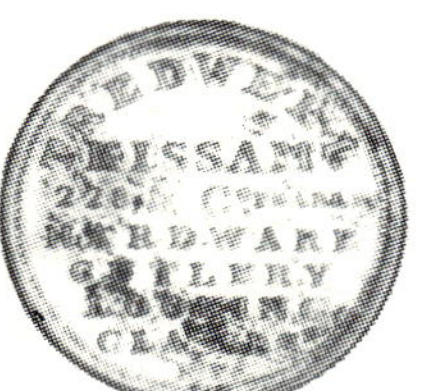

Rulau-E	Date	Metal	Size	VG	F	Unc
NY 921	(1825-26)	Brass	26mm	25.00	40.00	300.00
		Similar, but "228 PEARL ST." added to reverse, flanking "&" CO." (Wright 1156)				
NY 921A	(1825-26)	Copper	26mm	30.00	45.00	—
		As 921.				
NY 921B	(1825-26)	S/Br	26mm	32.50	47.50	300.00
		As 921.				

S. L. TREDWELL
New York, N.Y.

Rulau-E	Date	Metal	Size	VG	F	EF
NY 919	(1833)	Copper	29mm	—	200.00	—
		Both sides same: S.L. Tredwell, 228 PEARL ST. CHINA GLASS & EARTHENWARE.				

Seabury L. Tredwell and Joseph Kissam formed Tredwell, Kissam & Co., hardware, located at 245 Pearl Street, 1821-1825, and at 228 Pearl Street 1825-1833. They moved to 228 Pearl Street before November in 1825.
Seabury Tredwell was in business alone as S.L. Tredwell at 228 Pearl Street in 1833 and later.
NY 920 without address can be assigned to 1823, the date on the token. NY 921 to 921B at 228 Pearl St. emanated from the 1825-1826 period. NY 919 of S.L. Tredwell was issued, apparently, in 1833, so it really belongs in the Hard Times period.

RICHARD TRESTED
New York, N.Y.

Rulau-E	Date	Metal	Size	Denomination	VG	F	VF
NY 925	(1823-24)	Copper	27mm	(Cent)	—	—	Unique
		Eagle displayed, radiant Liberty Cap above. Rv: TRESTED 68 WIL-LIAMS ST. Struck over a U.S. cent. (Die trial)					

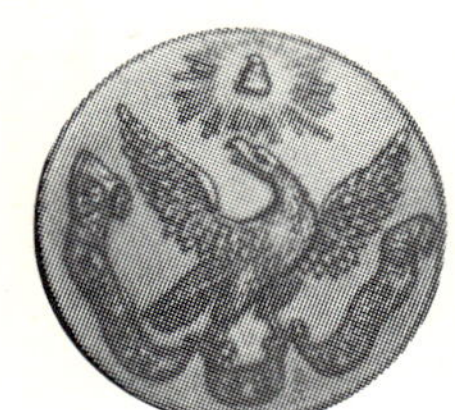
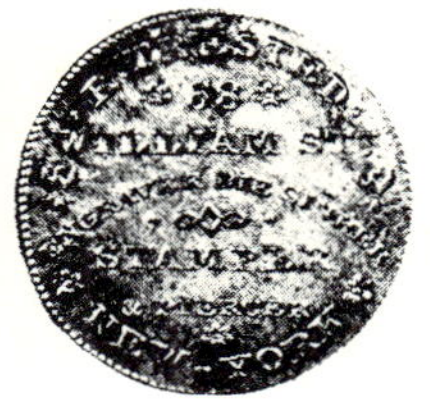

Rulau-E	Date	Metal	Size	Denomination	VG	F	VF
NY 924	(1823-24)	Brass	27mm	(Cent)	—	—	5000.
		Similar to 925, but R. TRESTED. Rosettes flank NEW YORK.					

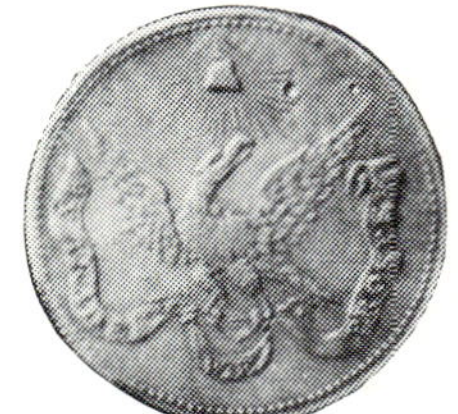
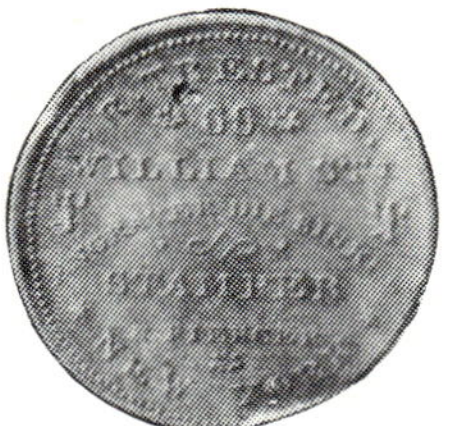

Rulau-E	Date	Metal	Size	Denomination	VG	F	VF
NY 924A	(1823-24)	Brass	27mm	(Cent)	—	—	Ex. Rare
		As 924, but small stars flank NEW YORK.					

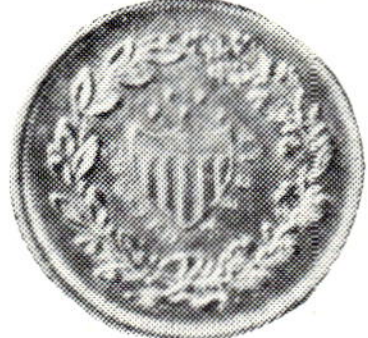
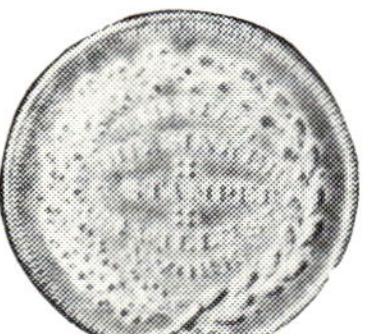

Rulau-E	Date	Metal	Size	Denomination	VG	F	VF
NY 922	(1825-29)	Brass	24mm		500.00	1250.	2000.
		U.S. Shield within wreath, TRESTED FECIT below. Rv: TRESTED / DIE SINKER / AND STAMPER / 68 WILLM. ST. / N. YORK within wreath. (Wright 1159)					
NY 923	(1825-29)	Brass	24mm	6 Cents	300.00	500.00	750.00
		Obverse similar to 922. Rv: SIX / CENTS, three rosettes and two stars.					

Trested, an Englishman, is first traced as an engraver in 1821 at 70 William St. From 1823-1827 he was at 68 William Street, and occupied quarters at both 68 William Street and 76 Maiden Lane 1828-1829. He died Jan. 13, 1829. The cause of death was complications resulting from an amputated finger. On May 25, 1829, his widow Ann sold his engraving and diesinking business to Charles Cushing Wright and James Bale. Bale had been Trested's apprentice.
Trested, one of New York's earliest token-makers, cut his own and the Castle Garden cards, and may have done the earliest Doremus, Suydam & Nixon tokens. He also seems to have done token work for the Scovills in Waterbury, Conn.

WASHINGTON MARKET CHOWDER
CLUB
New York, N.Y.

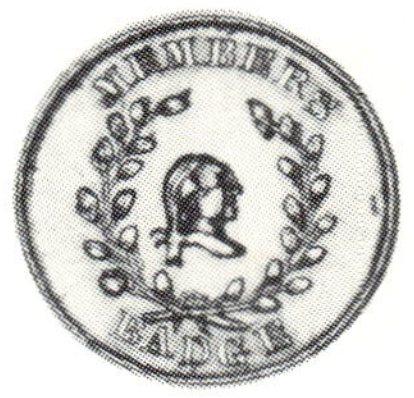
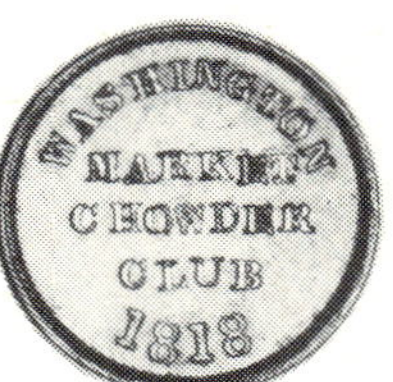

Rulau-E	Date	Metal	Size	Denomination	VG	F	EF
NY 930	1818	Silver	24mm	Admission	—	—	4 known
		Small George Washington head right within olive wreath, MEMBERS above, BADGE below. Rv: WASHINGTON/ MARKET / CHOWDER / CLUB / 1818. (Baker 338)					
NY 931	1818	Gold	24mm	Admission	—	—	25,000.
		As last. (Baker 338). The only traceable specimen was in the Johns Hopkins University collection. It was ex-J.N.T. Levick collection.					

The club may have been a fraternal group, or a marching or singing organization. Nothing is known of it.

WELLES & GELSTON
New York, N.Y.

Rulau-E	Date	Metal	Size	VG	F	EF
NY 933	(1840)	Copper	29mm	—	40.00	—
		..... D & GELSTON ctsp on U.S. 1819 Large cent.				

It was once thought this partial inscription stood for silversmiths Gould & Gelston of Baltimore, but that firm was always known only as Gelston & Gould (circa 1816-1820). Most likely the 'D' is a misreading by Maurice M. Gould or others for 'S'.

WILLIS & BROTHERS
New York, N.Y.

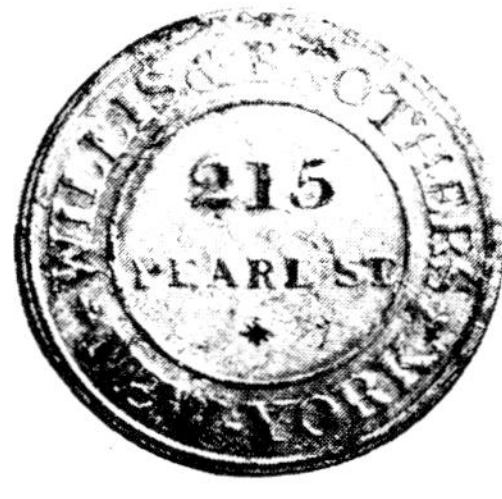 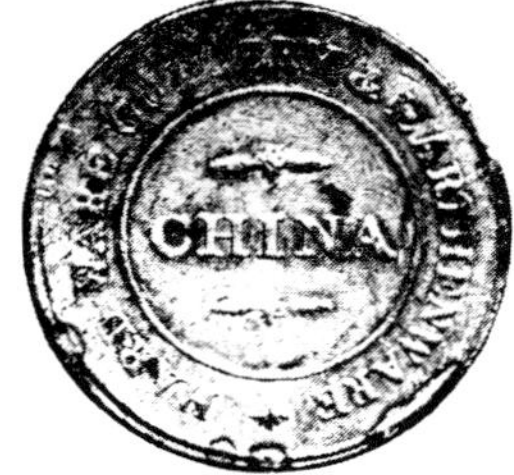

Rulau-E	Date	Metal	Size		G	VG	F
NY 954	(1830-32)	Tin	33mm		200.00	500.00	1000.

WILLIS & BROTHERS / 215 / PEARL ST / NEW-YORK. Rv: HARD-WARE CUTLERY & EARTHENWARE around, CHINA in center.

John R. Willis, the senior partner, and Alfred Willis and William H. Willis, were ironmongers and sold hardware and crockery at 276 Pearl St., 1829-1833.

C. & I.D. WOLFE
New York, N.Y.

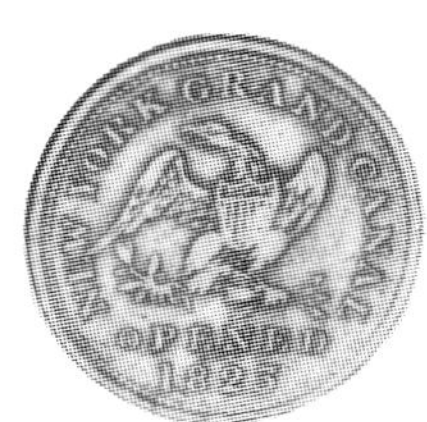 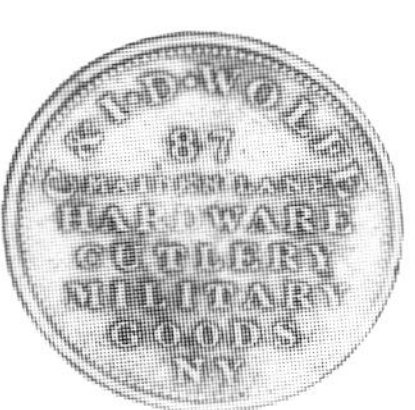

Rulau-E	Date	Metal	Size		VG	F	EF
NY 957	1823	Brass	26mm		15.00	22.50	50.00

Eagle displayed, NEW YORK GRAND CANAL / OPENED / 1823. Rv: C. & I. D. WOLFE / 87 / MAIDEN LANE / HARDWARE / CUT-LERY / MILITARY / GOODS / N.Y. (Wright 1263) Plain edge.

NY 957A	1823	Sil Br	26mm	—	20.00	30.00	50.00

As 957. Reeded edge.

NY 957B	1823	Brass			—	—	50.00

Reeded edge. As 957.

The exact same obverse die (Eagle displayed, head turned left, U.S. shield on breast GRAND CANAL 1823) was used also on cards of C. Wolfe, Spies & Clark; and Tredwell, Kissam & Co.

C. WOLFE, CLARK & SPIES
New York, N.Y.

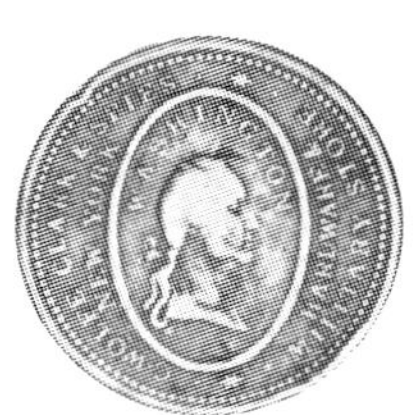 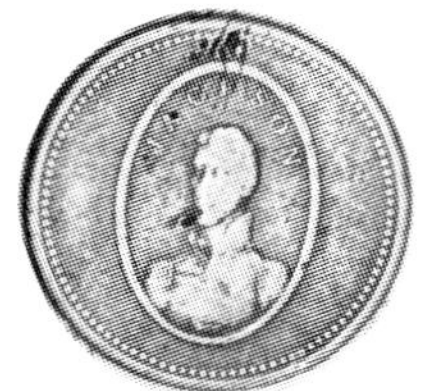

Rulua-E	Date	Metal	Size		VG	F	EF
NY 958	(1829)	Brass	26mm		500.00	1250.	2000.

Washington head right in central oval, WASHINGTON above; C. WOLFE CLARK & SPIES NEW YORK HARDWARE & MILITARY STORE around. Rv: Jackson head facing three-quarters left, JACKSON above; plain field. Reeded edge. (Baker 588)

NY 958A	(1829)	Copper	26mm		—	—	—

Same as 958. Reeded edge. All known 958A in copper are counterfeits.

At this late juncture, it seems unlikely we'll find out why this firm proceeded to change the ranking of its partners to C. Wolfe, Spies & Clark as in the examples which follow.

C. WOLFE, SPIES & CLARK
New York, N.Y.

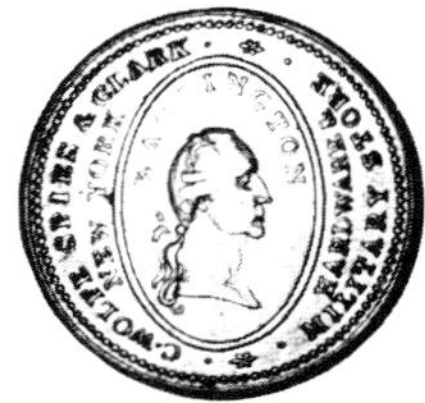 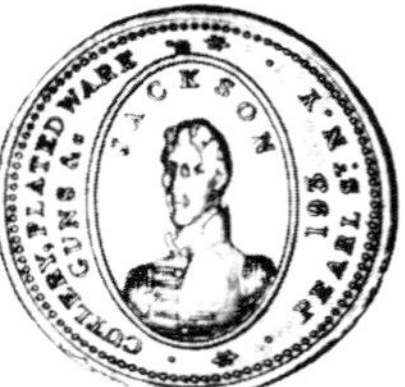

Rulau-E	Date	Metal	Size		VG	F	EF
NY 962	(1829-30)	Brass	26mm		500.00	1250.	2000.

Similar to obverse of NY 958 but name change. Rv: Central oval with Jackson military bust facing as on 958, but field now carries: CUTLERY, PLATED WARE / GUNS &C / 193 / PEARL ST. N.Y. Reeded edge. (Baker 589)

NY 962A	(1829-30)	Sil Br	26mm		550.00	900.00	Rare

As 962. Reeded edge.

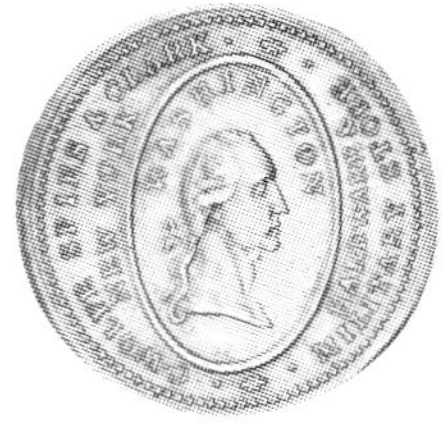 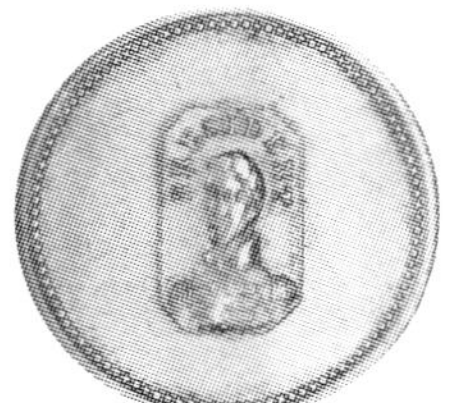

NY 959	(1829-30)	Brass	26mm		750.00	1250.	2000.

Obverse as 962. Rv: Jackson military bust facing three-quarters left in octagonal frame, PRESIDENT above; plain field. (Baker 590)

NY 960	(1829-30)	Copper	26mm		—	—	—

Same as 959. All copper pieces examined have been electrotype copies.

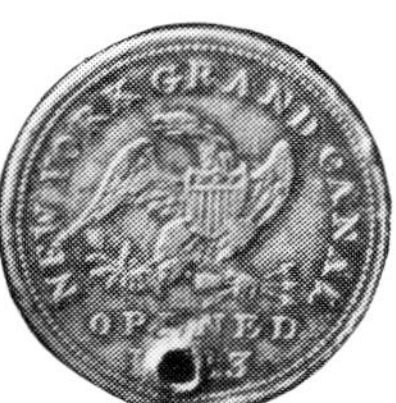

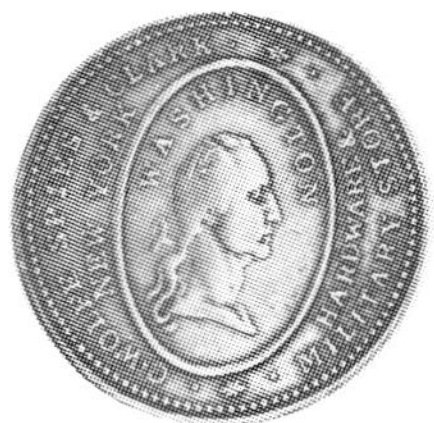 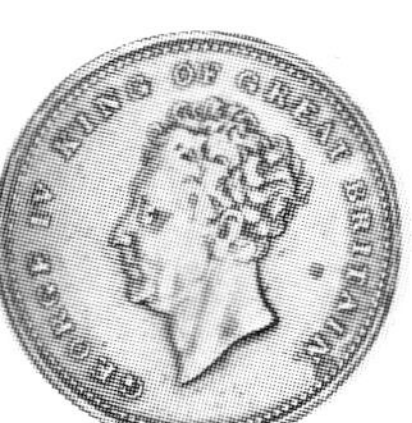

NY 961	1823 (1829)	Brass	26mm		550.00	1500.	—

Obverse as 962. Rv: Eagle and NEW YORK CANAL GRAND OPENED 1823. (Wright 1261; Baker 591)

NY 963	(1829-30)	Brass	26mm		550.00	2500.	—

Obverse as 962. Rv: Head left, GEORGE IV, KING OF GREAT BRIT-AIN. (Baker 592)

Andrew Jackson campaigned for the presidency in 1824, losing to John Quincy Adams. He won the presidency in 1828. George IV ascended the British throne in 1820.

The firm of C. & J. D. Wolfe (it reads C. & I. D. Wolfe on its tokens) traces its origins back before the war of 1812. It sold military and naval supplies, hardware and cutlery.

The 'C.' was Christopher Wolfe and the 'I. D.' was John D. Wolfe. The firm was located at 87 Maiden Lane opposite Clark & Brown's Coffee House; the business was located at the corner of Maiden Lane and Gold Street. John D. Wolfe married Miss. Lorillard of the tobacco family and was reputed to be very wealthy.

C. & J. D. Wolfe appears in New York city directories at 87 Maiden Lane 1821-1828. About 1829 the firm dissolved.

Christopher Wolfe joined with Adam W. Spies and R. Smith Clark to form Wolfe, Clark & Spies in 1829, quickly changing the name to Wolfe, Spies & Clark, hardware, cutlery and military goods, at 193 Pearl Street, 1829-1833.

John D. Wolfe formed J. D. Wolfe, Bishop & Co., hardware and military goods, still located at 87 Maiden Lane, 1829-1833.

NY 957 and 957A, dated 1823, could have been in use as late as 1828. They were probably struck by Thomas Kettle.

NY 958 and 958A, without address, may have been struck by Kettle in 1829. NY 959 through 963 were struck, apparently, in the 1829-1830 period. NY 961 uses an 1823-dated die in an early example of U.S. muling, but directory evidence now shows this token could not have appeared before 1829. (See *Coin Collector's Journal* for January, 1935)

WRIGHT & BALE
New York, N.Y.

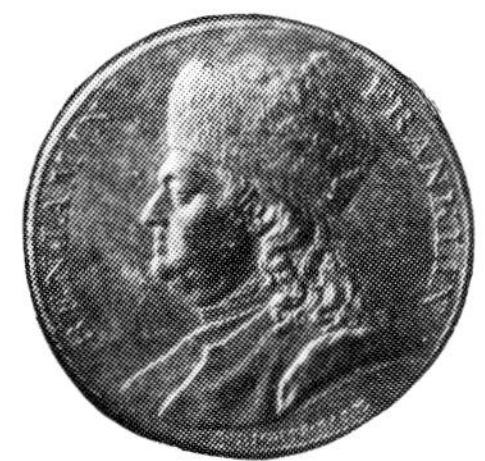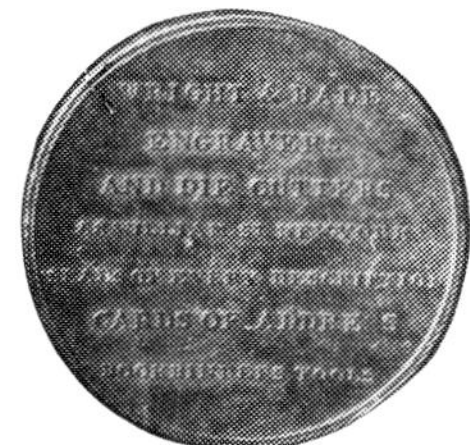

Rulau-E	Date	Metal	Size		F	VF	Unc
NY 1001	(1829-30)	Copper	30mm		2000.	—	Rare

Fur capped bust of Franklin left, BENJAMIN FRANKLIN around. Below: WRIGHT & BALE. Rv: WRIGHT & BALE / ENGRAVERS / AND DIE CUTTERS / 68 WILLIAM ST. NEW YORK / . . . . . OF EVERY DESCRIPTION / CARDS OF ADDRESS / BOOKBINDERS TOOLS. (Low 329)

Rulau-E	Date	Metal	Size		F	VF	Unc
NY 1000	(1829-30)	Brass	30mm		2000.	—	—

As 1001. (Low 330)

Rulau-E	Date	Metal	Size		F	VF	Unc
NY 1002	(1832-33)	Copper	19mm		150.00	300.00	750.00

Head of George Washington right within large oak wreath. Rv: WRIGHT & BALE / ENGRAVERS / & DIE / CUTTERS / 68 NASSAU STREET / PLATES & ROLLS / FOR EMBOSSING / DIES & SEALS OF / EVERY / DESCRIPTION / NEW-YORK. Thick planchet. (Wright 1275; Low 331)

Rulau-E	Date	Metal	Size		F	VF	Unc
NY 1003	(1832-33)	Copper	19mm		200.00	350.00	750.00

Same as 1002, but thin flan. (Low 332; Baker 594)

HENDERSON & LOSSING
Poughkeepsie, N.Y.

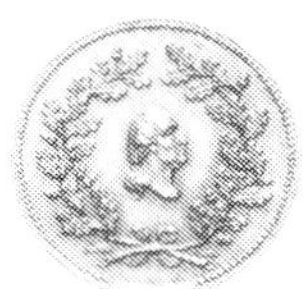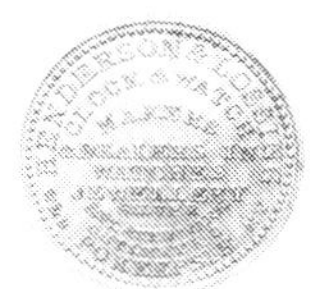

Rulau-E	Date	Medal	Size		F	VF	Unc
NY 1017	(1829-33)	Copper	15mm		300.00	750.00	1750.

Washington head right within oak wreath. Rv: HENDERSON & LOSSING / CLOCK & WATCH / MAKERS / & DEALERS IN / WATCHES / JEWELLERY / SILVER / W&B POKEEPSIE NY. Plain edge. (Low 317)

This card was cut by Wright & Bale, whose initials W&B NY appear on the text side; a Washington head in oak wreath adorns the obverse.

Benson J. Lossing gave up the cares of business in 1835, at age 22, to study art and literature. He became a well known historian. The date of the token is hard to fix, but it likely appeared in the 1830-1833 period.

WATERVLIET ARSENAL
Watervliet, N.Y.

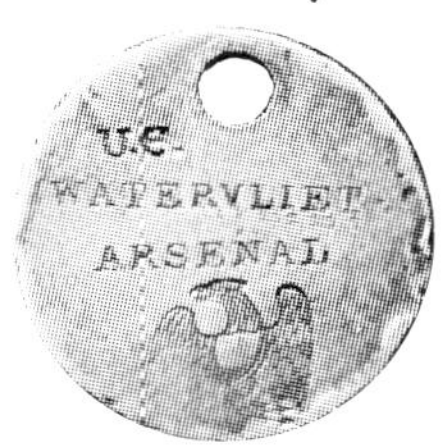

Rulau-E	Date	Metal	Size		VG	F	EF
NY 1050	(1816-30)	Copper	29mm		—	100.00	—

U.S. / WATERVLIET / ARSENAL / (eagle with shield on its breast) in four lines, ctsp on worn U.S. 1794 Large cent. Issued holed. (Frank Kovacs coll.)

Watervliet, in Albany County on the Hudson River, is a cross-river community from Troy.

The Watervliet Arsenal's activities peaked in the 1820's and 1830's, according to Ed Green, curator of the Army Museum at the Presidio of San Francisco, Calif. By the Civil War Watervliet was making only leather items for the Army, but it was noted earlier for cannon and coastal guns. It stopped using the name 'U.S.' Watervliet Arsenal in 1872.

Curator Green dated the token above definitely to earlier than 1835. The style of eagle, he pointed out, is very similar to that impressed on 1816 muskets, and this style was changed in 1835. He said the piece probably was used as a key tag.

The museum curator said many items such as this counterstamp have surfaced in excavations, etc., and that these were used as key tags, identification discs, etc. by armory personnel.

For a discussion on counterstamped coins found on Army installations, see *Material Culture Study of Fort Bowie* by Dave Herskovicz.

A. C. OF HEBRON
(Associate Church of Hebron)
West Hebron, N.Y.

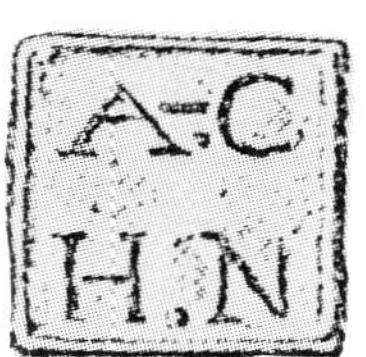

Rulau-E	Date	Metal	Size				
NY 1060	1807	Lead	sq 22x22mm		—	—	—

A. - C. / H. N in two lines. Rv: 1807. Raised border. Plain edge. (Warner 54)

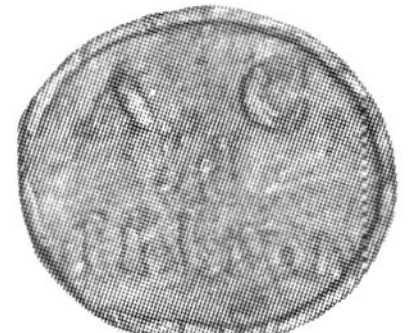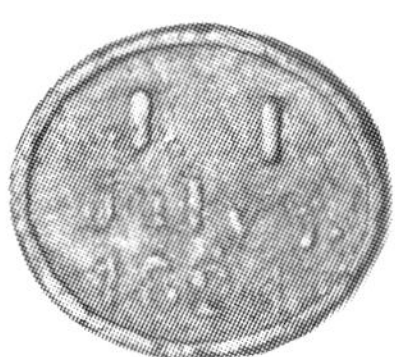

Rulau-E	Date	Metal	Size				
NY 1062	1824	Lead	oval 24mm		—	—	—

A. C. / OF / HEBRON. Rv: J. I. / JULY 7. / 1824. Raised rim. Plain edge. (Warner 55)

The 'A. - C. H.N' stands for 'Associate Church Hebron'. This church was organized in 1785. The 'J.I.' on the second token is for John Irvine, pastor 1824-1831.

NORTHWEST TERRITORY

R D I Co
(Robert Dickson Indian Company ?)
Northwest Territory

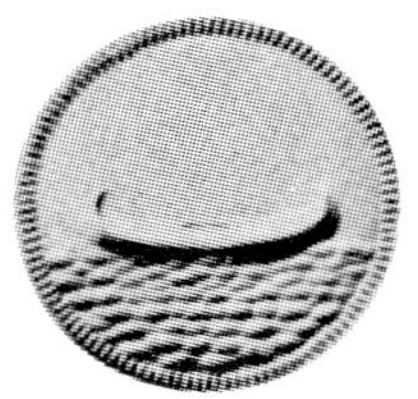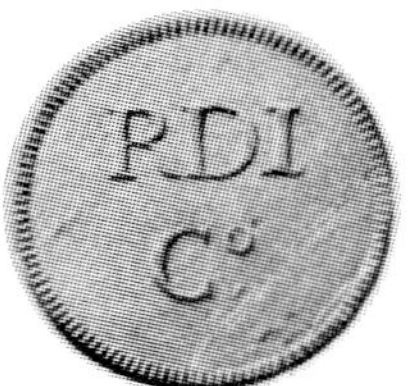

Rulau-E	Date	Metal	Size		VG	F	VF
NWT 1	(1786-1812)	Copper	26mm			2 or 3 Known	
		Canoe on choppy water. Rv:RDI / Co. Dentilated rims on both sides. Plain edge.					
NWT 2	(1786-1812)	Copper	21mm			2 or 3 Known	
		Similar to last, but smaller flan.					

These tokens were attributed to Robert Dickson by Prof. Arthur S. Morton of the University of Saskatchewan. Dickson was a well known fur trader in Northwest Territory and surrounding areas from 1785 through 1812, with his headquarters at Fort Michilimackinac (now Mackinac, Mich.) and Fort Niagara (New York). His men were active along the Wisconsin and Missouri Rivers.

One difficulty with this attribution is that the official name of the enterprise was Robert Dickson and Company, and the word ''Indian'' does not appear in existing records. Two trunkloads of Dickson's records were captured in the American raid on Michilimackinac in 1814 during the War of 1812.

Both Michilimackinac and Niagara were British posts on American territory after the Revolutionary War. These and other posts were not finally abandoned by the British until the end of the War of 1812. Dickson was British, and the tokens, if they prove to be his, would have been of British or Canadian manufacture.

The token type was first reported as lot 395 in the Caldecott sale of 1912. The *British Numismatic Journal* covered them in its 1936-37 volumes, and J. Verner Scaife catalogued them in his Aug. 1953 article in *The Numismatist* titled ''British Colonial Coins and Tokens.'' As recently as 1978 Warren Baker, the Canadian numismatist, called them fur trade tokens of Robert Dickson Indian Co.

They are catalogued here with utmost reserve. Tempting as it might be to admit them as fur trade pieces, there are many unanswered questions.

(See ''Robert Dickson Indian Company'' by Harley W. Rhodehamel in *TAMS Journal* for April 1979). George Fuld calls these pieces Canadian.

OHIO

P. EVENS
Cincinnati, Ohio

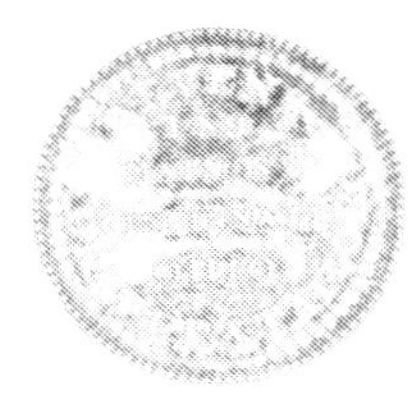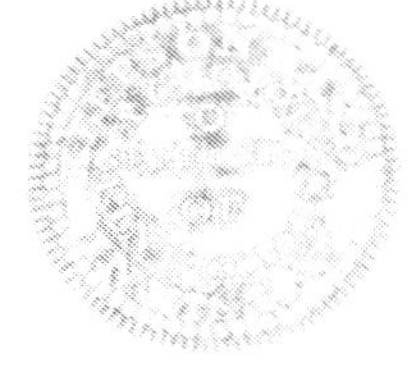

Platt Evens is recorded as having been at these addresses:
    1815-19 138 Main St.
    1829-40 149 Main St.
    1842-23 Main between 3rd & 4th (Evens and Farnham)
See The Numismatist, May 1917, page 198, for the Waldo C. Moore research on this issuer.

Issues of Evens signed BALE N.Y. are from the 1833-1835 period, listed in *Hard Times Tokens* as Low 313, 313A and 313B.

Rulau-E	Date	Metal	Size		VG	F	VF	EF
Oh 12	(1829-32)	GS	24mm		200.00	300.00	750.00	1000.
		Rarity 6. (Low 312)						
Oh 12A	(1829-32)	Brass	24mm		100.00	250.00	600.00	1000.
		Rarity 6. (Low 312A)						

E. WOODRUFF
Cincinnati, Ohio

Rulau-E	Date	Metal	Size	VG	F	EF
Oh 50	(1820's)	Silver	32.5mm	—	175.00	—

E. WOODRUFF script in relief within rectangular depression ctsp on U.S. 1809 Bust half dollar. (Roy Van Ormer coll.)

Enos Woodruff does not appear in the 1819 Cincinnati directory. He does appear in the 1825 directory as a watchmaker and silversmith at 58 Main Street. In the 1829 directory the firm had become Woodruff & White, watchmakers and clockmakers, still at 58 Main Street.

This counterstamped piece was discovered by the late Sol Kaplan of Cincinnati and is now in the collection of Roy Van Ormer. Its date of issue can be narrowed to the 1824-1828 period. (Research by Roy Van Ormer)

OREGON COUNTRY

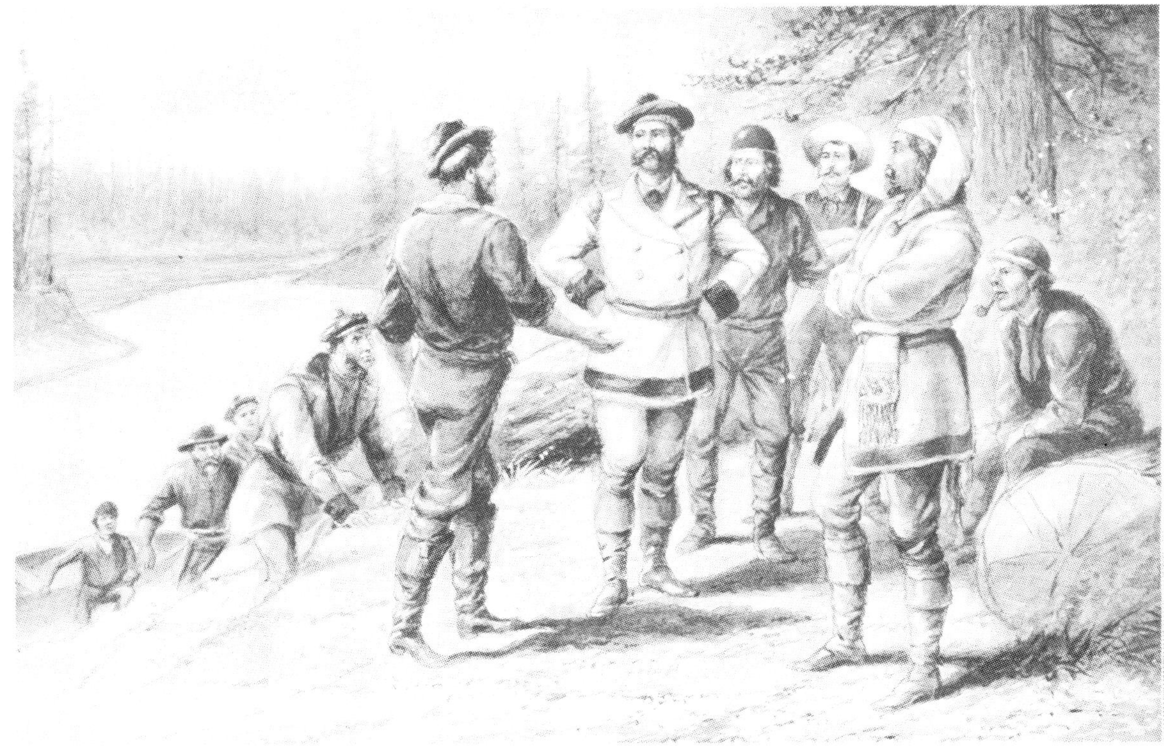

Canadian fur traders seized Astoria from the Americans in the War of 1812. The war provided the Hudson's Bay Company and the North West Company an opportunity to fight American traders in Oregon country. But the U.S. and British governments heard nothing of the transfer and the Treaty of Ghent in Dec. 1814 did not mention Astoria. This painting, by W. Montague Cary, depicts the Canadians in typical fur trader garb of the 19th century's second decade.

NORTH WEST COMPANY
Oregon Country

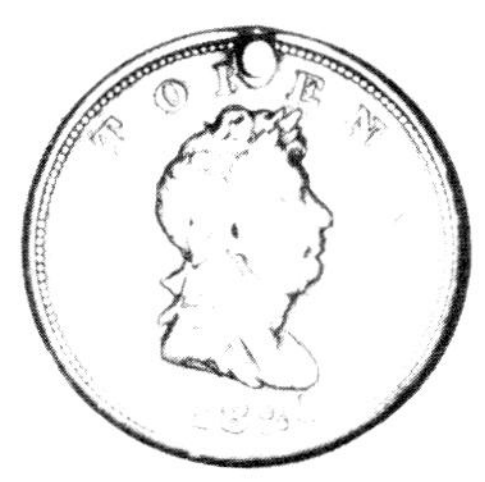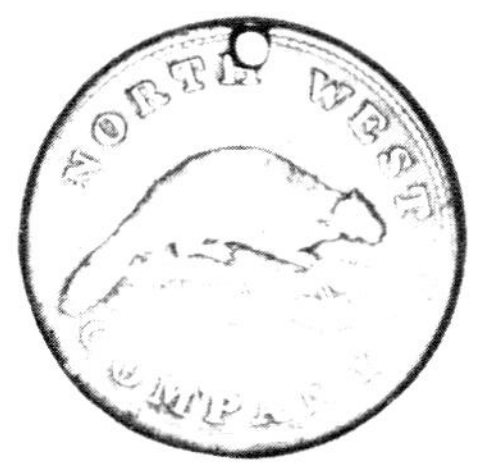

Rulau-E	Date	Metal	Size	Denomination	G	VG	F
Ore 1	1820	Brass	28mm	(1 Beaver)	—	225.00	375.00
		Laureate bust of George IV right, TOKEN / 1820. Rv: Beaver right, NORTH WEST above, COMPANY below. Plain edge. (RB) (Breton 925)					
Ore 2	1820	Copper	28mm	(1 Beaver)	—	250.00	425.00

These tokens were probably struck in 1820 in Birmingham, England, by John Walker & Co. Their value is "One Made Beaver." All but one known specimen are holed, and all have been found in the region of the lower Columbia River and Umpqua River valleys in Oregon. In 1821 the North West Company merged into the Hudson's Bay Company, another British firm.

The only unholed specimen known was owned by Doug Ferguson of Canada, having been purchased in the 1952 ANA auction. A full story on the North West Company was written by Donald Stewart and appeared in the *TAMS Journal*. An extract of James J. Curto's story on the same firm follows:

THE NORTH WEST COMPANY

The saga starts about 1759, at the fall of Quebec when a group of private traders — French Canadians, American frontiersmen and Scottish Highlanders — first moved into fur trade history. They were called the "Master Pedlars," the Lords of Lakes and Forests.

Always on the offensive, they banded together in 1775 to form The North West Company, to challenge and fight the great Hudson's Bay Company and its Royal Charter. Directed by men who knew every portage and rapid between the St. Lawrence and the Saskatchewan, they immediately emerged as a power great and formidable.

The leaders of the Company during the early years were Isaac Todd, James McGill, Benjamin and Joseph Frobisher, Simon McFavish, Robert Grout and Peter Pond.

They were the first white men to cross the North American continent. The Mackenzie River, greatest of northern rivers owes its name to the famous leader of that North West Company expedition, Alexander Mackenzie.

Grand Portage at the head of Lake Superior was the field headquarters of the company, the great depot where trade goods from the east were unloaded to begin their final journey over rivers, lakes, portages, and through forests to their ultimate destination to be exchanged for furs. After 1800 when the international boundary placed Grand Portage in United States Territory, the headquarters was shifted to Kaministiqua, now Fort Williams, Ontario.

With approximately 2,000 employees, its own cargo and freight canoes, organized portage transport crew, lake schooners and ocean ships, it was equipped to carry goods to and from England and to the markets of the Orient. It profits were estimated during the 15 years of its peak at 1,185,000 pounds.

In 1804, The North West Company attempted to purchase the Hudson's Bay Company outright, offering £103,000. The transaction was not completed chiefly because part of the stock was held by infants and other persons incapable of giving title or making transfer.

The ambition and boldness of the company eventually led to ruthlessness and lawlessness in inherent clashes between traders and settlements. To avoid exposure and prosecution as a result of such lawlessness, the leaders of The North West Company gradually fell apart. With disunion resulting in reduced means, loss of trade and jeopardized credit, the company opened negotiations for a merger with the Hudson's Bay Company in December, 1820. The merger was completed in 1821, ending the saga which lakes and forests will never see the likes of again.

At the time of this merger, the Hudson's Bay Company had 76 posts, The North West Company, 97.

THE BEAVER CLUB

Besides the token, The North West Company contributed another symbol, which also tied the early days of the fur trade to numismatics, its Beaver Club medal.

The Beaver Club was founded in Montreal in 1785. Originally composed of 19 members, it was formed by men of The North West Company, who qualified for membership by having spent at least one winter in the great Northwest.

The club met fortnightly in winter in brilliant and expensive style. Members wore the large gold club medals on club nights, and toasts to the fur trade and all its branches were continuously in order.

PHOENIX BUTTONS
Oregon Country

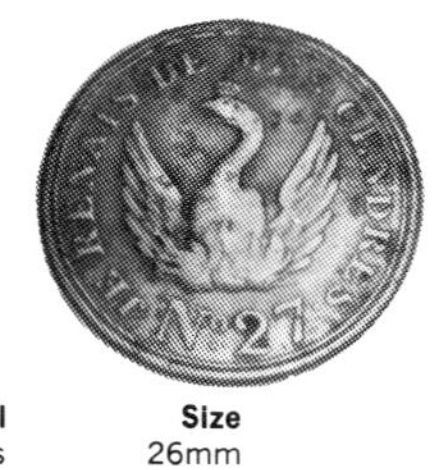

Rulau-E	Date	Metal	Size	G	VG	F
Ore 5	ca 1832-33	Brass	26mm	—	—	—

Crowned phoenix bird arising from flames at center. JE RENAIS DE MES CENDRES (I rise from my ashes) around; .NO. 27. below. Rv: Blank, with button shank.

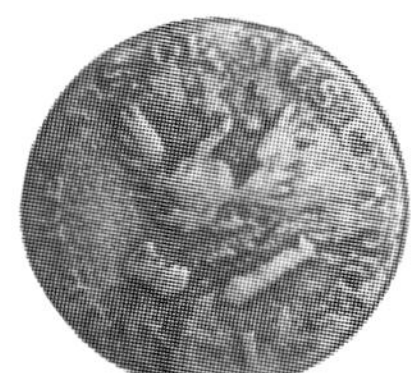

Rulau-E	Date	Metal	Size	G	VG	F
Ore 6	ca 1832-33	Brass	25mm	—	—	—

Similar to last, but crossed cannon under smaller phoenix, and NO. 1 beneath the cannon.

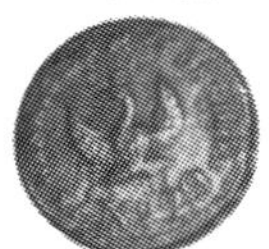

Rulau-E	Date	Metal	Size	G	VG	F
Ore 7	ca 1832-33	Brass	17mm	—	—	—

Similar to first button described above, but smaller, and NO. 29 under phoenix bird.

Rulau-E	Date	Metal	Size	G	VG	F
Ore 8	ca 1832-33	Brass	17mm	—	—	—
		Similar to last, but NO. 4 under phoenix.				
Ore 9	ca 1832-33	Brass	17mm	—	—	—
		Similar to last, but NO. 5 under phoenix.				
Ore 10	ca 1832-33	Brass	17mm	—	—	—
		Similar to last, but NO. 7 under phoenix.				
Ore 11	ca 1832-33	Brass	17mm	—	—	—
		Similar to last, but NO. 27 under phoenix.				
Ore 12	ca 1832-33	Brass	16mm	—	—	—
		Somewhat similar to preceding, but BALL-TYPE button; NO. 1 under phoenix.				

Cataloged above are eight tokens in four of the five or more styles of Phoenix button known. They are included here, though this is not a button catalog, because of their close association with the Northwest trading activities exemplified by the North West Company tokens. All examples illustrated are from the Byron Johnson collection; in all, some 600 of these buttons of all types are known.

Phoenix buttons are buttons of brass and bronze bearing a crowned Phoenix bird, a motto in French, and a numeral. They have been found in quantity in historic sites along the lower Columbia River, and less commonly throughout western North America. The buttons were not made for Napoleon, as is often claimed, but were manufactured by an English firm (probably Bushby of London) circa 1810-1820 for King Henri Christophe of Haiti.

The Phoenix and the motto are taken from Christophe's coat of arms; the numbers refer to army regiments. These military uniform buttons were brought to the Northwest about 1832-1833 as trade goods by an independent trader, most likely Nathaniel Wyeth, who probably used uniform coats which he may have obtained earlier when shipping ice to the West Indies, to trade for fish for his salmon packing plant at Fort William on Sauvies Island. The buttons are found most extensively on Sauvies Island, along the Cowlitz and Clackamas Rivers, at the falls at Oregon city, and at the Cascades.

They have also been found near California missions at San Juan Capistrano, San Luis Rey, Santa Barbara and Santa Ynez.

It has been ruled out that the Hudson's Bay Company or North West Company brought these buttons in. A few small ball-type buttons were originally silver-plated.

(See "Phoenix Buttons" by Emory Strong in the magazine *American Antiquity* for Jan., 1960)

PENNSYLVANIA

I.N.
(1st United Presbyterian Church)
Butler, Pa.

Rulau-E	Date	Metal	Size	VG	F	EF
Pa 3	(1819-64)	Lead	Rec 16x13mm		Rare	

I. N. within rectangular frame. Rv: Blank. Plain edge.

I.N. - Isaiah Niblock, pastor of the First United Presbyterian Church for 45 years, 1819 to 1864. The tokens probably were made early in his pastorship.

Lancaster County

The history of the development of transportation in North America has been marked by metal tokens which have been used to pay toll or fare. The idea of using tokens for this purpose originated in Germany in the 16th Century. During the Middle Ages, cities were surrounded by walls, which were closed after dark for the protection of the inhabitants of the cities.

But a means had to be found to identify citizens who, for one reason or another, could not enter the city until night time.

To identify these citizens on nocturnal business, special "gate tokens" were made, which were sold to persons who had to enter through the gates after dark. These tokens also helped pay the salary of the gatekeepers. As walls lost their military significance for protecting cities, the practice of using gate tokens continued as a sort of tax, and all who entered had to purchase tokens to gain access to the town.

Sometimes it was necessary to cross a moat, or stream, to enter the town, and appropriate "bridge toll" tokens were made for this purpose. The first such token was used to pay toll on a bridge at Regensburg in Bavaria in 1549.

With a tradition of using metal tokens for toll payment, the Germans who came to America brought this idea with them. Thus the earliest use of transportation tokens in America was in Lancaster County, Pennsylvania, where an elaborate system of toll roads was built by the "Pennsylvania Dutch" settlers of that beautiful countryside. These earliest transportation tokens used in the United States date from the 1790's.

Other turnpikes in Ohio, Kentucky and Virginia, followed suit. These early toll roads were generally called "turnpikes," because of a row of spikes which faced the traveler and were then turned when he paid his toll: "Turned spikes." Hence, "turnpike."

Frequently these roads were paved with planks, and for that reason were known as "plank roads." The planks provided a bumpy ride, but they were far better than the alternative, which was a mire of mud in the rainy season, and a cloud of dust in the dry season.

PHILADELPHIA AND LANCASTER TURNPIKE ROAD

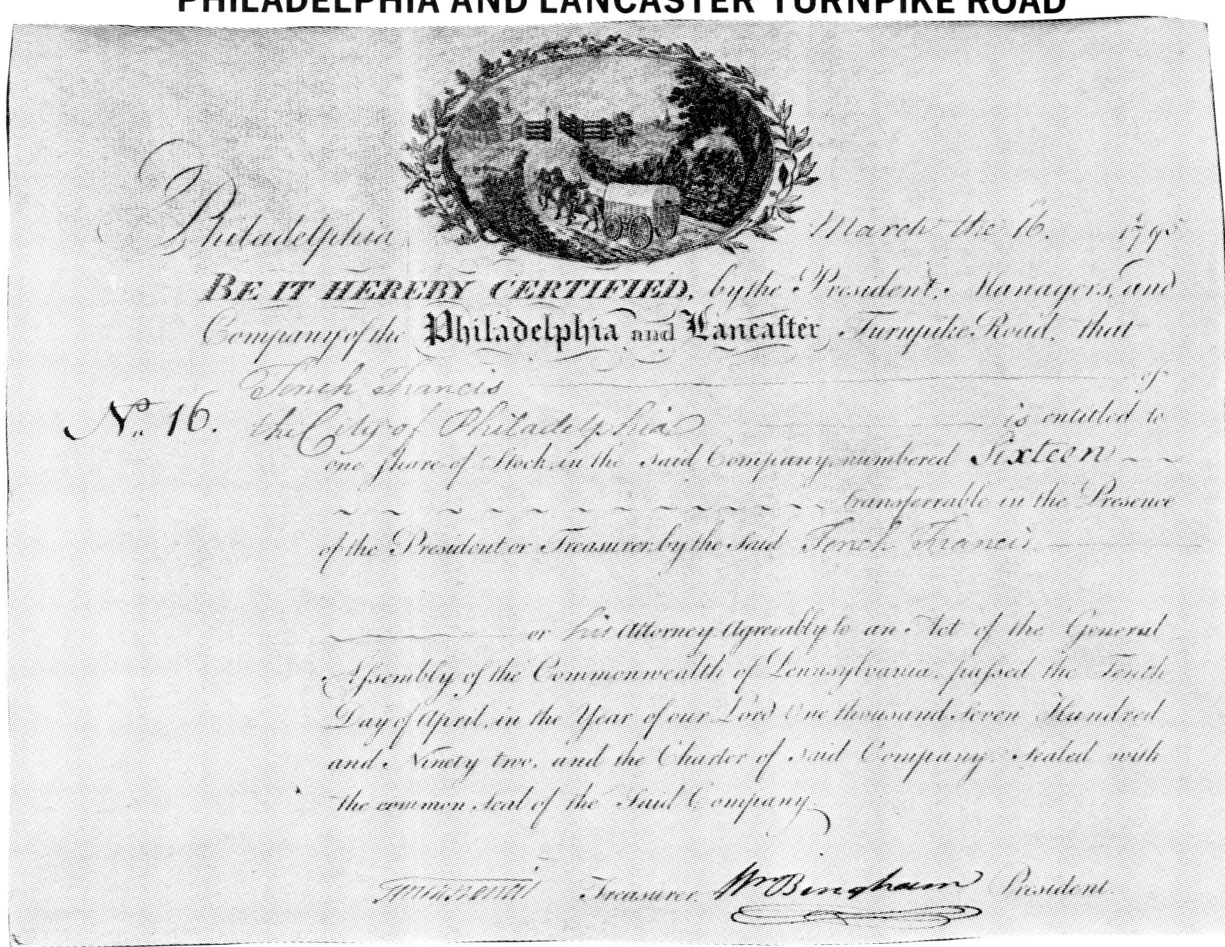

This share certificate is on parchment. It is signed by William Bingham, president, and Tench Francis, treasurer. The illustrated certificate, number 16, is made payable to Tench Francis for one share. Tench Francis was the cashier of the Bank of North America, Philadelphia, 1781 to 1792. From 1793 on he was also treasurer of the Delaware & Schuylkill Canal Navigation Co. Francis was also an associate of Robert Morris, financier of the Revolution.

The vignette shows a covered wagon approaching a tollgate house. The certificate is dated March 16, 1795. The Turnpike apparently was chartered by Pennsylvania on April 10, 1792.

The reverse of the illustrated certificate shows it was transferred by Francis on Aug. 17, 1801 to one William Weston.

This is supposedly the earliest known U.S. share certificate bearing a vignette. It was issued for the first major turnpike in the U.S.

William Bingham, the turnpike's financier and manager of its construction, was a director of the First Bank of the United States (chartered 1792). He was the father-in-law of a Baring Brothers founder, and was one of the — if not the — wealthiest landowner of his time. (Information courtesy Anthony Hetherington, editor *Scrip Magazine*, Ilford, Essex, England)

The Philadelphia & Lancaster Turnpike became part of the Philadelphia-to-Pittsburgh road.

C & H TURNPIKE
Lancaster County, Pa.

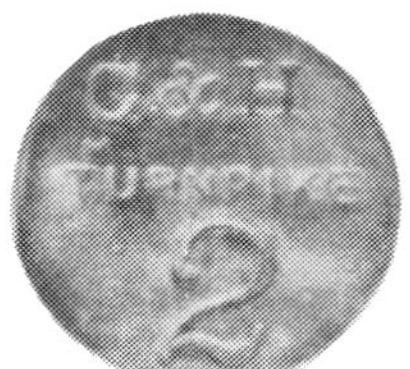

Pa 526 B

Rulau-E	Date	Metal	Size	VG	F	EF
Pa 526 Aa	(1806-20)	Br	Oct 27mm	—	150.00	—
		C & H / TURNPIKE / 1 incused, relief beaded border around Rv: Blank. Plain edge. Issued hole.				
Pa 526 Ab	(1806-20)	Br	Oct 25mm	—	150.00	—
		Similar, but plain flan. Rv: Blank. Plain edge. Issued holed.				
Pa 526 C	(1806-20)	Brass	24mm	—	150.00	—
		As 526B, but issued holed.				
Pa 526D	(1806-20)	Br	C-leaf 31mm	—	150.00	—
		As 526 Ab, but numeral 3. Plain flan. Plain edge. Issued holed.				

The Clay & Hinkeltown Turnpike was a part of the Downington, Ephrata & Harrisburg Turnpike, and went into operation sometime in the 1806-1816 period. Toll gates were probably at Clay, Ephrata and Hinkeltown.

L & E TURNPIKE
Lancaster County, Pa.

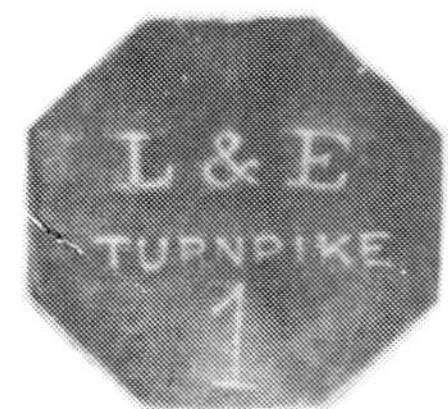

Rulau-E	Date	Metal	Size	VG	F	EF
526 AA	(c.1816?)	Br	Oct 26mm	—	150.00	—
		L & E / TURNPIKE / 1 incuse on plain field. Rv: Blank. Plain edge.				

Lancaster & Ephrata Turnpike.
Tokens of the various Lancaster County toll roads were either good for payment, or else were used as zone checks in indicate how much toll (how many gates) was paid, or was due.

L. E. & M. PIKE
Lancaster County, Pa.

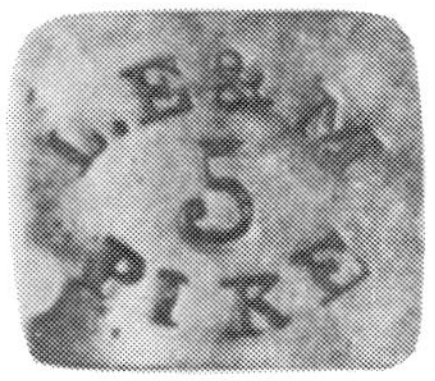

Pa 526 BD

Rulau-E	Date	Metal	Size	VG	F	EF
526 BA	(1812-45)	Br	Sq 25mm	—	250.00	—
		L. E. & M. / 2 / PIKE incuse on plain flan. Rv: Blank. Plain edge. Corners are rounded.				
526 BB	(1812-45)	Br	Sq 23mm	—	250.00	—
		Similar, but sharp corners. Numeral 4 instead of 2.				
526 BC	(1812-45)	Br	Sq 25x22mm	—	250.00	—
		Similar, numeral 4, rounded corners.				
526 BD	(1812-45)	Br	Sq 26x44mm	—	250.00	—
		Similar to 526 BC, but numeral 5 instead of 4.				
526 BE	(1812-45)	Br	Par 44x23mm	—	250.00	—
		L. E. & M. 5 / PIKE incuse on plain field. RV: H incuse on plain flan. Plain edge.				
526 BE	(1812-45)	Br	Sq, size?	—	250.00	—
		L. E. & M. PIKE 6 on plain field. Plain edge.				

Lancaster, Elizabethtown & Middletown Turnpike, 26 miles long, opened in 1812 and stopped collecting tolls in 1845. Probably the tokens were already by then out of use. The road, following Route 230 today, was used until 1920.

L. & F. TURNPIKE
Lancaster County, Pa.

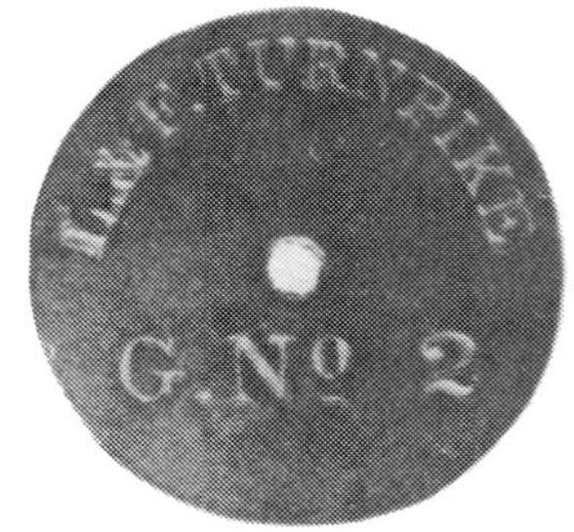

Pa 526 CD

Rulau-E	Date	Metal	Size	VG	F	EF
526 CA	(c.1816?)	Brass	32mm	—	150.00	—
		L. & F. TURNPIKE / G. No. 1 incuse on plain field. Rv: Blank. Plain edge.				
526 CB	(c.1816?)	Brass	34mm	—	125.00	—
		Similar, but issued holed.				
526 CC	(c.1816?)	Brass	36mm	—	150.00	—
		Similar, issued holed.				
526 CD	(c.1816?)	Brass	35mm	—	150.00	—
		Similar, but numeral 2 instead of 1.				

Lancaster & Fruitville Turnpike. The 'G' is 'Gate.'

L. & S. TURNPIKE CO.
Lancaster County, Pa.

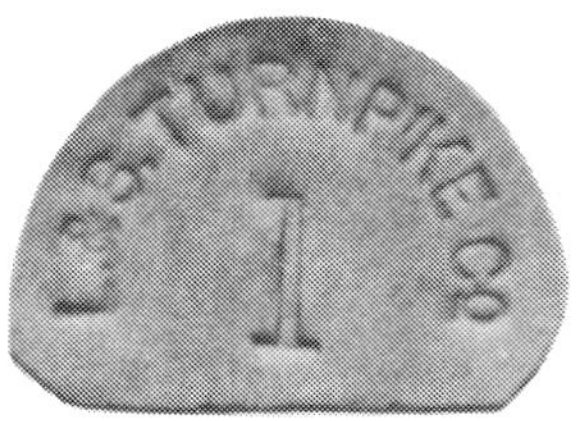

Pa 526 DA

Rulau-E	Date	Metal	Size	VG	F	EF
526 DA	(1807-20)	Br	½-sp 34x25mm	—	150.00	—
		L. & S. TURNPIKE CO. / 1 incuse on plain flan. Plain edge.				
526 DB	(1807-20)	Br	Rec 39x26mm	—	150.00	—
		Similar. Clipped corners. Numeral 4 instead of 1.				
526 DC	(1807-20)	Br	½-sp 35x25mm	—	150.00	—
		Similar to 526 DB. Clipped corners.				

Lancaster & Susquehanna Turnpike was incorporated in 1794 and opened in 1807. There were four toll gates: the road went from Lancaster to Wright's Ferry (now Columbia) on the Susquehanna River. In 1918 the state of Pennsylvania took over the road.

LANC. & E. TURNPIKE
Lancaster County, Pa.

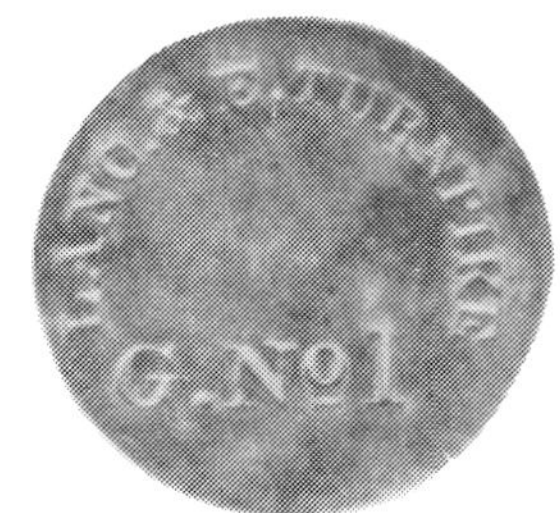

Pa 526 EA

Rulau-E	Date	Metal	Size	Gate	VG	F	EF
526 EA	(c.1816?)	Brass	31mm	1	—	125.00	—
526 EB	(c.1816?)	Br	Obl 34x29mm	1	—	150.00	—
526 EC	(c.1816?)	Br	½-Sp 39x35mm	1	—	150.00	—
526 ED	(c.1816?)	Br	½-Sp 33x29mm	1	—	150.00	—
526 EE	(c.1816?)	Br	Sq 30mm	2	—	150.00	—
526 EF	(c.1816?)	Br	½-Sp 40x32mm	2	—	150.00	—
526 EG	(c.1816?)	Brass	30mm	2	—	150.00	—
526 EH	(c.1816?)	Br	Sq 33mm	2	—	150.00	—
526 EI	(c.1816?)	Br	½-sp 32x28mm	3	—	150.00	—

Lancaster & Elizabethtown Turnpike.

MY. MA. PIKE
Lancaster County, Pa.

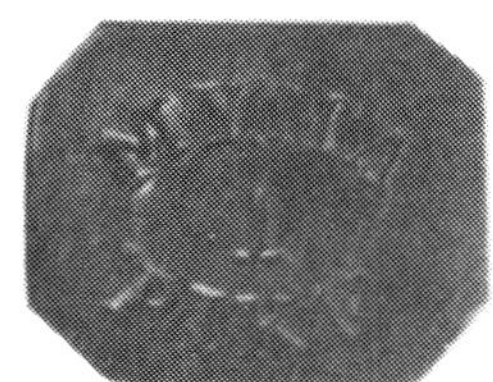

Rulau-E	Date	Metal	Size	Gate	VG	F	EF
Pa 526 HA	(1815-22)	Br	Obl 29x24mm	1	—	250.00	—
Pa 526 HB	(1815-22)	Br	Obl 31x27mm	2	—	250.00	—
Pa 526 HC	(1815-22)	Br	Obl 30x28mm	2	—	250.00	—

Mount Joy & Marietta Pike opened in 1815 and continued in operation at least until 1822.

ASHMEAD
Philadelphia, Pa.

Rulau-E	Date	Metal	Size	VG	F	EF
Pa 20	(1810?)	Copper	29mm	—	200.00	—
		ASHMEAD / PHILA ctsp on U.S. 1806 Large cent. (Hallenbeck 1.761; Brunk collection)				
Pa 21	(?)	Copper	29mm	—	—	—
		ASHMEAD ctsp on U.S. 1818 Large cent.				

William Ashmead was a silversmith active circa 1797-1810 or longer. Ashmead does not appear in the 1819 or 1823 directories.
The second counterstamp above, Pa 21, may possibly not be connected.

J. BEAM
Philadelphia, Pa.

Rulau-E	Date	Metal	Size	Denomination	VG	F	EF
Pa 23	(1818-22)	Copper	29mm	(Cent)	—	50.00	—
		J. BEAM ctsp on U.S. Large cent.					

Jacob C. Beam was active as a silversmith circa 1818-1822 in Philadelphia.

BRIDESBURG BARREL MANUFG. CO.
Philadeplhia, Pa.

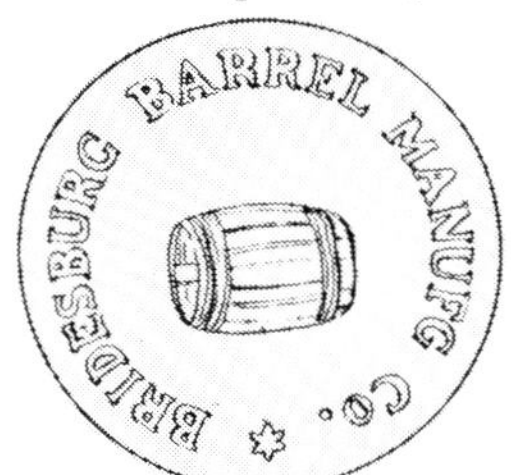

Rulau-E	Date	Metal	Size	VF	EF	Unc
Pa 54	(?)	Brass	32mm	—	200.00	400.00
		Barrel in center, six-pointed star at bottom BRIDESBURG BARREL MANUFG CO. Rv: Blank. Very Rare.				
Pa 54A	(?)	Brass	32mm	—	200.00	400.00
		As 54, but numeral '1' stamped on back.				
Pa 55	(?)	Brass	32mm	—	200.00	400.00
		As 54, but numeral '2' stamped on back.				
Pa 56	(?)	Brass	32mm	—	200.00	400.00
		As 54, but numeral '5' stamped on back.				
Pa 57	(?)	Brass	32mm	—	200.00	400.00
		As 54, but numeral '10' stamped on back.				
Pa 58	(?)	Brass	32mm	—	200.00	400.00
		As 54, but numeral '50' stamped on back.				

These may be from the 1850-60 period.

R. DUNLEVY
Philadelphia, Pa.

Rulau-E	Date	Metal	Size	VG	F	EF
Pa 60	(1831)	Copper	29mm	—	40.00	—
		R. DUNLEVY in relief within rect. depression ctsp twice on obverse of U.S. 1803 Large cent. (Frank Kovacs coll.)					

Robert Dunlevy was a silversmith active about 1830-37. He was located at Lodge Alley in 1832-37. From 1843-46 he was part of the Dunlevy & Dowell firm (George G. Dowell), and from 1847-50 in Dunlevy & Wise (George K. Wise).

W. LEVIS
Philadelphia, Pa.

Rulau-E	Date	Metal	Size	VG	F	EF
Pa 70	(1810-18)	Copper	29mm	—	50.00	—
		W. LEVIS in relief on a curving ribbon depression ctsp on U.S. Large cent. (Hallenbeck 12.504)					

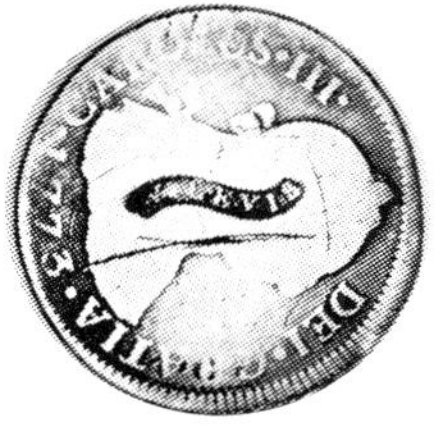 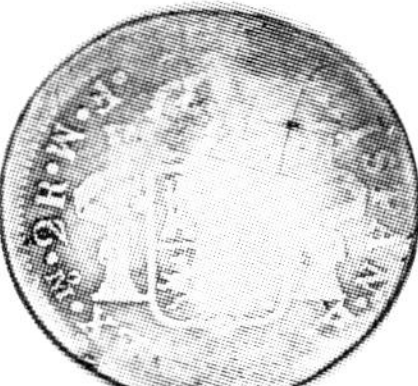

Rulau-E	Date	Metal	Size	VG	F	EF
Pa 72	(1810-18)	Silver	27mm	—	85.00	—
		Similar ctsp on Spanish-American 1773-Mo-FM 2-reales. (Chester Krause coll.)					
Pa 73	(1810-18)	Silver	27mm	—	85.00	—
		W. LEVIS on a ribbon ctsp on Spanish-American 1781-Mo 2-reales. (Duffield 1365: Brunk 91)					
Pa 75	(1810-18)	Silver	32.5mm	—	200.00	—
		Similar ctsp on U.S. 1807 half dollar. (Duffield 1410)					
Pa 77	(1810-18)	Silver	32.5mm	—	200.00	—
		Similar ctsp on U.S. 1818 Bust half dollar. (Kenneth Bressett coll.)					
Pa 79	(1810-18)	Copper	28mm	—	65.00	—
		Similar ctsp on Spanish-American 1819 quarter-real. (Donald Partrick coll.)					
Pa 80	(?)	Copper	29mm	—	—	—
		W.L. ctsp on U.S. Large cent. (Duffield 1451; Hallenbeck 23.011). This set of initials may not be connected with Levis.					
Pa 81	(1832-37)	Copper	29mm	—	60.00	—
		W. LEVIS in relief within rectangular depression ctsp on U.S. 1827 Large cent. (Hartzog coll.)					

Unlike Pa 70, Pa 81's counterstamp is in an oblong rather than a ribbon-shaped depression.
William Levis is a man of mystery. In 1796-97 he is listed as a paper maker at 6 No. 8th St. He does not appear in the 1816, 1819 or 1823 directories. Despite the absence of listings in 1816-23 directories, he functioned as a silversmith and applied his counterstamp to coins circa 1810-1818.
The same man (or a son?) appears in 1832-33 as a currier at 292 Filbert. We meet him next in 1836-37 at 228 No. 3rd St., where he is listed as an oil and leather merchant. (His home in 1836-37 was at 242 Filbert.)

PHILADELPHIA MUSEUM
Philadelphia, Pa.

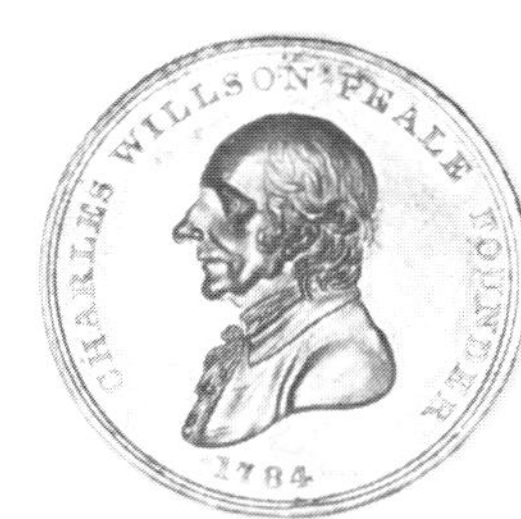 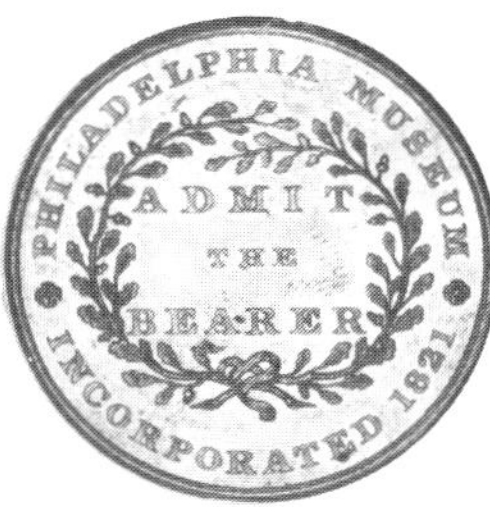

Rulau-E	Date	Metal	Size	Denomination	VG	F	EF
Pa 398	1821	Copper	32mm	1 Admission	12.50	25.00	65.00
		Bust left, CHARLES WILLSON PEALE FOUNDER 1784. Rv: ADMIT / THE / BEARER within wreath. PHILADELPHIA MUSEUM INCORPORATED 1821 around. (Wright 6)						
Pa 397	1821	Silver	32mm	1 Admission	—	—	—
		Same as 397.						
Pa 394	1821	Copper	32mm	1 Admission	—	—	—
		Similar to NY 397, but blank space within wreath on reverse.						

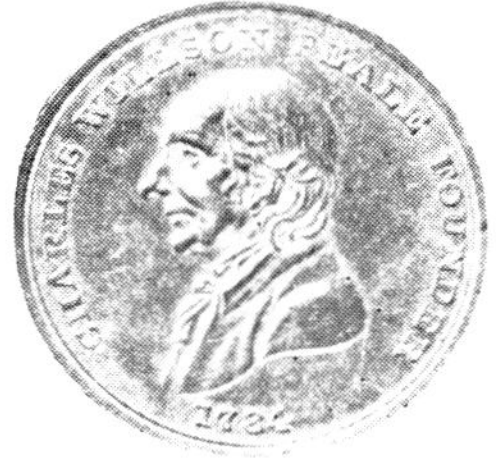 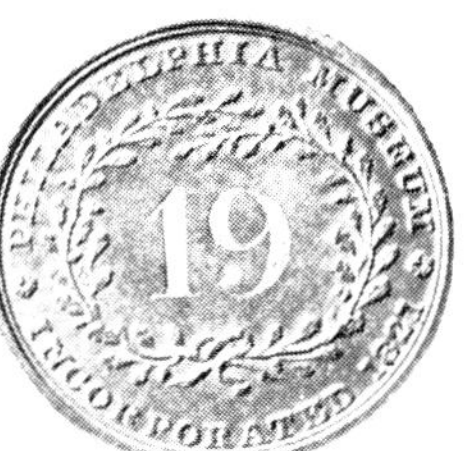

Rulau-E	Date	Metal	Size	Denomination	VG	F	EF
Pa 395	1821	Copper	32mm	1 Admission	—	—	—
		As 394, but number incused inside the wreath.						

Rulau-E	Date	Metal	Size	Denomination	VG	F	EF
Pa 396	1821	Gilt Copper Same as 394.	32mm	1 Admission	—	—	—

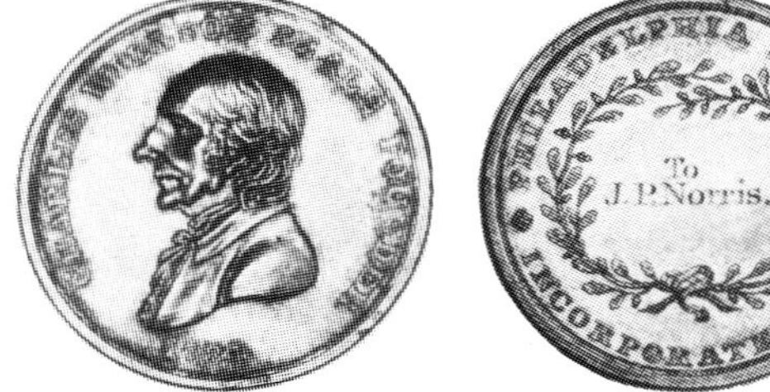

Pa 399	1821 (1830)	Silver	32mm	Medal	—	—	—
	As NY 394. 12 known. (Freeman 414; Storer 2780)						
Pa 400	1821 (1830)	Gold	32mm	Medal	—	—	Unique
	As NY 394. Only 1 struck. (Freeman 414a)						

Designed by Christian Gobrecht and struck at the U.S. Mint, Philadelphia, about 1830. The silver and gold medals were designed as an award for service to the Museum or for advancement of science, in memory of the late founder.

In May, 1833, silver medals were presented to Mint Director Dr. Samuel Moore, Mint Engraver William Kneass and Mint Chief Coiner Adam Eckfeldt. Also each of the five Museum directors and two former directors — Dr. Robert Patterson and Joseph Parker Norris — were to receive silver medals. Each was engraved with the name of the recipient. On the John Work Garrett specimen at Johns Hopkins University in Baltimore, the engraving within the wreath reads; TO / J.P. NORRIS.

The May, 1833, authorization awarded the single gold version to Silas E. Burroughs, who helped finance the 1831-32 Titian Peale expedition to Colombia.

CHARLES WILLSON PEALE

Charles Willson Peale was perhaps the most celebrated portrait painter of his day in the U.S. Many of the men in public life of Revolutionary times were painted by him, and he painted George Washington six times — in 1772, 1778, 1781, 1783, 1786 and 1795.

He was born of English parents at Chestertown, Kent County, Maryland, on April 16, 1741. He moved to Annapolis in 1762 where he carried on trade as saddler, harnessmaker, silversmith, watchmaker and engraver. In 1767, at age 26, he received instructions in painting from Hesselius of Annapolis, and afterwards from Copley in Boston and West in England. He moved to Philadelphia in 1776, where he got caught up in patriotic fervor and became a captain of volunteers under Washington, fighting at Trenton and Germantown.

In 1784 Peale opened his museum at his residence, corner Third and Lombard Streets in Philadelphia. He displayed his own large collection of paintings, and added many natural curiosities. In 1794 the Philosophical Society granted him the use of its Hall on Fifth Street below Chestnut, and the museum was transferred there in Sept. 1794. Peale became also a taxidermist and maker of dentures, including, reportedly, a set for George Washington.

By act of the Pennsylvania Legislature of March 17, 1802, Peale was authorized to occupy the east room of the lower story of the State House (now known as Independence Hall), and all the upper story. In 1809 Peale petitioned the Legislature for perpetual use of the upper part of the State House for his museum. At this time the Philadelphia Museum contained 200 stuffed animals, 1,000 specimens of birds, 4,000 specimens of insects, a mineral collection, cabinets of serpents, fishes, etc., plus over 100 portraits of statesmen and soldiers painted by Peale. There was also a skeleton of a mammoth excavated in Ulster County, N.Y.

In Feb., 1821, the museum was incorporated as The Philadelphia Museum, the incorporators being Pierce Butler, Raphael Peale, Rembrandt Peale, Coleman Sellers and Rubens Peale. Only Butler was not a Peale family member. In 1827 the museum was removed to the Philadelphia Arcade on the north side of Chestnut Street between 6th and 7th Streets, where it remained until 1838. In that year it was moved to the northeast corner of 9th and Sansom Streets, in a new building which cost $130,000 to erect. The company's enterprise was not successful from 1838 on, and in 1844 the museum was closed and the collections sold.

Peale died in Philadelphia on Feb. 27, 1827, aged 85 and active until the end. He had six sons and named five of them after painters — Raphael, Rembrandt, Vandyke, Titian and Rubens. His eldest daughter was named Angelica Kauffman Peale.

Rubens Peale established his own museum in New York City in 1825. (See Peale's Museum tokens under New York.)

The sixth son, Franklin Peale (named after Benjamin Franklin, whom C.W. Peale admired almost as much as he did painters), was appointed melter and refiner of the Philadelphia Mint in Jan., 1836. In 1839 he succeeded Adam Eckfeldt as chief coiner at the mint.

After the Philadelphia Museum was incorporated in 1821, admission tokens were issued with Charles Willson Peale's portrait on them. Some of the token numbers which have survived in collections include 1, 18, 19, 22, 30, 41, 42, 43, 46, 48 and 53. Duffield thought there were about 50 numbered tokens distributed by management as passes to special friends, with the ADMIT THE BEARER type probably sold by annual subscription.

In the Bushnell sale one piece in silver was offered, engraved TO J.P. NORRIS. (This piece later went to Johns Hopkins University.) In the same Bushnell sale a lead trial piece was also offered.

Charles Willson Peale also opened a museum in Baltimore in 1784, and this passed into the hands of Charles peale Polk and closed in 1796. No tokens are known from this institution.

Soon after 1796 Raphael and Rembrandt Peale opened the Baltimore Museum in the same building as the closed institution. In 1813 Rembrandt Peale erected a building on Holiday Street north of Lexington in Baltimore for a museum, which was called Peale's Museum. Many years later this building became City Hall. These institutions also had no known tokens issued.

In 1831-1832 Titian Peale led an expedition to Colombia in search of natural curiosities.

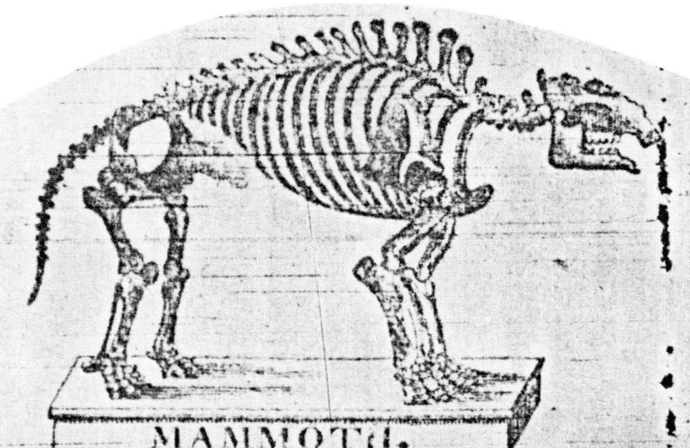

Philadelphia Museum,

IN THE UPPER PART OF THE

ARCADE,

CHESNUT STREET, (ABOVE SIXTH.)

Open throughout the day, and ILLUMINATED every Evening.

ADMITTANCE 25 CENTS.

This Museum is the oldest and largest establishment in the United States, and contains immense collections of the Animal and Mineral Kingdoms of nature, from all parts of the world. These are all beautifully arranged, so as to enable the visitor to study the objects with the greatest advantage. The collection of implements and ornaments of our aboriginal tribes is very extensive and interesting, and the Cabinet of Antiquities, and Artificial Curiosities, is not less worthy of attention. In addition to the ordinary attractions of a Museum, there is in this a very large collection of the Portraits of American Statesmen and Warriors of the Revolution, and of the most distinguished scientific men of Europe and America.

The Founder, C. W. Peale, desirous of securing the Museum permanently in this city, obtained an act of Incorporation, by which the stability of the Institution is insured. The act of Incorporation secures the use of the Museum in perpetuity to the city, and authorizes the Stockholders to appoint annually five trustees, who meet quarterly to regulate the business of the Institution. Nothing can be removed from the Institution under a penalty, and forfeture of double the value of the thing removed; hence donations may be made with certainty on the part of the donors, that the articles placed in the Museum will always remain for the public good.

RICKETTS' CIRCUS
Philadelphia, Pa.

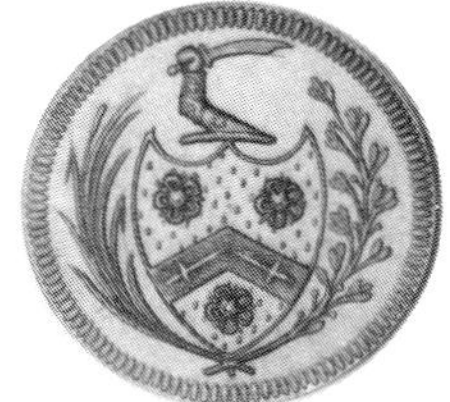 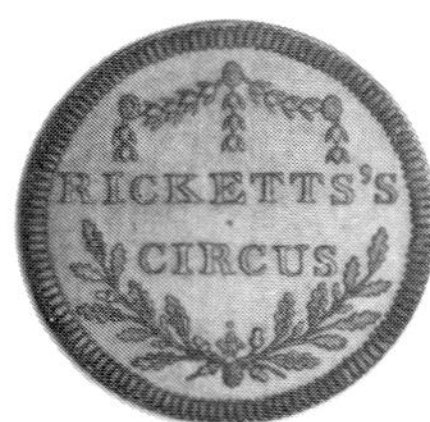

Rulau-E	Date	Metal	Size	Denomination	F	VF	Unc
Pa 430	(1793-99)	Copper	29mm	(1 Admission)	—	—	Ex. Rare

Crested shield of arms within palm and olive branch. Rv: RICK-ETTS'S / CIRCUS at center, festoon of leaves above, oak branches below. Dentilated rims on both sides. Plain edge. (Wright 894)

Rulau-E	Date	Metal	Size	Denomination	F	VF	Unc
Pa 429	(1793-99)	Bronze	29mm	(1 Admission)	—	—	Ex. Rare

Similar to 430, but reeded edge.

Rulau-E	Date	Metal	Size	Denomination	F	VF	Unc
Pa 428	(1793-99)	Silver	29mm	(1 Admission)	—	—	Ex. Rare

Similar to 430, but reeded edge.

The arms shown on the tokens are those of Sir Cornwallis Ricketts, of The Elms, Gloucester. The arms are: Two swords on a chevron azure. Three roses, two in chief, one in base, on a field or (or ermine). The crest is an arm wielding a scimitar. Palm branch on left, olive branch right.

John Bill Ricketts, a Scottish horseman, emigrated to America in 1792. He first appeared in Philadelphia, where he erected a building for a riding school for instruction of ladies and gentlemen, which opened in October 1792. Later he erected a circus for equestrian performances which was opened April, 1793.

Ricketts' Circus was attended by fashionable people of the day, and by notables — George Washington on April 22, 1793, and French ambassador Citizen Genet on June 5, 1793.

On May 12, 1795 Ricketts opened at a new amphitheater he built in Boston (box seats $1, pits 50 cents). Later he returned to Philadelphia, where he remained active until his circus was destroyed by fire Dec. 17, 1799. Afterward he attempted to retrieve his fortunes but ill luck dogged him and he returned to England.

The Ricketts' Circus tokens most likely are from the 1793-1795 days in Philadelphia. A May 15, 1793, newspaper ad tells us the box seats were $1 and the pits 50 cents, the same as he charged later in Boston. Ricketts was a skilled equestrian, and in one June, 1793, performance he sponsored a Mr. Blanchard who dropped a dog, cat and squirrel by parachute from a balloon one mile high. The animals survived! It was the first parachute test in North America, according to a Philadelphia newspaper.

The Ricketts' tokens were a special study of the American Numismatic Society, which published researches on them in 1868 and 1878. *The Numismatist* tied all this research together in a 1912 article. They also were examined in Robert Julian's 1977 book, *Medals of the United States Mint.*

Franklin Peale, the coiner, in 1841 began a register of the dies in possession of the U.S. Mint at Philadelphia, and this included the Ricketts' Circus dies. Julian concludes that the tokens may have been made at the mint, engraver unknown, in the early 1790's. We favor 1793 as the date of mintage.

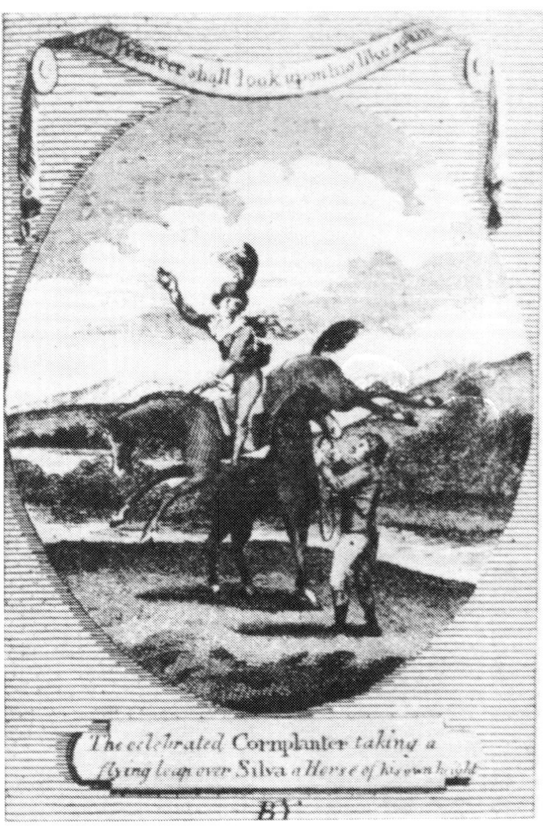

Shown above is an old print of Ricketts, mounted on his horse Cornplanter, leaping over another horse, Silva. The scroll reads: WE NEVER SHALL LOOK UPON HIS LIKE AGAIN. "Never" seems a long time, but it was undoubtedly effective advertising in 1793.

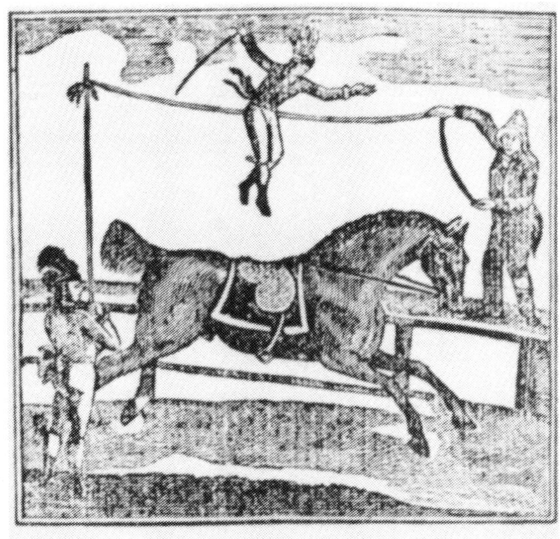

Also shown is a 1795 Boston handbill advertising Ricketts' triumphs there.

SOCIETATIS PHILALETHICAE
(Truth-lovers Society)
Philadelphia, Pa.

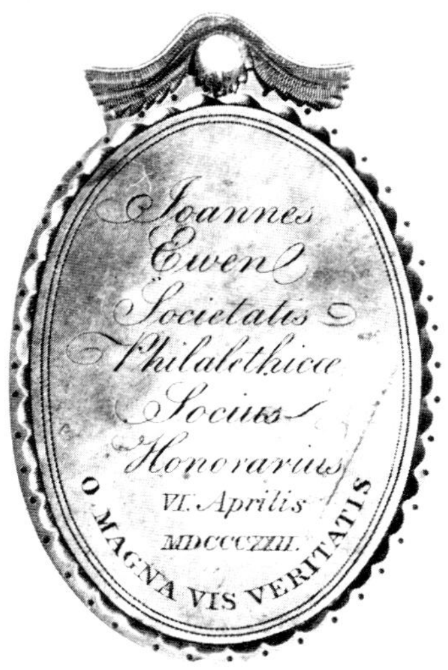

			F	VF	EF
Pa 440	1822	Silver Oval, 43x67mm	—	300.00	550.00

The oval badge is contained in a mirror-like frame. Obverse: (all engraved incuse) JOANNES / EWEN / SOCIETATIS / PHILALETH-ICAE / SOCIUS / HONORARIUS / VI. APRILIS / MDCCCXXII. / O MAGNA VIS VERITATIS. (John Ewen, honorary member, Truth-lovers Society, 6 April 1822, Oh great strength of the Truth). Rv: Hallmark: WL.

The hallmark WL is for William Little, silversmith in Philadelphia, 1813-1819 or later.

This badge is previously unpublished; it first appeared in the NASCA Providence collection sale, July 16-17, 1981.

WHARTENBY
Philadelphia, Pa.

Rulau-E	Date	Metal	Size	F	VF	EF
Pa 442	(1829)	Copper	29mm	—	50.00	—

WHARTENBY / PHI A. in relief within two separate rectangular depressions ctsp on U.S. 1825 Large cent. (Hartzog 1982 sale)

Thomas Whartenby was a Philadelphia silversmith of note from 1811 to 1850 or later. The mark resembles his hallmark. Some of his known addresses are:

1815-16	196 So. 3rd and also 117 Cedar
1816-18	(Whartenby & Bumm)
1818-19	117 Spruce
1822-23	33 No. 3rd
1832-33	173 Pine
1836-37	Ridge Road near Buttonwood

The firm became Thomas Whartenby & Co. in 1847.

SOUTH CAROLINA

CHARLES TOWN SOCIAL CLUB
Charleston, S.C.

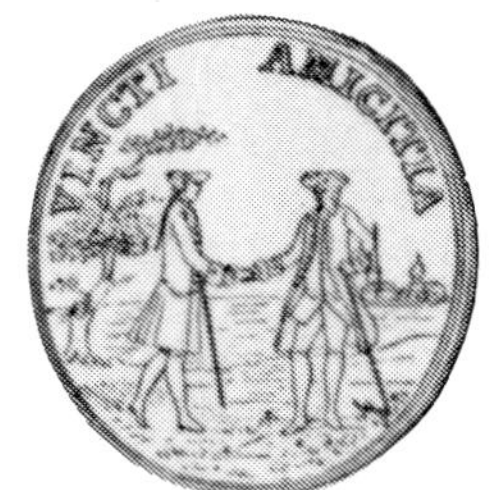 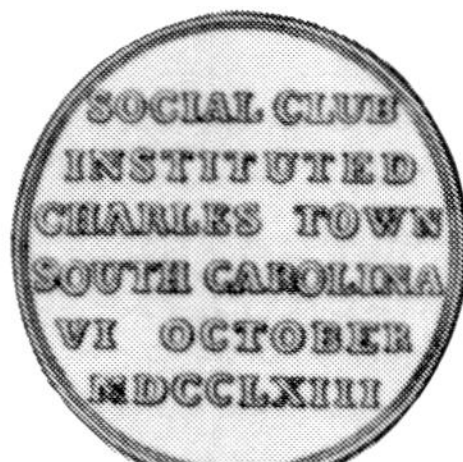

Rulau-E	Date	Metal	Size		VG	F	EF
SC 1	1763	Sil	Oval 33x37mm		—	—	Rare

Two men in 18th Century gentlemen's garb shaking hands in a field, a tree at left, church and houses in right back ground. VINCTI AMICITIA above. (Legend in Latin means "Bound in Friendship"). Rv: SOCIAL CLUB / INSTITUTED / CHARLES TOWN / SOUTH CAROLINA / VI OCTOBER / MDCCLXIII. (Betts 508)

Rulau-E	Date	Metal	Size		VG	F	EF
SC 2	1763	Bze	Oval 33x37mm		—	—	—

Same as last. Betts believed all bronze pieces were restrikes off original dies.

This little-known member's medal was struck on the Charles Town Social Club being instituted on Oct. 6, 1763. Specimens appeared in the Hollis sale (1817), the Bushnell sale, and the Chapmans' sale of the Warner collection. It was written up in the *American Journal of Numismatics*, Volumes V and XVII, and illustrated by a line drawing Betts' 1894 catalog.

HIBERNIAN SOCIETY
Charleston, S.C.

Rulau-E	Date	Metal	Size		VG	F	EF
SC 5	(1763?)	Silver	**		—	—	Rare

**Elliptical, ringed for suspension.

Harp of six strings formed of a winged female figure with fish's tail. Above: HIBERNIAN)|(SOCIETY. Below: CHARLESTON. SC. Rv: Harp intaglio. Both sides are engraved on a silver planchet. All devices and lettering are cut out from the flan. Plain edge. (Betts 507)

The size is not known. This is more a bangle than a medalet, apparently.

PRESBYTERIAN CHURCH
Charleston, S.C.

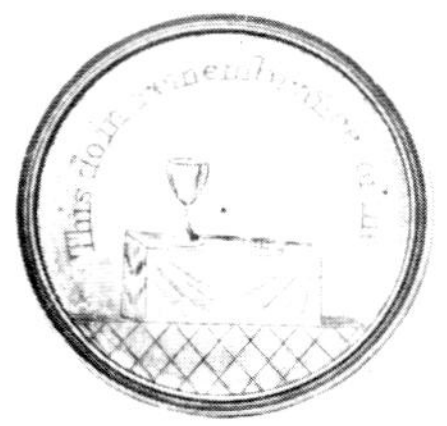 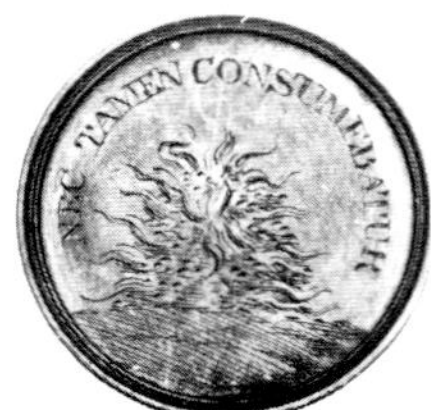

Rulau-E	Date	Metal	Size		VG	F	EF
SC 8	1800	Silver	28mm		—	Rare	—

Chalice and paten on Communion table, THIS DO IN REMEMBRANCE OF ME above. Rv: Burning bush, NEC TAMEN CONSUMEBATUR (nevertheless it was not consumed) above. On edge: PRESBYTERIAN CHURCH OF CHARLESTON, S.C. 1800.

The tokens are hand engraved. In the Civil War (1864), Union soldiers took the church's silver tokens, thinking they were some kind of Confederate money. Only about 10 pieces have survived.

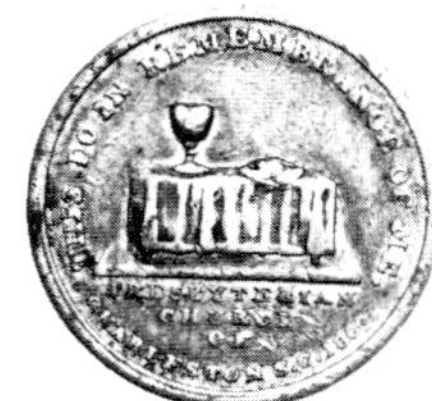 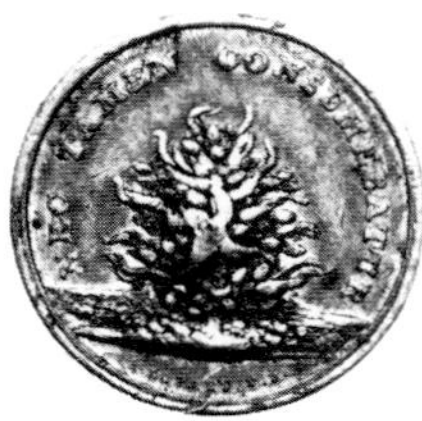

Rulau-E	Date	Metal	Size		VG	F	EF
SC 10	(1830's)	WM	28mm		—	Scarce	—

Similar to last, but struck from dies rather than engraved. Under the table, in four lines: PRESBYTERIAN / CHURCH / OF / CHARLESTON S.C. 1800. Under the burning bush: R. LOVETT N.Y.

This latter token was cut by Robert Lovett of New York for what was evidently a greatly expanded church membership later in the century. Though this piece may be from the wrong time frame for this catalog, we thought it best to include it here to enhance the earlier token's writeup. This piece may have been struck in the 1830-1850 period.

TENNESSEE

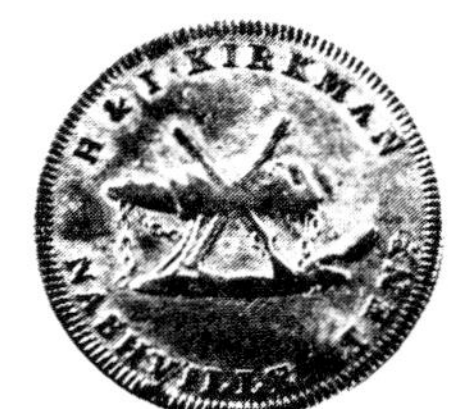 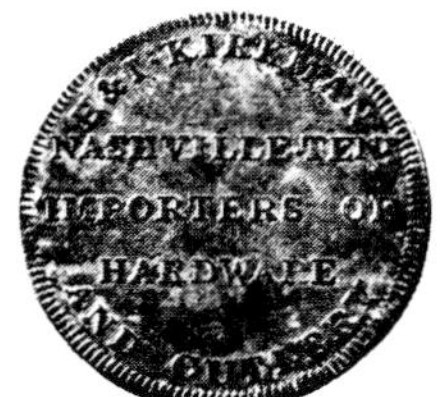

H. & I. KIRKMAN
Nashville, Tenn.

Rulau-E	Date	Metal	Size	Denomination	VG	F	EF
Tenn 59	(?)	Copper	28mm	(1 Cent)	350.00	750.00	2000.

Anvil and implements at center, H & I KIRKMAN above, NASHVILLE TENE. below. Rv: H & I KIRKMAN / NASHVILLE TENE / IMPORTERS OF / HARDWARE / AND CUTLERY.

Rulau-E	Date	Metal	Size	Denomination	VG	F	EF
Tenn 59A	(?)	Brass	28mm	(1 Cent)	350.00	750.00	2000.

As 59.

Rulau-E	Date	Metal	Size	Denomination	VG	F	EF
Tenn 60	(?)	Sil Cop	28mm	(1 Cent)	—	—	Unique

As 59.

Both Adams and Miller (see Bibliography) misspelled this name as KIRKHAM, possibly relying on auction catalog descriptions. However, Wayte Raymond accurately pictured the token in his 1942 *The Standard Catalogue of United States Coins and Tokens*. The specimen pictured is the John Work Garrett specimen sold by Bowers & Ruddy Galleries in 1980.

VERMONT

BRINSMAID'S
Burlington, Vermont

Rulau-E	Date	Metal	Size		VG	F	EF
Vt 3	(1830?)	Silver	40.1mm		—	500.00	—

BRINSMAID'S in relief within rectangular recessed punch ctsp on U.S. 1795 silver dollar. (Johnson & Jensen auction of March 28, 1982, lot 70)

Abram Brinsmaid was born in 1770 in Great Barrington, Mass. He died in Burlington, Vt. in 1811. The silversmith's mark used on this piece, by him and his successors, is widely known among collectors of antique silverware.

The only known specimen occurs on an About Good (well worn) dollar of Bolender type 8, reverse 7, with a bold counterstamp. It was consigned to the Nathan Eglit sale conducted by Johnson & Jensen in 1982.

A successor firm, Pangborn & Brinsmaid, was active circa 1833. An earlier firm, Brinsmaid & Hildreth, used the BRINSMAID'S mark circa 1830.

VIRGINIA

RIGAULT (&) DAWSON
Gloucester County, Va.

 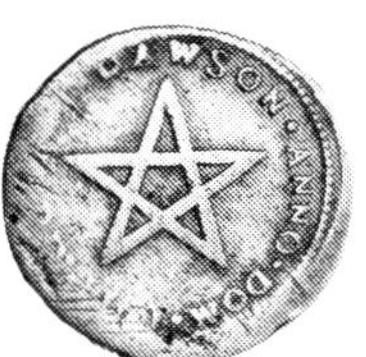

Rulau-E	Date	Metal	Size	Denomination	VG	F	VF
Va 1	1714	Brass	24mm	Shilling	—	—	36,000

Building (court house?) in center, GLOUCESTER COURT HOUSE VIRGINIA / XII around. Rv: Large 5-pointed star at center, RIGAULT DAWSON . ANNO DOM. 1714. Plain edge. (RB)

Va 3	1715	Brass	24mm	Shilling	—	—	Unique

As last, but 1715. Plain edge.

Two genuine specimens of the 1714 date are known, and a cast copy of the 1714 date. One genuine 1714 has a long pedigree — Mickley, Cram, Parmelee, Ten Eyck, Newcomer, Garrett, Don Kagin, Roper. Donald Kagin paid $36,000 for it in the Garrett sale, Oct. 1980, later reselling it.

The other 1714 genuine piece surfaced in March, 1981, and was first published in Nov. 1981. It had been in a family accumulation up to 200 years. It sold in a Bowers-Ruddy sale for $3,250.

The false copy was formerly in the Massachusetts Historical Society collection. It has a long pedigree — Clay, Seavey, Parmelee, Appleton, MHS, Stack's.

The 1715 piece was found with a metal detector in 1982. It has not yet been authenticated.

As tobacco was legal tender in Virginia at this period, the pieces may have been warehouse talleys or served some similar purpose, suggests Q. David Bowers.

Christopher Rigault (or Righault) was a large landowner on Craney Creek and Samuel Dawson was a landowner in Ware Parish, both near the Gloucester courthouse. Rigault and Dawson were apparently merchants in the courthouse area, possibly in the tobacco business.

A . S
(Associate Synod)
Lexington, Va.

Rulau-E	Date	Metal	Size	VG	F	EF
Va 5	(1781)	Lead	20mm			

A . S Rv: Blank. Plain edge.

The issuer is the Timber Ridge Associate Reformed Presbyterian Church, according to Autence A. Bason, in *TAMS Journal* for Feb. 1978.

RICHMOND LIGHT INFANTRY BLUES
Richmond, Va.

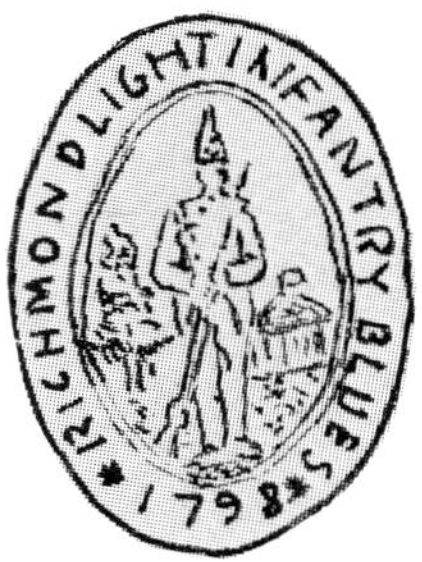

Rulau-E	Date	Metal	Size	F	VF	EF
Va 8	1798 (1830)	Copper	Oval by 37mm	—	—	—

Sentry in late 18th century uniform standing, facing, his musket with fixed bayonet at "port trail arms." Around: RICHMOND LIGHT INFANTRY BLUES / * 1978 *. Rv: Blank. (Wright 893)

It is difficult to fix the issuance date of this piece, which is evidently some early form of identification or membership medalet. It is almost certainly pre-Civil War and is probably much earlier than 1860. The date '1798' refers to the founding date of the Richmond Light Infantry Blues, a militia regiment.

MAVERICKS

A. & W.
Location Not Known

Rulau-E	Date	Metal	Size	VG	F	EF
Mav 1	(?)	Copper	29mm	—	—	—

A & W in relief in toothed rectangular depression ctsp on U.S. 1812 Large cent.

Possibly a silversmith's hallmark. Possibility: Avery & Willis, Salisbury, N.Y., circa 1820.

H. ABENSFELD
Location Not Known

Rulau-E	Date	Metal	Size	VG	F	EF
Mav 1E	(?)	Copper	29mm	—	60.00	—

H. ABENSFELD (in arc) / LOCKSMITH (straight) ctsp on each side of U.S. 180. Large cent. (Donald Partrick coll.)

W.W. AVERILL
Location Not Known

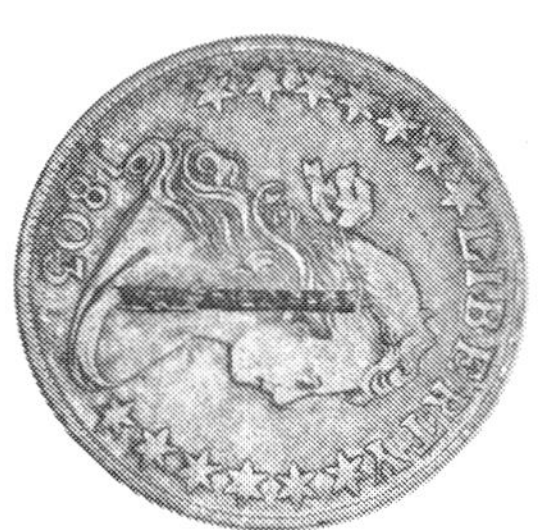

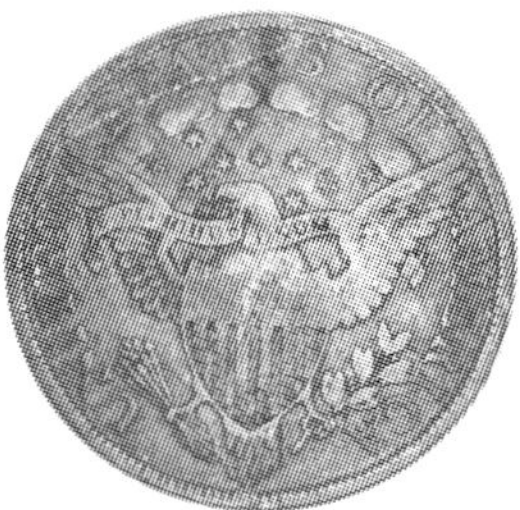

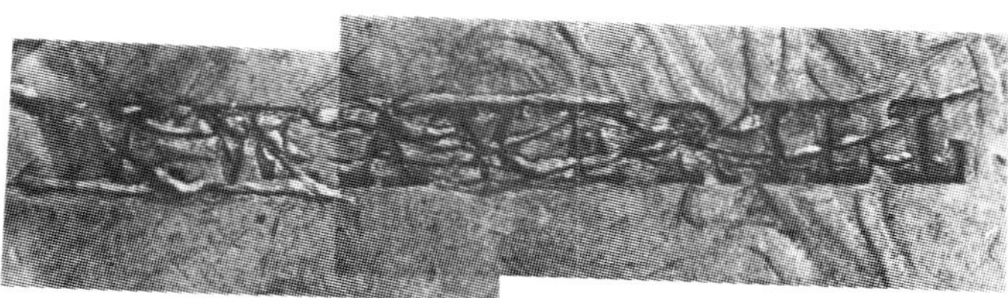

Rulau-E	Date	Metal	Size	VG	F	EF
Mav 2	(?)	Silver	32.5mm	—	135.	—

W.W. AVERILL ctsp on U.S. 1803 Half dollar. (Collection of Donald R. Lewis, Harvester, Mo.)

The blowup photographs of the counterstamp area were made by the American Numismatic Association Certification Service (ANACS) staff in 1982.

H.B
Location Not Known

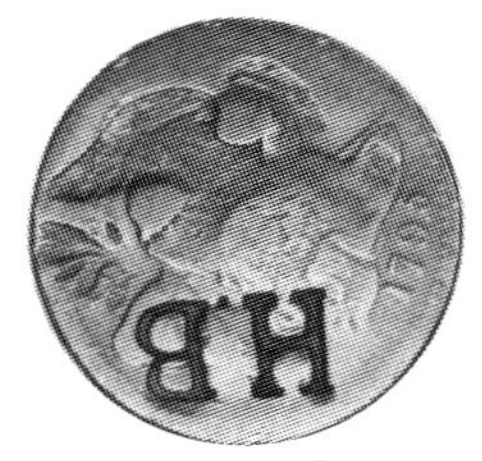

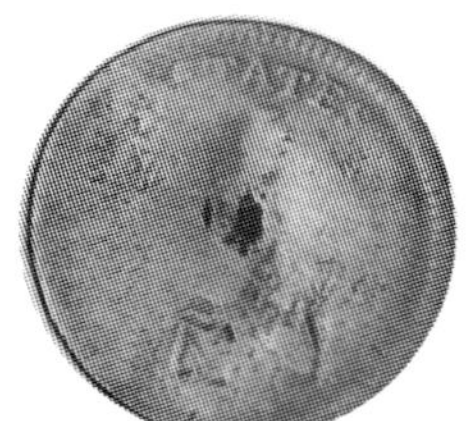

Rulau-E	Date	Metal	Size	VG	F	VF
Mav 3	(?)	Copper	29mm		Unique?	

Large incuse H . B ctsp on U.S. 1795 Large cent, which has first been overstruck with an eagle, head turned left, device over the Liberty head. Details of the head, neckline, Phrygian cap and date are still clearly visible. The overstriking, then the incusing blow, have obscured most reverse details except the word STATES and the dentilated border near it.

Possibilities: Henry Biershing, silversmith, Hagerstown, Md., circa 1815, or Henry Bailey, silversmith, Boston, circa 1780.

I B
Location Not Known

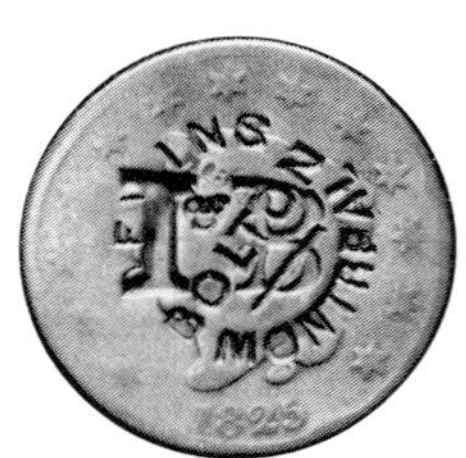

Rulau-E	Date	Metal	Size	VG	F	EF
Mav 5	(?)	Copper	29mm	—	—	—

I B (large) ctsp on U.S. 1825 Large cent. (This piece later was ctsp by Devins & Bolton of Montreal, Canada)

Rulau-E	Date	Metal	Size	VG	F	EF
Mav 6	(?)	Copper	29mm	—	—	—

Similar ctsp on U.S. 1823 Large cent. (Hallenbeck 9.001)

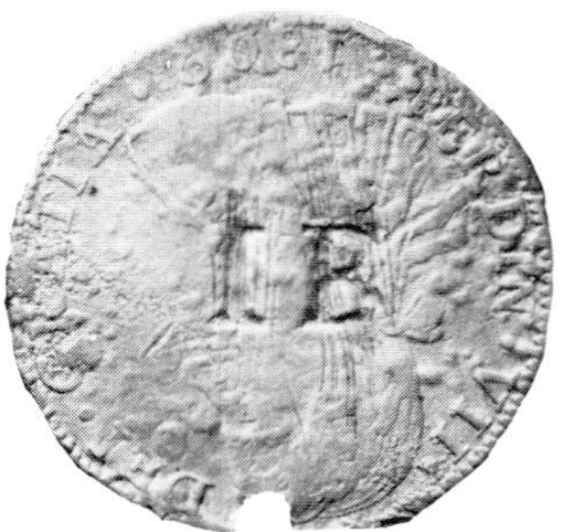

Rulau-E	Date	Metal	Size	VG	F	EF
Mav 7	(?)	Silver	39mm	—	—	—

Similar ctsp on Spanish-American 1809-Mo 8-reales.

Both coins in collection of Frank Kovacs, San Francisco.

J.P.B.
Location Not Known

Rulau-E	Date	Metal	Size	VG	F	EF
Mav 9	(?)	Silver	32.5mm	30.00	—	—

J P B monogram in relief within oval depression ctsp on U.S. 1812 Bust half dollar. (Frank Kovacs coll.)

P.J. BAKER
Location Not Known

Rulau-E	Date	Metal	Size		VG	F	VF
Mav 10	(?)	Copper	29mm		—	40.00	—

P.J. BAKER / A.R.M. CO. ctsp on worn 1787 New Jersey "Nova Caesarea" cent, holed. (John Cheramy coll.)

R B
Location Not Known

Rulau-E	Date	Metal	Size		VG	F	EF
Mav 10E	(ca 1780 ?)	Silver	24mm		—	400.00	—

Large R B ctsp on Massachusetts 1652-dated Oak Tree shilling which has been clipped down about 2mm and is holed. (Frank Kovacs coll., San Francisco)

The Massachusetts Oak Tree coinage was struck in the 1660-1667 period. It is possible this store card (if it is that) could have passed for a shilling late in the 18th century. The initials may also be frivolous.

S. BEWER
Location Not Known

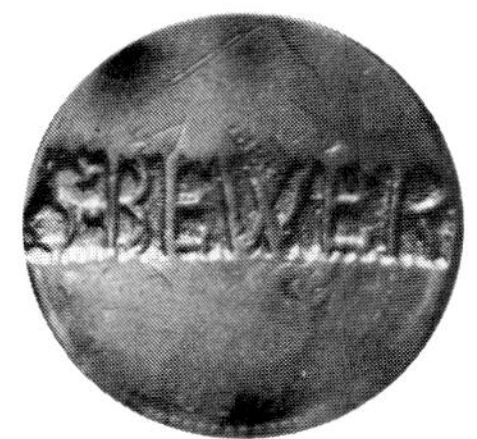

		Metal	Size		VG	F	VF
Mav 11	(?)	Copper	29mm		—	25.00	—

S. BEWER in relief within toothed recessed rectangle ctsp on U.S. 1818 Large cent. (Frank Kovacs coll.)

S. BOARDMAN
Location Not Known

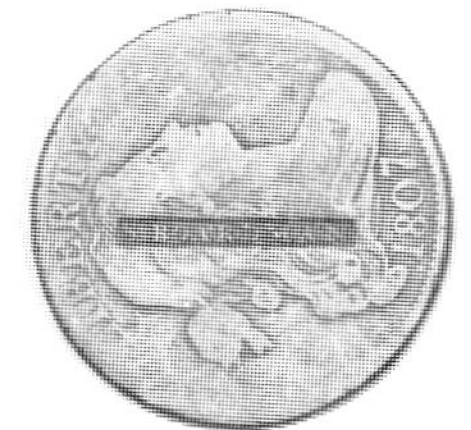 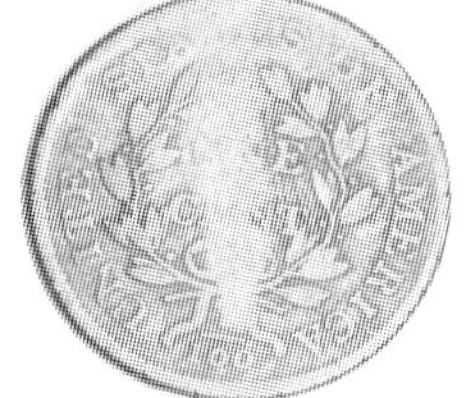

Rulau-E	Date	Metal	Size		VG	F	VF
Mav 11E	(?)	Copper	29mm		—	—	65.00

S. BOARDMAN in relief within rect. depression ctsp on U.S. 1807 over 6 Large cent.

JOHN Q. BOYCE
Location Not Known

Rulau-E	Date	Metal	Size		VG	F	EF
Mav 12	(?)	Copper	28mm		—	130.00	—

JOHN Q BOYCE CENT ctsp on U.S. 1783 Nova Constellatio cent. (Kagin 1978 GENA sale, lot 1623)

J. BURNS
Location Not Known

Mav 13	1829	Copper	29mm		—	20.00	—

J: BURNS (in relief within rectangular depression) / 1829 (incuse) / (Long bar) (incuse) / DN upside down (incuse) / J: BURNS (in relief within rect. depression) — all ctsp on U.S. 1821 Large cent. (Kovacs coll.)

Possibility: John H. Burns, silversmith, New York City, circa 1835.

M. C.
Location Not Known

Rulau-E	Date	Metal	Size		VG	F	EF
Mav 15	(?)	Copper	29mm (Cent)		—	25.00	—

M. C. ctsp on Connecticut AUCTORI CONNEC 1785-88 cent.

Once attributed to silversmiths Coit & Mansfield (1816-19 in Norwich, Conn.), but verification could not be achieved.

E. G. DRAKE
Location Not Known

Rulau-E	Date	Metal	Size		F	VF	EF
Mav 16	(?)	Copper	29mm		—	55.00	—

E. G. DRAKE in relief within toothed rect. depression ctsp on U.S. 1798 Large cent. (Donald Partrick coll.)

EVERDELL
Location Not Known

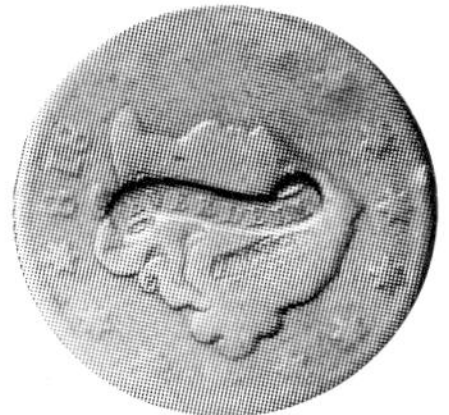

		Metal	Size				
Mav 17	(?)	Copper	29mm		—	60.00	—

EVERDELL in relief within curved scroll-shaped depression ctsp on U.S. 1818 Large cent. (Frank Kovacs coll.)

Every indication points to the Early American period for this stamp. The stamp resembles a silversmith's signature stamp.

J. G.
Location Not Known

		Copper	29mm		—	—	—
Mav 19	(?)						

J . G in relief within toothed rect. depression ctsp on U.S. 1798 Large cent (Kovacs coll.)

This may be James Gough, New York, circa 1769-1799.

J. O. G.
Location Not Known

Mav 19E	(?)	Copper	29mm				

J. O. G. in relief within toothed depression ctsp on U.S. 1810 Large cent.

GARDINER
Location Not Known

Mav 20	(?)	Copper	28mm (Cent)		—	50.00	—

GARDINER ctsp on Mott 1789 cent token of New York City. (Gould 1431)

This could be an unrecorded hallmark of silversmith Baldwin Gardiner, who worked in Philadelphia 1814-22 and New York 1827-40. The usual hallmarks were B GARDINER and B. G or variations with '& CO.' added.

A. H.
Location Not Known

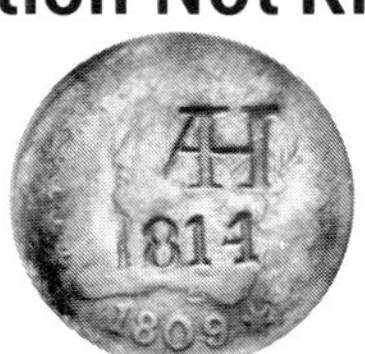

Mav 21	1814	Copper	23mm		—	30.00	—

AH monogram / 1814 ctsp on U.S. 1809 Half cent. (Frank Kovacs coll.)

V. HOLTBY
Location Not Known

Mav 22	(?)	Copper	29mm		—	—	—

V. HOLTBY ctsp on U.S. Large cent, date worn off.

W. W. IVES
Location Not Known

Rulau-E	Date	Metal	Size		VG	F	EF
Mav 24	(?)	Silver	32.5mm		—	30.00	—

W. W. IVES ctsp on obverse of U.S. 1810 Bust half dollar. Similar ctsp on reverse of coin. (Frank Kovacs coll.)

I K
Location Not Known

Rulau-E	Date	Metal	Size		VG	F	EF
Mav 27	(1810-19)	Copper	29mm		—	25.00	—

I K in toothed rectangular cartouche ctsp on England 1773 Halfpenny of George III (possibly a Machins Mill imitation). (Steinberg Jan. 1982 mail bid sale)

Possibly Joseph Keeler, who was a silversmith in Norwalk, Conn. Born 1786, died 1824. He was active about 1810.

ASA LAW
Location Not Known

Rulau-E	Date	Metal	Size		VG	F	EF
Mav 28	(ca 1800)	Copper	29mm		—	25.00	—

ASA 1783 LAW ctsp on U.S. 1797 Large cent. (Stanley Steinberg 1981 sale)

Attributed to Hartford, Conn., but this could not be verified.

P.M.
Location Not Known

Rulau-E	Date	Metal	Size		G	F	EF
Mav 30	1821	Copper	29mm	(Cent)	—	—	—

U.S. 1795 Large cent ctsp: P inside small oval depression at center. Above is ctsp P M, to right 1821, at bottom 1821. (It has been theorized that this may be an early Peale's Museum admission check of Philadelphia).

This could also be the mark of silversmith Peter Mood Sr. (1766-1821) of Charleston, S.C., or his son, Peter Mood Jr. (1796-1879).

M. MILLER
Location Not Known

Rulau-E	Date	Metal	Size		VG	F	EF
Mav 31	1822	Copper	29mm		—	25.00	—

1822 / M. MILLER / 26 ctsp. on U.S. Large cent.

E. L. NORFOLK (and)
T. PARKER
Location Not Known

Rulau-E	Date	Metal	Size		VG	F	EF
Mav 33	(?)	Silver	27mm		—	25.00	—

E. L. NORFOLK / T. PARKER ctsp on U.S. 1821 Bust quarter dollar. (Partrick coll.)

J. O.
Location Not Known

Rulau-E	Date	Metal	Size		VG	F	EF
Mav 35	1820	Copper	29mm		—	—	—

J O / 1820 ctsp on U.S. Large cent, date illegible. (Kovacs coll.)

B. P.
Location Not Known

Rulau-E	Date	Metal	Size		VG	F	EF
Mav 35E	(?)	Silver	27mm		—	35.00	—

B. P in relief within recessed square ctsp on Spanish-American 2-reales. (Gould 415ff)

It is possible this is the hallmark of silversmith Benjamin H. Pierpont of Boston, Mass., born 1730, died 1797.

A less probable silversmith's mark would be that of B. Peck, Connecticut, circa 1820.

P. PIERCE
Location Not Known

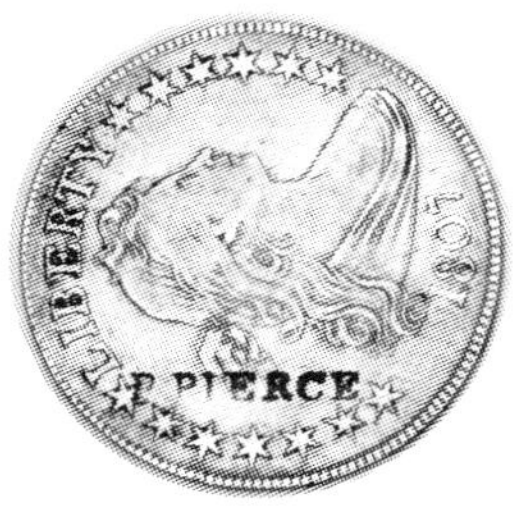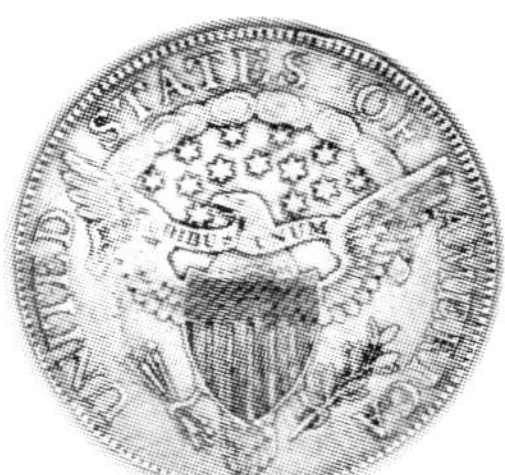

Rulau-E	Date	Metal	Size		VG	F	EF
Mav 36	(?)	Silver	32.5mm		—	—	85.00

P. PIERCE ctsp on U.S. 1807 Bust-Heraldic Eagle half dollar. (Krause collection)

S. W. REED
Location Not Known

Rulau-E	Date	Metal	Size		VG	F	EF
Mav 37	(?)	Copper	29mm		—	25.00	—

S. W. REED in relief within toothed rectangular depression ctsp on U.S. 1816 Large cent. Also crude Masonic device and TOOLMASTER on obverse. Rv: Same Reed cartouche ctsp on reverse of coin.

Reed is reputed to have been a Philadelphia silversmith, according to Stanley Steinberg, Malden, Mass. Not in 1837 city directory or in the Kovel or Wyler references on silversmiths.

J. T. S.
Location Not Known

Rulau-E	Date	Metal	Size		VG	F	VF
Mav 39	1830	Copper	25.5mm		—	—	Rare

J. T. S. / 1830 stamped on planchet. Rv: Same incused (intaglio?). (Wright 527)

C. SCOTT
Location Not Known

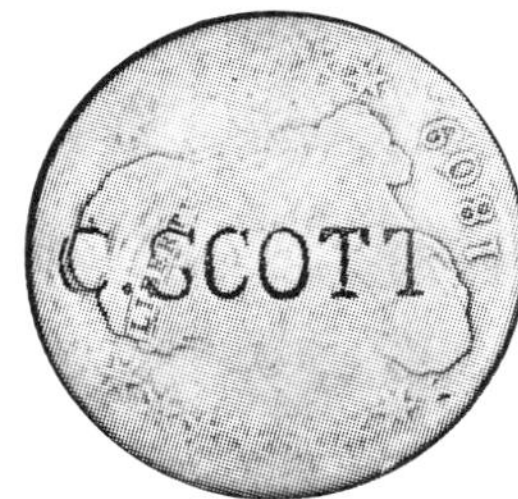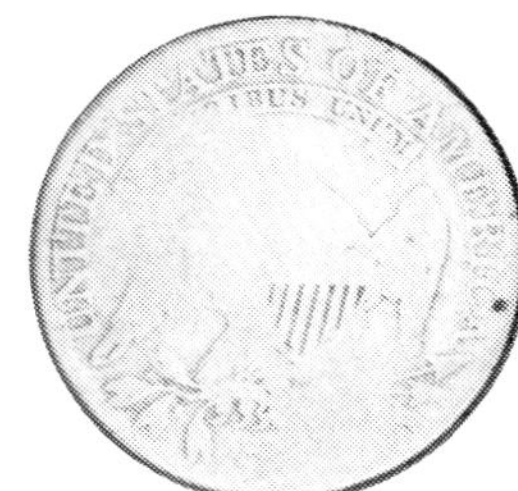

Rulau-E	Date	Metal	Size		VG	F	EF
Mav 41	(?)	Silver	32.5mm		—	45.00	—

C. SCOTT in large letters ctsp on U.S. 1809 Turban Head half dollar. (Rulau coll.)

Possibility: Charles Scott, silversmith, Penn Yan, N.Y., circa 1839.

P. STOW
Location Not Known

Rulau-E	Date	Metal	Size		VG	F	EF
Mav 42	(?)	Copper	29mm		—	20.00	—

P. STOW in relief within crude rectangular depression ctsp on U.S. 1801 Large cent. (Kurt Krueger coll.)

STROHECKER
Location Not Known

Rulau-E	Date	Metal	Size		VG	F	VF
Mav 44	(?)	Silver	40mm		—	—	2,000.

STROHECKER ctsp on each side of U.S. 1796 Small date, Large letters silver dollar. (Only known specimen reported 1983 by Harvey Gamer.)

T
Location Not Known

Rulau-E	Date	Metal	Size	VG	F	EF
La 11	(?)	Copper	29mm	—	—	—

'T' in toothed heart-shaped depression ctsp on U.S. 1822 Large cent. (Steinberg Jan. 1982 sale)

Stanley L. Steinberg says this is attributable to William Theofile of New Orleans, but gives no details on his rationale for this. Theofile was a silversmith active beginning about 1822.

C.T.
Location Not Known

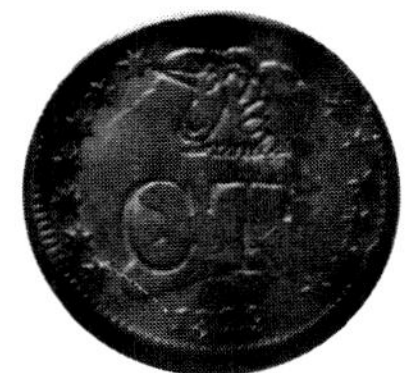

Rulau-E	Date	Metal	Size	VG	F	EF
Mav 46	(?)	Copper	23.5mm	—	20.00	—

Large C.T. in relief within toothed recessed rectangular depression ctsp on U.S. 1805 Half cent. (Hartzog coll.)

R.F.
Location Not Known

Rulau-E	Date	Metal	Size	VG	F	VF
Mav 18	(?)	Copper	29mm	—	20.00	—

R F in relief within recessed rectangular depression ctsp on U.S. 1801 Large cent. (Hartzog coll.)

H. TOWLE
Location Not Known

Rulau-E	Date	Metal	Size	VG	VF	EF
Mav 50	(1835)	Copper	29mm	—	25.00	—

H. TOWLE in relief within recessed rectangular depression ctsp on U.S. 1807 Large cent. (Rich Hartzog collection)

The style of countermark is that of a jeweler's hallmark. H. Towle's location and work is not known to silver experts.

It is possible there is a connection between the H. Towle of this mark and the Towle Mfg. Co., silversmiths of Newburyport, Mass., which was formed only in 1857 as Towle & Jones (by Anthony F. Towle and William P. Jones) and became A.F. Towle & Son in 1873 (Anthony F. and Edward B. Towle) and Towle Mfg. Co. in 1882.

A. WHITCOM
Location Not Known

Rulau-E	Date	Metal	Size	Denomination	VG	F	EF
Mav 55	1827	Copper	29mm	(Cent)			Ex. Rare
Mav 56	1827	Silver	32.5mm	(50 Cents)	—	—	75.00
Mav 57	1827	Silver	32.5mm	(50 Cents)	—	—	75.00

A. WHITCOM 1827 in script counterstamped on U.S. Large cent. (Hallenbeck 23.509)

Similar ctsp on U.S. 1806 half dollar. (Don Ketterling coll.)

Similar ctsp on U.S. 1826 Bust half dollar. (Harvey Gamer coll.)

H. WHITCOM
Location Not Known

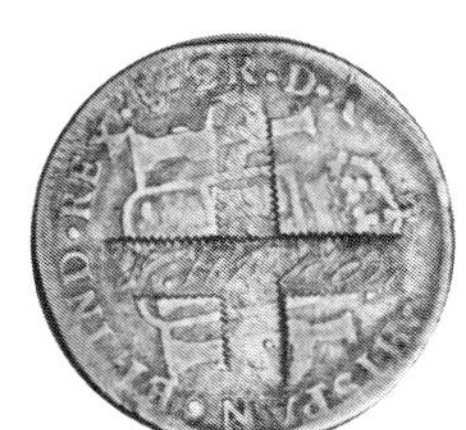
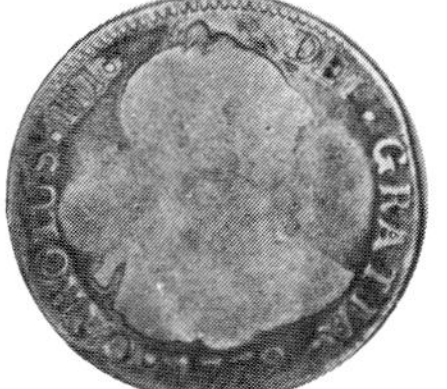

Rulau-E	Date	Metal	Size	VG	F	VF
Mav 58	1827	Silver	27mm	—	—	100.00

July 1827 / H. Whitcom (all in script) in relief within large finely-toothed rectangular depression, ctsp on Spanish-American 1779-So-DA 2-reales. The ctsp has been applied twice, at right angles to form a cross. The word 'July' is not clear; it could as easily be 'Jany'. (Holland Wallace coll. Sausalito, Calif.)

Brunk reports the A. WHITCOM 1827 stamp, noting that it occurs on an 1806 Large cent and half dollars dated 1800 and 1817. He also calls it a "commemorative advertising countermark." Some of the foregoing Whitcom token descriptions may be partially due to faulty reporting of the specimens.

J. WINNER
Location Not Known

Rulau-E	Date	Metal	Size	VG	F	EF
Mav 60	(?)	Copper	23mm	—	27.50	—
Mav 60E	(?)	Copper	29mm	—	27.50	—
Mav 60F	(?)	Copper	29mm	—	27.50	—

J. WINNER ctsp on U.S. 1805 Half cent. (Kurt R. Krueger coll.)

Similar ctsp on U.S. 1807 Large cent. (Donald Partrick coll.)

Similar ctsp on U.S. 1817 Large cent. (Partrick coll.)

HANN(A)H WINTER
Location Not Known

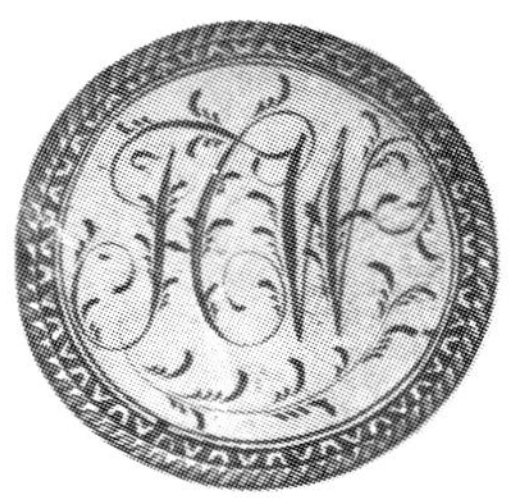
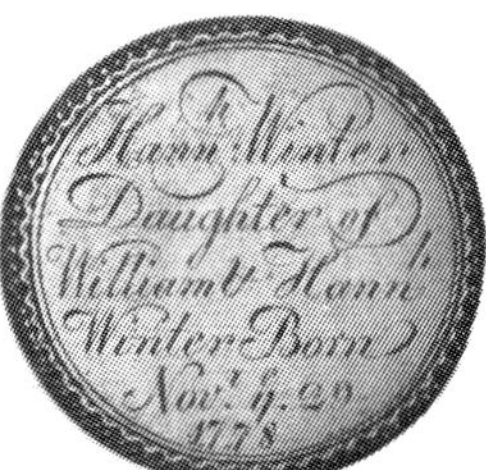

Rulau-E	Date	Metal	Size	VG	F	VF
Mav 61	1778	Silver	32mm			Unique

(Engraved on planed-off sides). Large ornate script monogram HW circled by double fret border at rim. Rv: (All script) within fret border at rim: HANNH: WINTER / DAUGHTER OF / WILLIAM & HANNH / WINTER BORN / NOVR. YE. 29 / 1778.

Generally engraved pieces (so-called "love tokens") are avoided in this reference. This piece is included as a classic example of the "birth token" prevalent among upper classes at this period. Though it has not been traced, this type of engraved coin would be easiest to attribute, since it contains so much precise information.

The underlying coin may have been a Spanish-American 4-reales or English half crown. The people involved could have been English rather than American.

K 1830
Location Not Known

Rulau-E	Date	Metal	Size	VG	F	VF
Mav 65	1830	Copper	29mm	—	20.00	—

K / 1830. 2. d. 9 ctsp on U.S. 1827 Large cent. (Stanley L. Steinberg 1983 sale)

It has been suggested the '2. d. 9' might be an English denomination, but this seems unlikely.

EAGLE, 18
Location Not Known

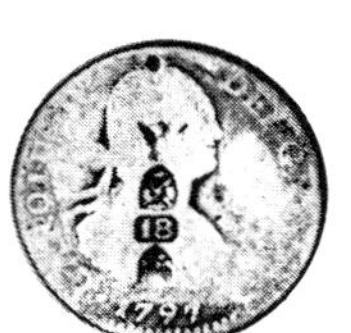
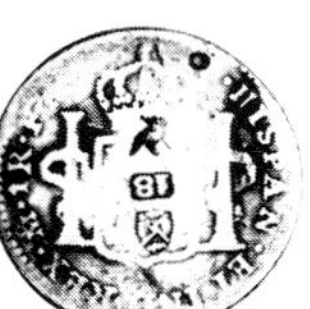

Rulau-E	Date	Metal	Size	VG	F	EF
Mav 80	(?)	Silver	21mm	—	50.00	—

Series of four hallmarks arranged vertically, ctsp on Spanish-American 1797-Mo-FM 1-real. On obverse: Eagle-Windmill-18-Scales. On reverse: Windmill-18-Eagle. (Kurt Krueger Sept. 7, 1983 sale, lot 153)

The hallmarks seem to be American or European, but no trace of them can be found in the standard references on silver and pewter ware by Kovel, Wyler or others. The eagle seems distinctly American.

NON-LOCAL PIECES

WASHINGTON — LIBERTY AND SECURITY TOKENS

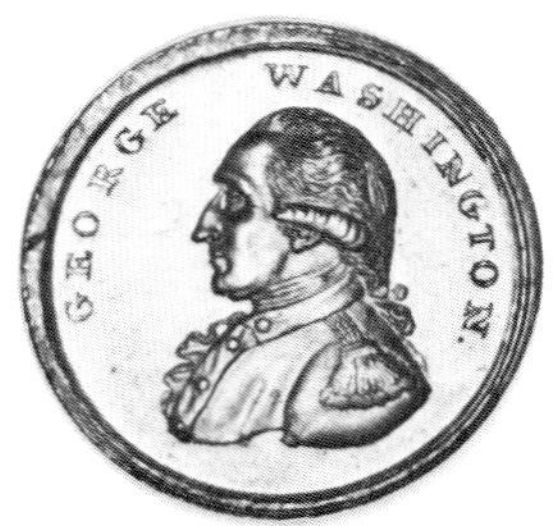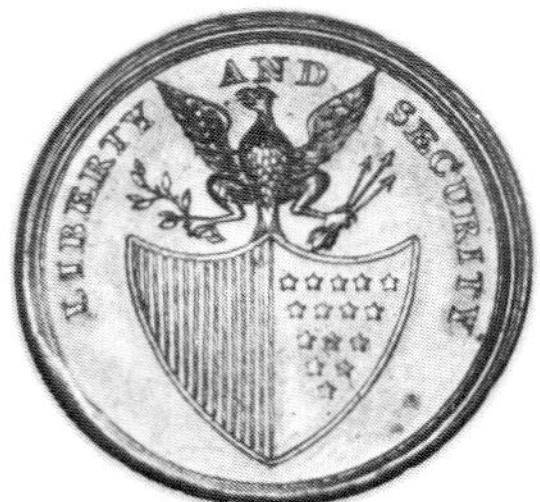

Rulau-E	Date	Metal	Size	Denomination	F	VF	Unc
Non 1	(1795)	Copper	33mm	(Penny)	150.00	275.00	1000.

Uniformed bust left, GEORGE WASHINGTON around. Rv: U.S. arms in spade-shaped shield, above which is an eagle with wings outspread, clutching an olive branch and five arrows in its talons. LIBERTY AND SECURITY around. Two concentric rings around rim. Edge lettered: AN ASYLUM FOR THE OPPRESS'D OF ALL NATIONS X:X. (D&H Middlesex 243; Atkins Middlesex 42) (Also known with plain and corded edges)

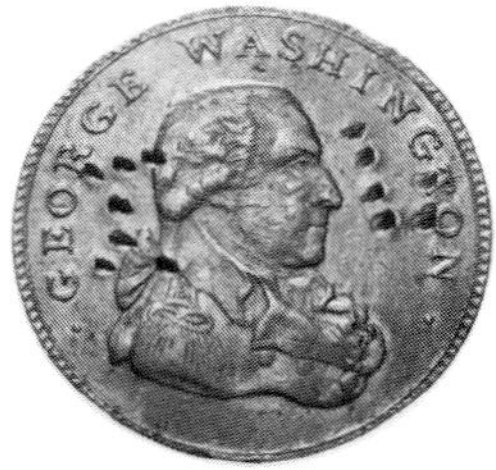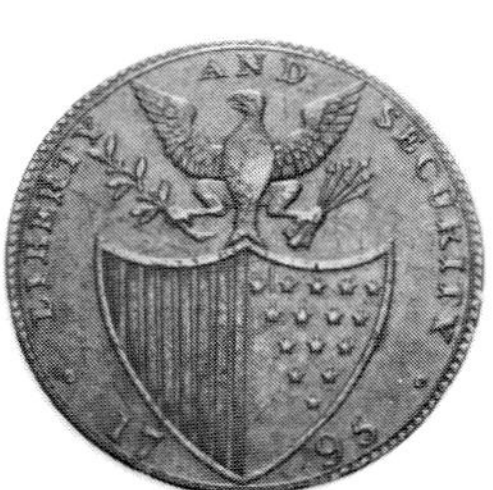

Rulau-E	Date	Metal	Size	Denomination			
Non 2	1795	Copper	33mm	(Penny)			Ex. Rare

Uniformed bust right, GEORGE WASHINGTON around. Rv: Similar to last, but larger shield, and date 17 — 95 divided by shield's point. Single rim around rim, which is dentilated. Edge same as last (AN ASYLUM). (D&H Middlesex 244; Atkins Middlesex 43). Extremely rare.

Non-2A	1795	Copper	33mm	(Penny)	—	—	Unique

As 2. Plain edge. (Aston collection)

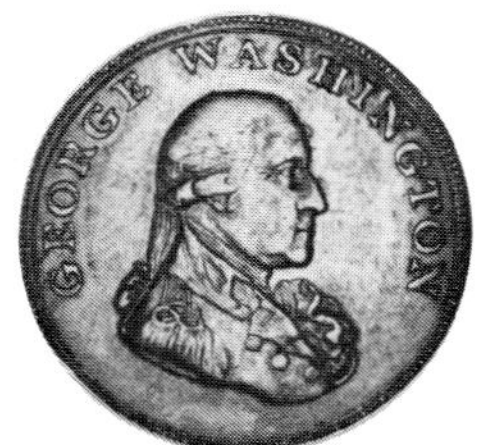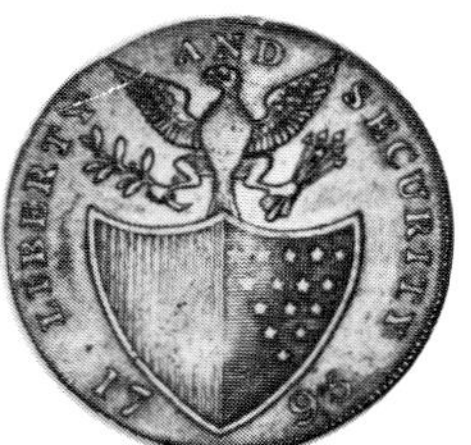

Rulau-E	Date	Metal	Size	Denomination	VG	F	EF
Non 3	1795	Copper	29mm	(½ Penny)	60.00	100.00	325.00

Uniformed bust right, GEORGE WASHINGTON around. Rv: As D&H Middlesex 244, in smaller size. Edge lettered: PAYABLE AT LONDON LIVERPOOL OR BRISTOL. (D&H Middlesex 1052a; Atkins Middlesex176a)

Non 4	1795	Copper	29mm	(½ Penny)	125.00	300.00	675.00

As last, but edge reads: AN ASYLUM FOR THE OPPRESS'D OF ALL NATIONS. (D&H Middlesex 1052b; Atkins Middlesex 176b)

Non 5	1795	Copper	29mm	(½ Penny)	85.00	150.00	450.00

As last, but edge is plain. (D&H Middlesex 1052c; Atkins Middlesex 176c)

Non 6	1795	Copper	29mm	(½ Penny)	75.00	125.00	400.00

As last, but edge lettered with BIRMINGHAM legend.

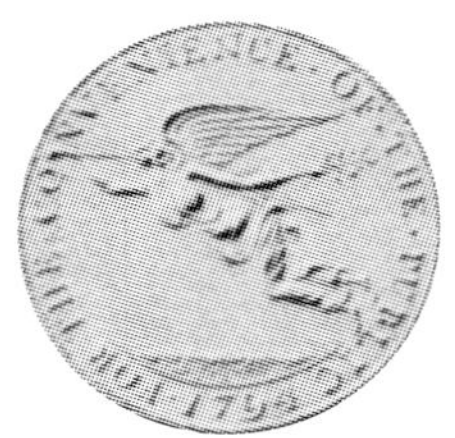

Rulau-E	Date	Metal	Size	Denomination	VG	F	EF
Non 7	1795	Copper	29mm	(½ Penny)	—	—	Ex. Rare

Figure of Fame flying left, blowing a trumpet. FOR. THE. CONVENIENCE. OF. THE PUBLIC / .1794. Rv: Same as D&H Middlesex 1052a, above. Plain edge. (D&H Cork 13; Atkins Cork 12). Extremely rare.

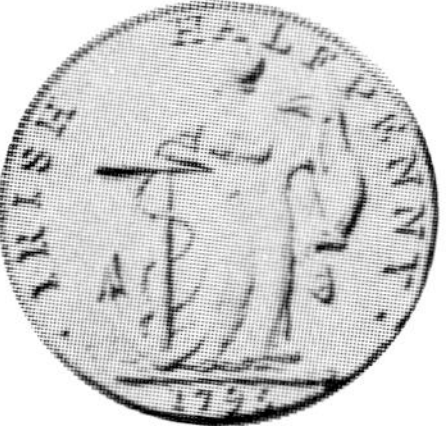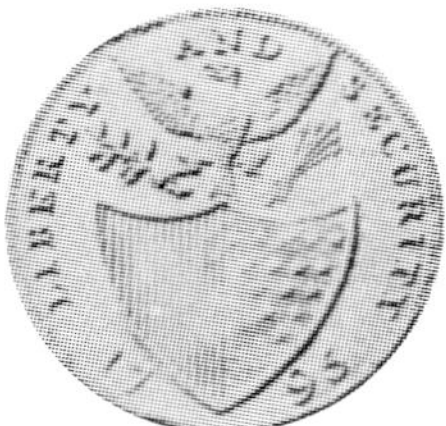

Rulau-E	Date	Metal	Size	Denomination	F	VF	Unc
Non 8	1795	Copper	29mm	(½ Penny)	100.00	200.00	300.00

Figure of Hope standing, leaning on an anchor. Around: . IRISH HALFPENNY . / 1795. Rv: Same as last. Edge lettered: PAYABLE AT LONDON LIVERPOOL OR BRISTOL. (D&H Dublin 9; Atkins Dublin 8)

These Washington pieces were excluded from the First Edition of this book. However, so much misunderstanding about these English-made tokens is accepted that we thought it best to include the Liberty and Security series in this reference.

According to Thomas Sharp *Catalogue of the Provincial Copper Coins, Tokens and Medalets . . . in the Collection of Sir George Chetwynd, Bart.),* the issuer of the "Cork mules" was Matthew Denton, a coin dealer of West Smithfield, London. In this instance Denton apparently had the Liberty and Security mulings struck by William Lutwyche of Birmingham.

Denton or Thomas Prattent, another coin dealer of West Smithfield, London, may have been responsible for the Washington-head tokens; if so they copied the military bust device of Thomas Wyon, whose Washington portrait on the so-called "Grate halfpenny" was the model.

All the Liberty and Security tokens were apparently made for sale in America as well as in England. The Washington halfpenny reached the U.S. in moderate quantities.

WASHINGTON — GRATE TOKENS
London, England

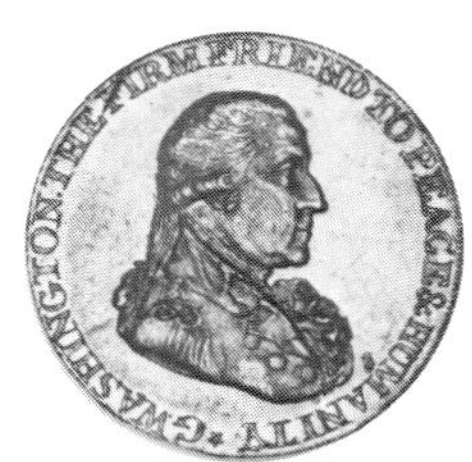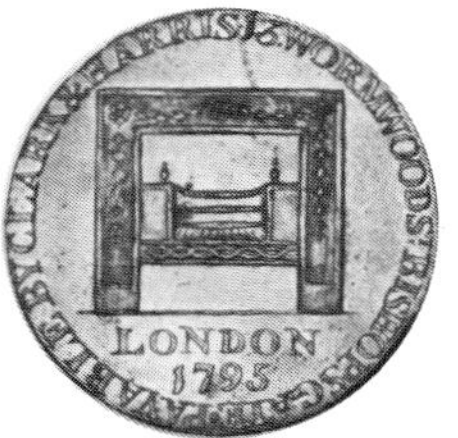

Rulau-E	Date	Metal	Size	Denomination	VF	EF	Unc
Non 10	1795	Copper	29mm	(½ Penny)	350.00	650.00	1300.

Washington bust right. Large buttons on coat. Around: G. WASHINGTON. THE FIRM FRIEND TO PEACE & HUMANITY *. Rv: Open stove, LONDON / 1795 below. Around: PAYABLE BY CLARK & HARRIS 13. WORMWOOD ST. BISHOPSGATE. Edge lettered: PAYABLE AT LONDON LIVERPOOL OR BRISTOL. (D&H Middlesex 283; Atkins Middlesex 201) (Also known in Brass)

Non 11	1795	Copper	29mm	(½ Penny)	75.00	150.00	450.00

As last, but edge reeded diagonally right. (D&H Middlesex 283a; Atkins Middlesex 201a)

Non 12	1795	Copper	29mm	(½ Penny)	—	Rare	—

As last, but edge reeded diagonally left. (D&H Middlesex 283b; Atkins Middlesex 201b)

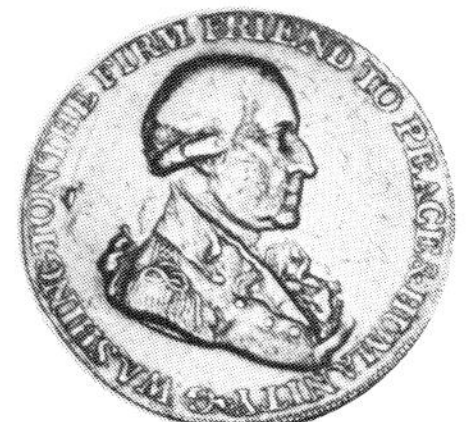

Rulau-E	Date	Metal	Size	Denomination	VF	EF	Unc
Non 13	1795	Copper	29mm	(½ Penny)	160.00	325.00	800.00

Similar to last, but small buttons on coat. End of the obverse legend is nearer the star, and the bust. Edge reeded to right. (D&H Middlesex 284; Atkins Middlesex 202)

Designed by Thomas Wyon and struck by James Good, both in Birmingham, England.

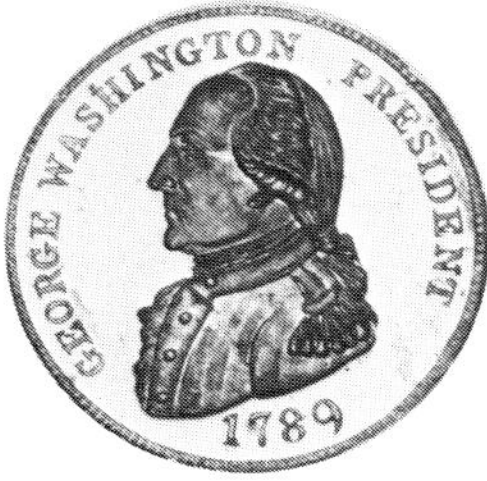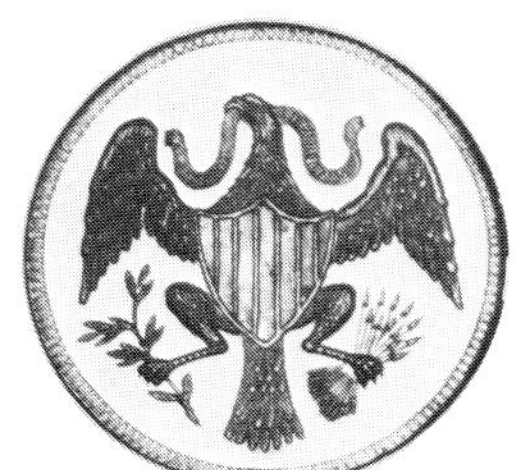

Rulau-E	Date	Metal	Size	Denomination	F	VF	Unc
Non 15	1789	Copper	32mm	(Penny)	—	—	—

Military bust left, GEORGE WASHINGTON PRESIDENT around, 1789 below. Rv: Eagle displayed, shield on its breast with six vertical lines on it. Plain edge. (D&H Middlesex 242; Baker 14)

This is a fantasy piece by Alfred Robinson (1836-1876). It is also known in bronze and silver. No genuine originals exist.

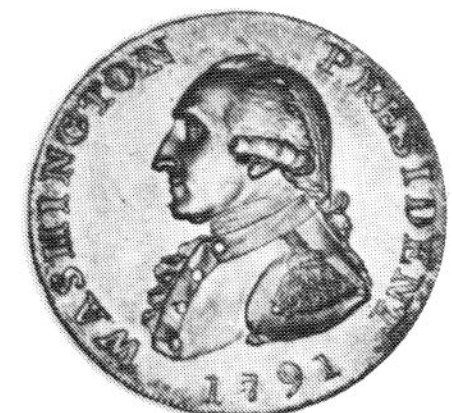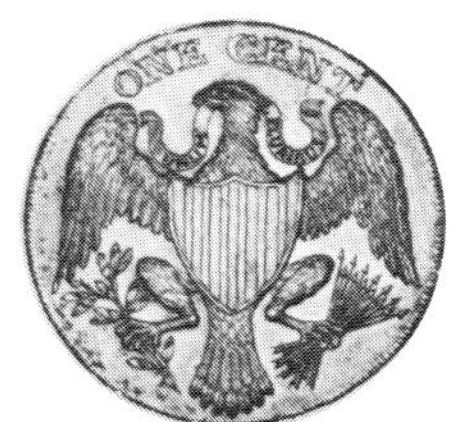

Non 18	1791	Copper	30mm	Cent	150.00	450.00	1000.

Military bust left, WASHINGTON PRESIDENT around, 1791 below. Rv: Large eagle displayed. ONE CENT above. Edge lettered: UNITED STATES OF AMERICA . X . (D&H Middlesex 1049)

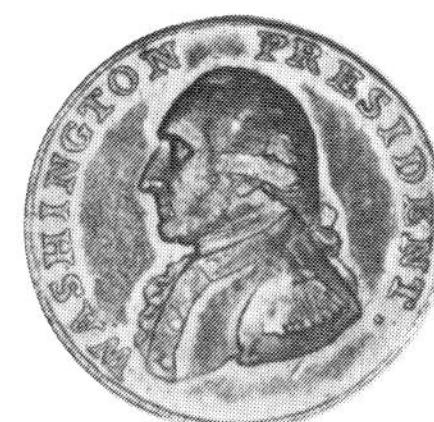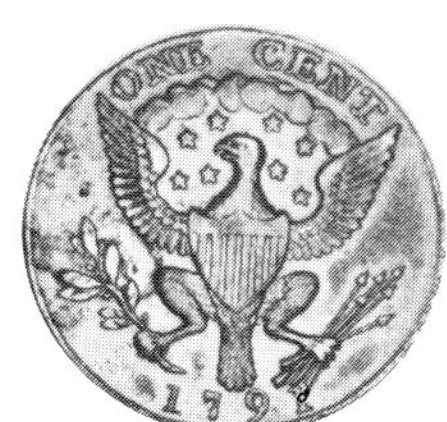

Non 19	1791	Copper	30mm	Cent	150.00	450.00	1100.

Obverse similar to 18, no date under bust. Rv: Small eagle displayed, cloud and eight stars above, ONE CENT at top, 1791 at bottom. Edge as 18. (D&H Middlesex 1050)

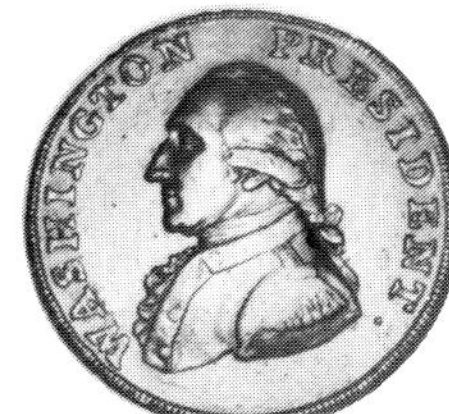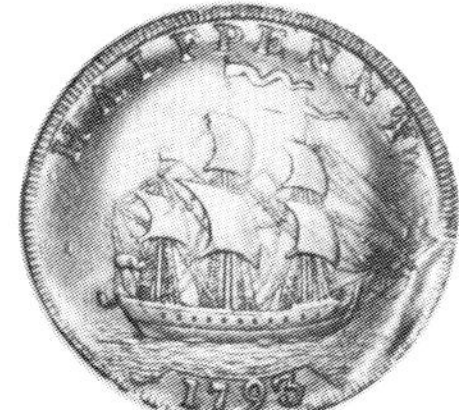

Non 20	1793	Copper	30mm	(½ Penny)	400.00	1000.	2000.

Obverse as 19. Rv: Three-masted ship sailing right, HALFPENNY above, 1793 below. Edge lettered: PAYABLE IN ANGLESEY LONDON OR LIVERPOOL . X . (D&H Middlesex 1051)

Number Non 20 was designed by John Gregory Hancock Sr., according to Charles Pye, a contemporary writer on tokens. Hancock was a Birmingham maker and probably is also responsible for 18 and 19 as well.

The three pieces (Non 18, 19 and 20) were samples for a private coinage which never eventuated, according to Anthony Terranova and Steve Tanenbaum.

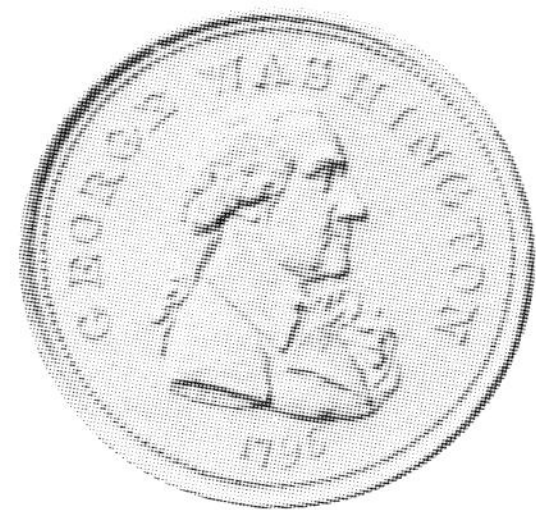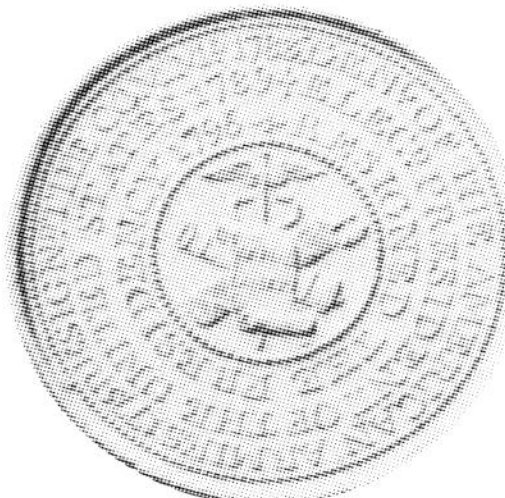

Rulau-E	Date	Metal	Size	Denomination	F	EF	Unc
Non 22	1796	Copper	33mm	(Penny)	—	—	—

Bust right, WYON on truncation. GEORGE WASHINGTON around, 1796 below. Rv: Caduceus, crossed cannon and fasces, and scroll within central circle. Three concentric lines of text around, beginning: GENL OF THE AMERICAN ARMIES. (D&H Middlesex 245)

As stated, Wyon was the designer of this handsome piece in England.

(WASHINGTON BUST)

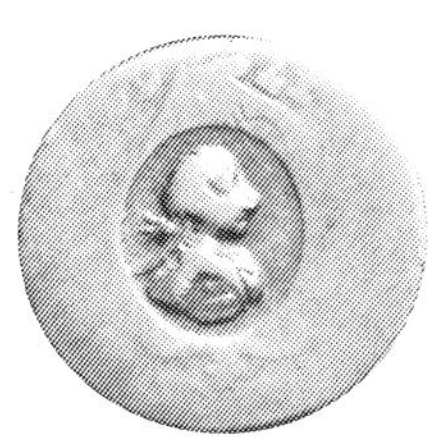

Rulau-E	Date	Metal	Size	VG	F	EF
Non 100	(?)	Copper	28mm	—	100.00	—

Military bust of Washington (?) right, in relief within 12 by 15mm oval depression, ctsp on Ireland imitation 1766 halfpenny. (Kovacs coll.)

Discovered in London recently by Frank Kovacs, who calls this bust Washington rather than George III because of its similarity to Crosby plate X, 17, the military jacket with epaulette and broad lapel.

There are several other Washington busts counterstamped on U.S. coins, all listed in the 1965 Fuld revision of Baker's *Medallic Portraits of Washington*. They are listed below.

Rulau-E	Date	Metal	Size	VG	F	EF
Non 101	(1799)	Copper	29mm	—	—	Unique?

Washington bust left (relief, within upright oval depression) ctsp on U.S. Large cent. The bust is from the hub of the Funeral medal, Baker 169 etc. (See illust. under Funeral medals in Baker-Fuld revision)

Rulau-E	Date	Metal	Size	VG	F	EF
Non 101A	1824	Copper	29mm	—	—	Scarce

Head of Washington left, GEORGE WASHINGTON around, in relief within circular depression, ctsp on obverse of U.S. Large cent. Rv: Head of Lafayette right, GENERAL LA FAYETTE 1824 around, in relief within circular depression, ctsp on reverse of the coin. Dates examined: 1820. (This is Baker die 198, Raymond 35)

Other items known: Tiny Washington head right in oval depression, ctsp circa 1825 on U.S. 1820 Bust dime.

Washington military bust left in circular depression ctsp on planed-off U.S. silver dollar. Reverse side engraved script monogram ALS (?) — the so-called 'Stickney' Perkins dollar.

(RADIANT EAGLE)

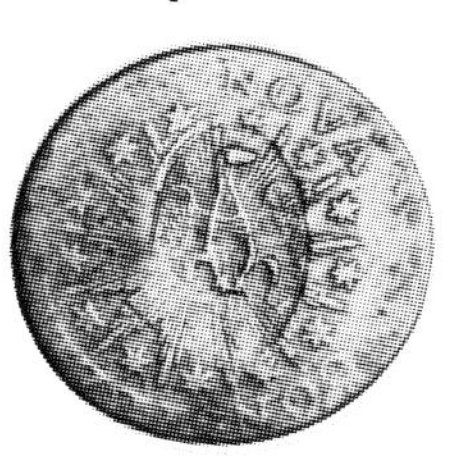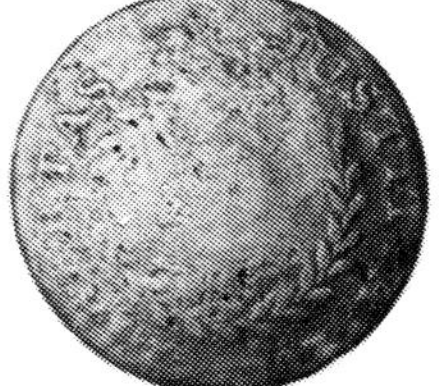

Rulau-E	Date	Metal	Size	VG	F	EF
Non 102	(1790's)	Copper	28mm	—	—	Unique?

Radiant, scrawny eagle in relief within upright oval depression ctsp on 1783 Nova Constellatio cent (pointed rays).

(EAGLE ON ANCHOR)

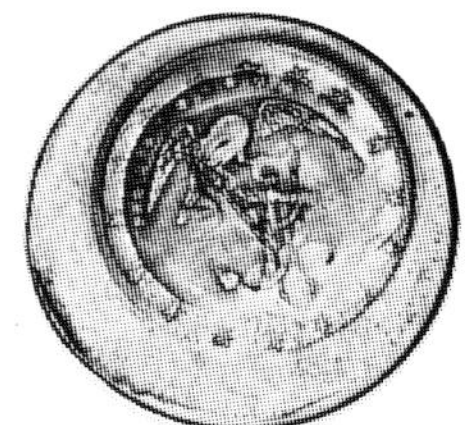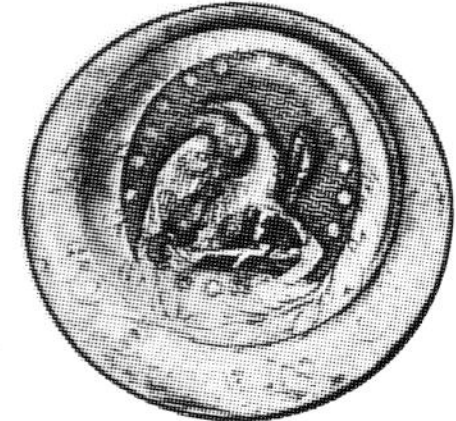

Rulau-E	Date	Metal	Size		VG	F	EF
Non 104	(1812-22)	Copper	29mm		—	Rare	—

Eagle with wings upraised perched on fouled anchor, all within starred circle, in relief, ctsp on U.S. 1802 Large cent. Rv: Eagle with folded wings perched on horizontal anchor, all within starred oval, in relief, ctsp on other side of the coin. (George Fuld report)

The devices used are those on marine buttons of the 1812-1822 period, according to Alphaeus Albert, the button authority.

ELTON'S
(Non-Local Fantasy)

Rulau-E	Date	Metal	Size	Denomination	VG	F	EF
Non 110	1757	Copper	36mm	(Penny)	—	—	Unique

Trader buying skins from an Indian, within central circle. Around: THE RED MEN COME TO ELTONS DAILY. Rv: A deer (?) lying under a tree, within a central circle. Around: SKINS BOUGHT AT ELTONS, 1757. Plain edge. (Designs and lettering are *etched* on English 1797 cartwheel penny which was first smoothed off on each side.) (Betts 397; AJN VII.90)

Howland Wood in *The Numismatist* for Jan. 1913 branded the Elton card a "counterfeit." He meant a fantasy piece which did not have the benefit of a genuine precursor.

The single specimen known appeared in the Thomas Birch & Sons sale in Philadelphia, Dec. 18, 1872, and from there went into the Williams S. Appleton collection, and thence to the Massachusetts Historical Society holdings in Boston.

Wood examined the MHS specimen and declared it had been acid-etched on an English 1797 penny. The only known piece is holed at 7 o'clock on obverse. By whom the piece was made, and why, is not known. The "when" seems easier, probably about 1870.

ELECTION MEDALETS

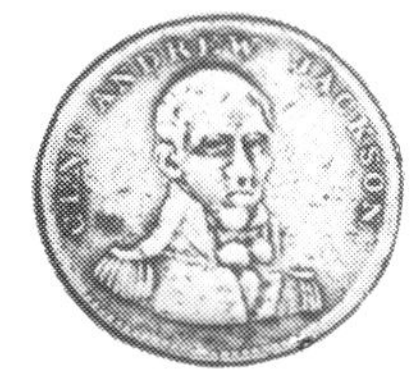 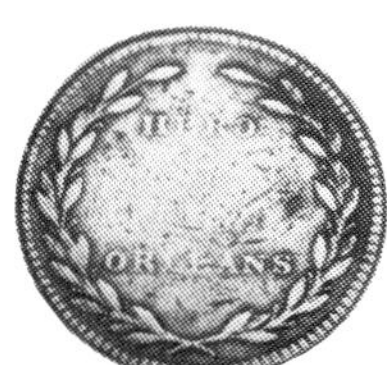

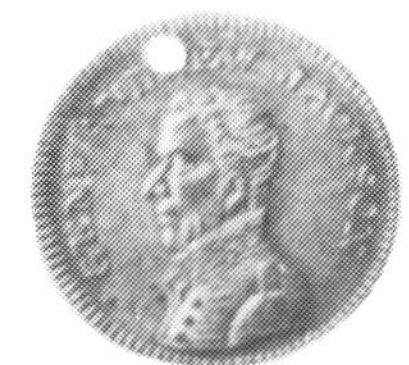 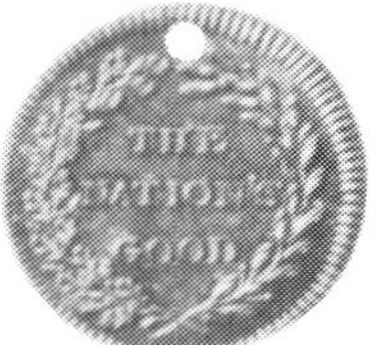

Rulau-E	Year	Metal	Size	F	VF	Unc
Med 1	(1828)	Brass	25mm	—	35.00	—

Facing military bust of Jackson, GENL. ANDREW JACKSON around. Rv: HERO / OF / NEW / ORLEANS within olive wreath. Wreath has 37 leaves and 20 berries. Reeded edge. (DeWitt AJACK 1824-1)

| Med 2 | (1828) | Sil Brass | 25mm | — | 45.00 | — |

As last. Reeded edge. (DeWitt AJACK 1824-1)

| Med 3 | (1828) | Brass | 25mm | — | 35.00 | — |

As last, but 38 leaves and 18 berries. Reeded edge. (DeWitt AJACK 1824-2)

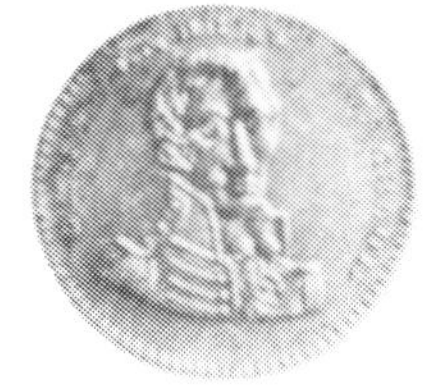 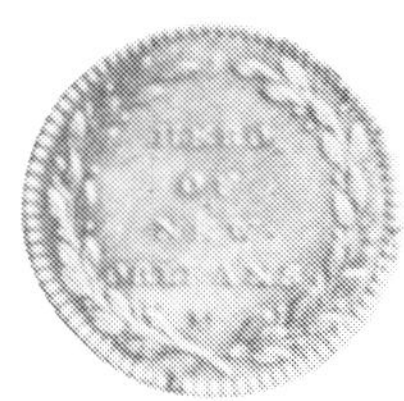

| Med 4 | (1824) | Brass | 25mm | — | 50.00 | — |

As last, but 34 leaves and 25 berries. Plain edge. (DeWitt AJACK 1824-3)

Rulau-E	Year	Metal	Size	F	VF	Unc
Med 5	(1824)	Brass	24mm	—	35.00	—

Left-facing military bust of Jackson, GENL ANDREW JACKSON. Rev: THE / NATION'S / GOOD within oak and olive wreath. Plain edge. (DeWitt AJACK 1824-4)

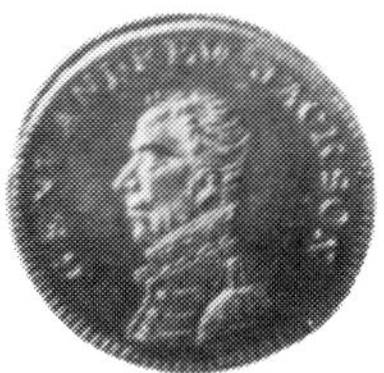 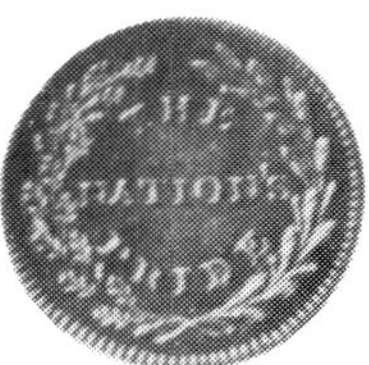

| Med 6 | (1824) | Brass | 24mm Medalet | — | 50.00 | — |

Obverse as last. Rev: THE / NATION'S / PRIDE within oak and olive wreath. Plain edge. (DeWitt AJACK 1824-5)

| Med 7 | (1824) | Brass | 24mm Medalet | — | 100.00 | — |

Obverse similar to last, but leaf decorations on collar and coat ornaments. Rev: Similar to last, but 5-pointed stars added above and below NATION'S. Plain edge. (DeWitt AJACK 1824-6)

A new phenomenon, the election medalet or campaign badge, emerged in the bitter John Quincy Adams-Andrew Jackson-Henry Clay election contest. Three basic types of Jackson medalet appeared in this year, each suggested by the Congressional medal awarded to the general for his 1815 victory at New Orleans. All were struck at Waterbury, Conn., according to J. Doyle DeWitt. Since these pieces were often worn on clothing, they sometimes occur holed.

MASONIC MEDALETS

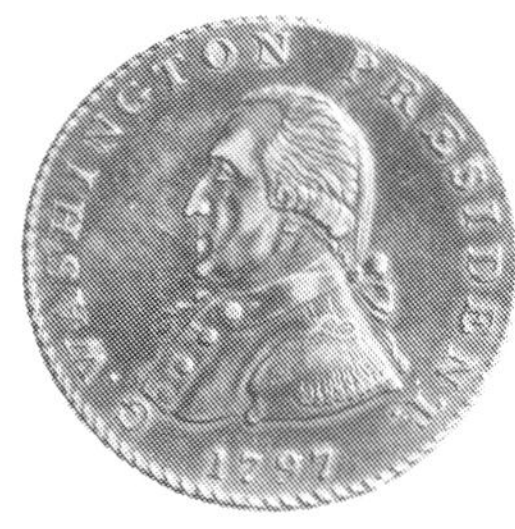 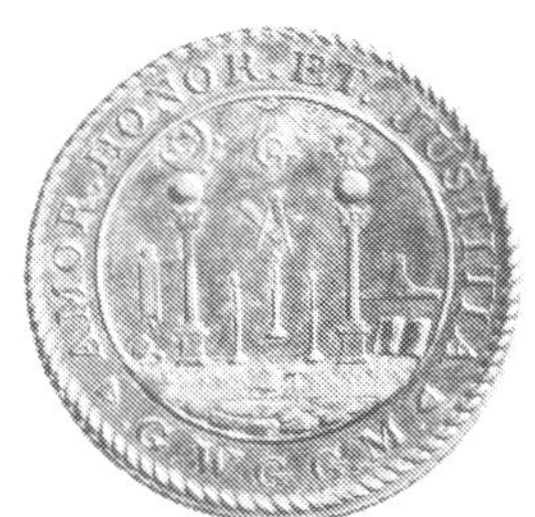

Rulau-E	Year	Metal	Size	VG	F	EF
Med 11	1797	Brass	34mm	—	3500. Ex. Rare	

Uniformed bust of Washington left, G. WASHINGTON PRESIDENT around, 1797 below. Rv: Two pillars topped by globes; All-seeing eye, G, square and compasses, open book, three burning candles, level, plumb and gavel, trowel - all within central circle. Around: AMOR. HONOR. ET. JUSTITIA. Below: - G.W.G.G.M. -. Engrailed edge. (Baker 288)

Rulau-E	Year	Metal	Size	VG	F	EF
Med 12	1797	Silver	34mm	—	—	45,000.

As last. Engrailed edge. (Baker 288)

| Med 13 | 1797 | Brass | 34mm | — | 750.4-known | |

Obverse as last. Rv: Blank.

A Masonic "penny." AMOR. HONOR. ET JUSTITIA – Love, Honor and Justice. G.W.G.G.M. – George Washington General Grand Master (of the United States). George Washington was initiated a Mason Nov. 4, 1752 into Fredericksburgh Lodge, Va. In 1788 he was chosen Master of Alexandria Lodge, Va. — later Alexandria Washington Lodge No. 22.

At a meeting Jan. 13, 1780, the Grand Lodge of Pennsylvania elected him General Grand Master of the United States. This did not meet with favor from other Grand Lodges, and the office was never established. But this action and its attendant publicity created the impression there was such a Masonic office and Washington occupied it, and this 1797 medallic token reinforced this belief. Struck in 1797, the low relief bust after Pierre Eugene du Simitiere's sketch closely resembles the 1792 Washington half dollars by Peter Getz of Lancaster, Pa. A silver specimen in the Bushnell sale passed through R. Coulton Davis of Pa. to the Garrett collection at Johns Hopkins University.

BENJAMIN FRANKLIN

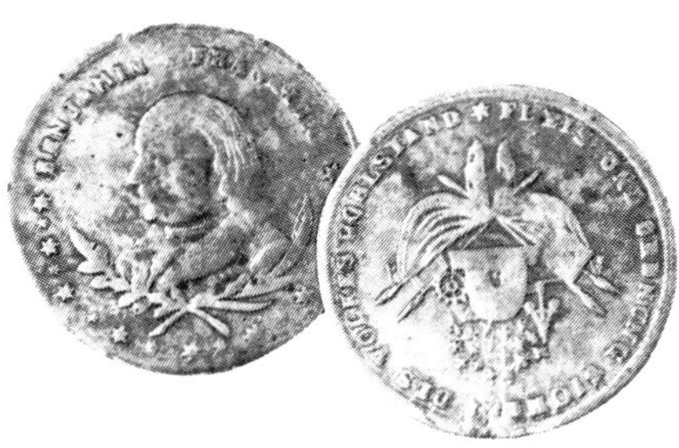

| Med 16 | (1800-15) | Brass | 37mm | — | — | Rare |

Described by George Fuld in Franklin and Numismatics as FR.M.NL.9, this token bears a portrait of Benjamin Franklin, two olive sprigs, 17 stars, and the name BENJAMIN FRANKLIN on its obverse. The reverse depicts a group of beehives, flags, machinery, and the legend FLEISS UND ORDNUNG SEGNET DES VOLVES WOHLSTAND ("Industry and Order Bless the Welfare of the People"). Struck in brass, this very rare 37mm token was first exhibited by Thomas Elder in 1917. Originally Elder thought it was struck between 1800 and 1815.

(THE SENTIMENTAL)
London, England

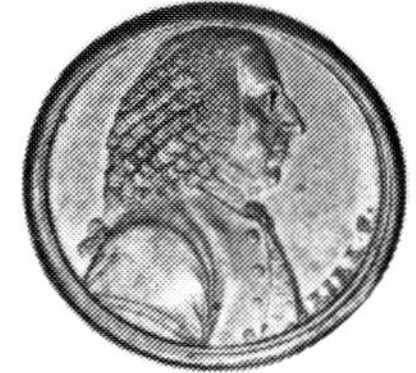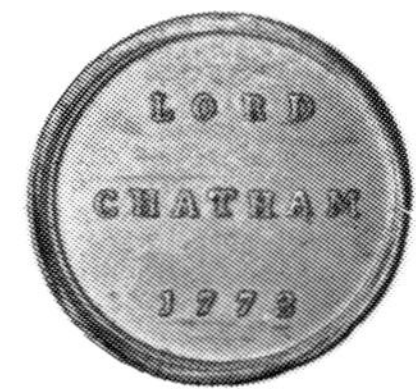

				VG	VF	Unc
Med 18	1773	Copper	25mm (Medalet)	11.50	30.00	60.00

Bust of William Pitt the Elder right, in wig and coat. Tiny KIRK F. under bust. Rv: LORD / CHATHAM / 1773 in three lines. Plain edge. (Betts 522)

				VG	VF	Unc
Med 19	1773	Silver	25mm (Medalet)	—	—	Rare

As last. (Betts 522A)

The copper token was given away with numbers of a magazine called *The Sentamental*, published 1773-1775. Apparently a silver version also was struck, and was given away as prizes by the owners. Betts says the copper pieces are also known silver-plated.

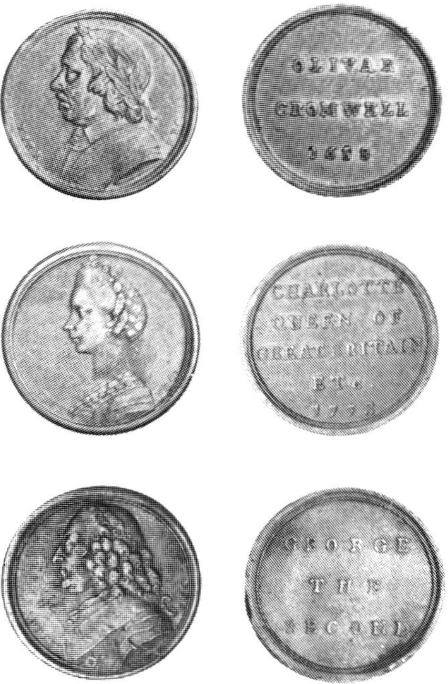

According to *The Numismatic Chronicle* of London for 1890 (page 54) the Pitt token was one of a series of 13 tokens given away with as many numbers of the magazine. These other tokens depict George II, Oliver Cromwell, David Garrick, Queen Charlotte and other English figures, but only Pitt (died 1778) has an American connection.

John Kirk of London (1724-1778), a pupil of James Anthony Dassier, and a maker of many coin weights of this period, cut the dies for this series of tokens. Most of his work is from the 1740-1776 period. (See "The Sentimental Magazine and its Medalets" by Sidney K. Eastwood in *Numisma* for 1939).

FUGIO
(E.J. Theisen)
East Orange, N.J.

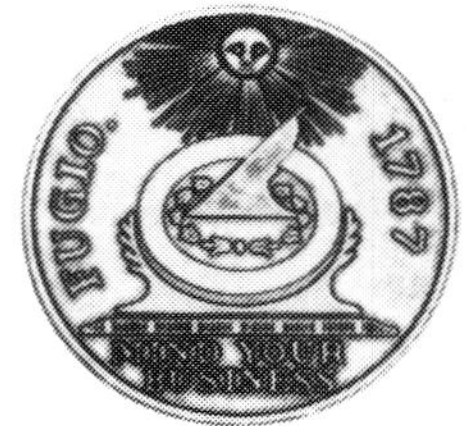

Rulau-E	Date	Metal	Size	VF	EF	Unc
Med 25	(1957)	Bronze	29mm (Token)	—	7.00	10.00

Imitation of Fugio cent. Radiant sunface above sundial, FUGIO 1787 around, MIND YOUR / BUSINESS in two lines in exergue. Rv: THE / FOUNDERS / ISOLATIONISM / DEVELOPED U.S. / FOR IT IS A / BASIC LAW / OF LIFE. Plain edge.

Rulau-E	Date	Metal	Size	VF	EF	Unc
Med 26	(1957)	Gilt/Bz	29mm (Token)	—	8.50	12.50

As last. Plain edge.

Rulau-E	Date	Metal	Size	VF	EF	Unc
Med 27	1961	Bronze	29mm (Token)	—	7.75	11.00

Obverse as last (Sundial). Rv: FORTITUDE PRUDENCE DEF. BYE J (backward) T / 1961 / TEMPERANCE / JUSTICE (under bridge) / (blank space across center) / THE FOUR CARDINAL VIRTUES / DEPICTED ON FIRST COIN / OF THE UNITED STATES / COIN AUTH. BY CONGRESS / JULY 6, 1787. Plain edge.

Rulau-E	Date	Metal	Size	VF	EF	Unc
Med 28	1961	Bronze	29mm (Token)	—	7.00	10.00

Obverse as last. Rv: As last, but DEF. E.J.T. replaces DEF. BYE. J (backward) T, which was poor die work on the earlier piece. Also, blank space across center now reads: ". . . THE U.S.A. OUGHT TO RELY / ON THEIR OWN VIRTUE." / (VOL. 22. PG. 339 JRNLS. C.C.). Plain edge.

These tokens use the 1787 Fugio cent design in an attempt to recapture the Founding Fathers' neutrality and isolationism. They are included here because the date and style fit into the Early category and may cause confusion among collectors.

The first pieces were issued by Eugene J. Theisen of East Orange, N.J. in an effort to convince Congress to issue a commemorative honoring the Fugio cent of 1787 on its coming (1962) 175th anniversary. To publicize the 1957 issue, Theisen offered a $250 reward to anyone who identified the designer of the 1787 coin and the author's interpretation of the Sundial design and legends, payable until Oct. 24, 1957. There were no winners.

The author possesses much original Theisen literature of the 1957 period, advancing his peculiar view of where America should be, politically and socially. The 1961 issues expound some of these views. He theorized the Fugio cent showed America the right path.

ILLINOIS

MOORMAN MFG. CO.
Quincy, Ill.

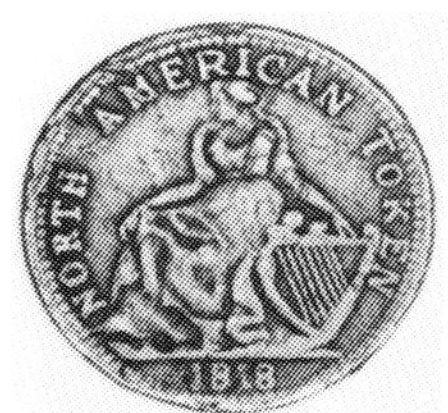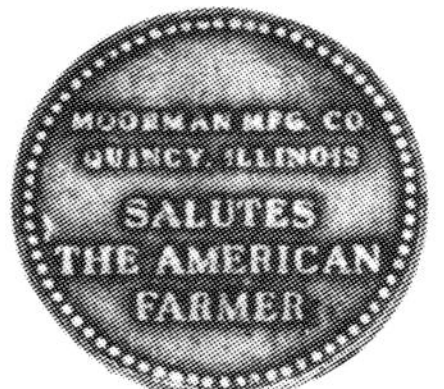

Rulau-E	Date	Metal	Size		VG	EF	Unc
		Copper-plated					
Med 33	1818	Pewter	26mm		—	8.00	11.00

Seated female left, with harp. NORTH AMERICAN TOKEN around, 1818 in exergue. Rv: MOORMAN MFG. CO. / QUINCY, ILLINOIS / SALUTES / THE AMERICAN / FARMER.

The obverse is an imitation of the Irish-American token dated 1781 which is associated with the American Colonial series. The piece was probably made circa 1968 in connection with the Illinois Sesquicentennial that year. Since it bears a date and a style fitting the Early American token category and could be mistaken, it was thought best to catalog it here.

STAMPS,

AT A GREAT DISCOUNT.

S. & M. ALLEN,

No. 2 South Third-street,

HAVE constantly for sale, a **complete** assortment of STAMPS, *wholesale or retail.* To those who purchase for retailing, a very *liberal discount* will be made.

☞ *Lottery Tickets* and *Shares* for sale.

☞ All kinds of *Bank Notes* and *Specie* bought and sold.

☞ A liberal premium paid for *Treasury Notes.* Also, for New-York, Boston, Charleston, North Carolina, and Virginia Bank Bills.　　nov. 23—¶

There was a brisk trade after the War of 1812 in bank notes, Treasury notes, lottery tickets, shares, embossed tax stamps and specie by dealers such as S. & M. Allen of Philadelphia, whose ad (above) appeared in the Nov. 25, 1816 issue of The Freeman's Journal and Philadelphia Mercantile Advertiser. Notice that bills on New York, Boston, Charleston, etc. banks were favored.

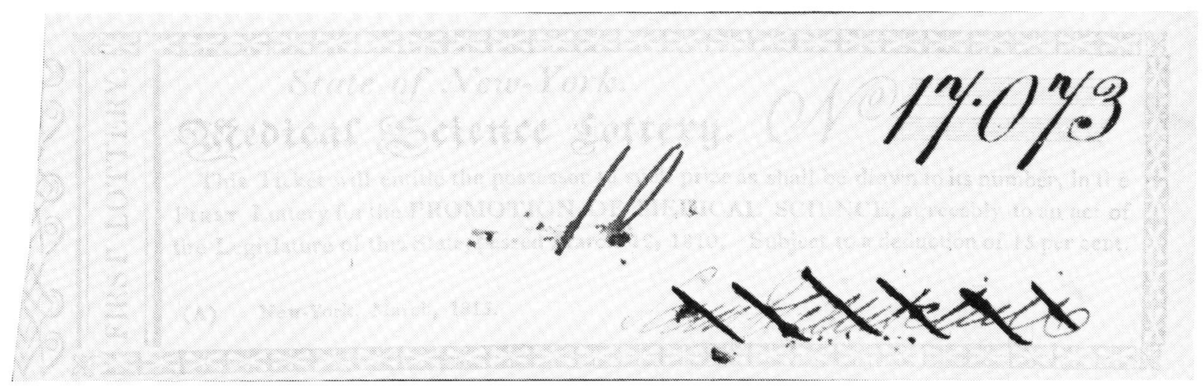

Lotteries abounded in the early United States — lotteries for many different causes, from the building of turnpikes and canals to the advancement of medical science (such as this 1815 orange and black ticket of New York state promoted.)

CONNECTICUT COURANT.

Daily newspapers in the Early period of our country were unlike those of today, with ads on the front page and dispatches months old appearing as news. This Connecticut Courant (Hartford) for Sept. 11, 1811, warns of imminent war with England and reports on the summer campaign in Spain, while advertising several lotteries, shares of stock in the Hartford Bank, and the new dry goods store of Joseph Wheeler. This paper (13 by 19¼ inches in format) consisted of four pages.

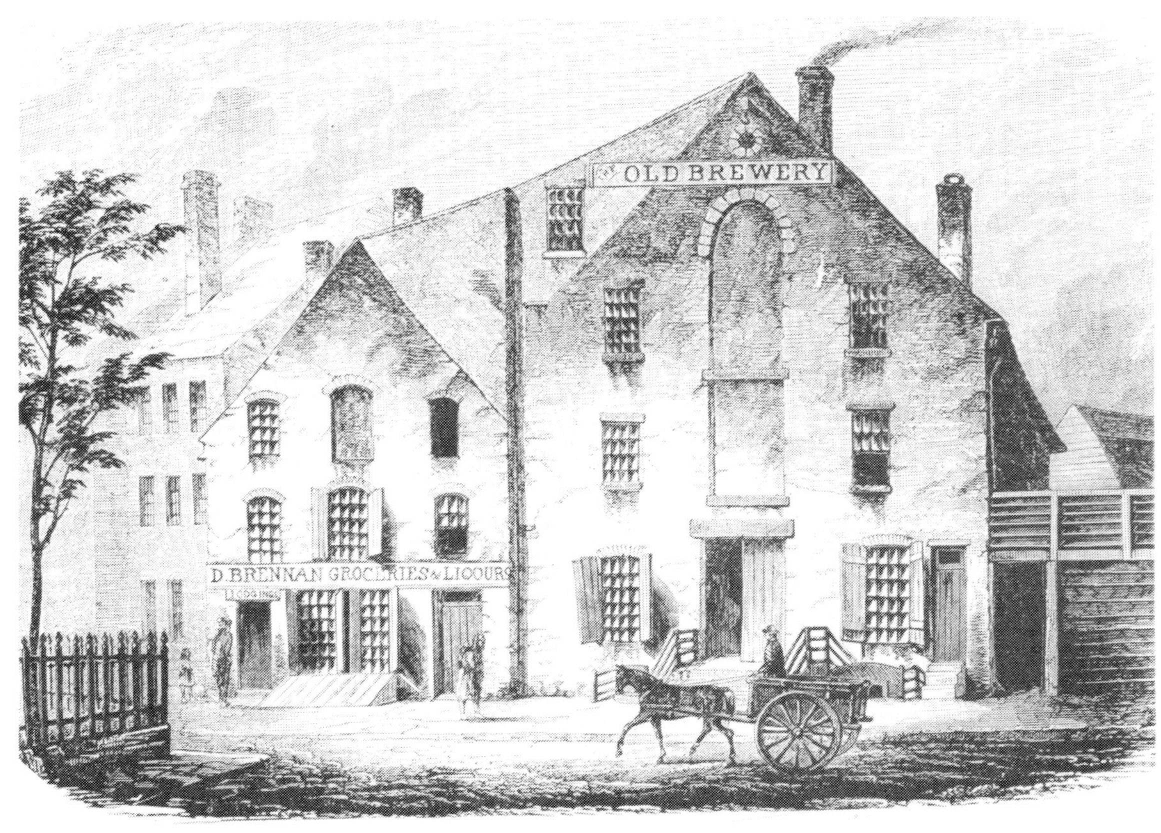

Etching of "The Old Brewery" at Five Points, New York City. Next door may be seen D. Brennan's grocery, liquor store and lodgings. (Counsel collection)

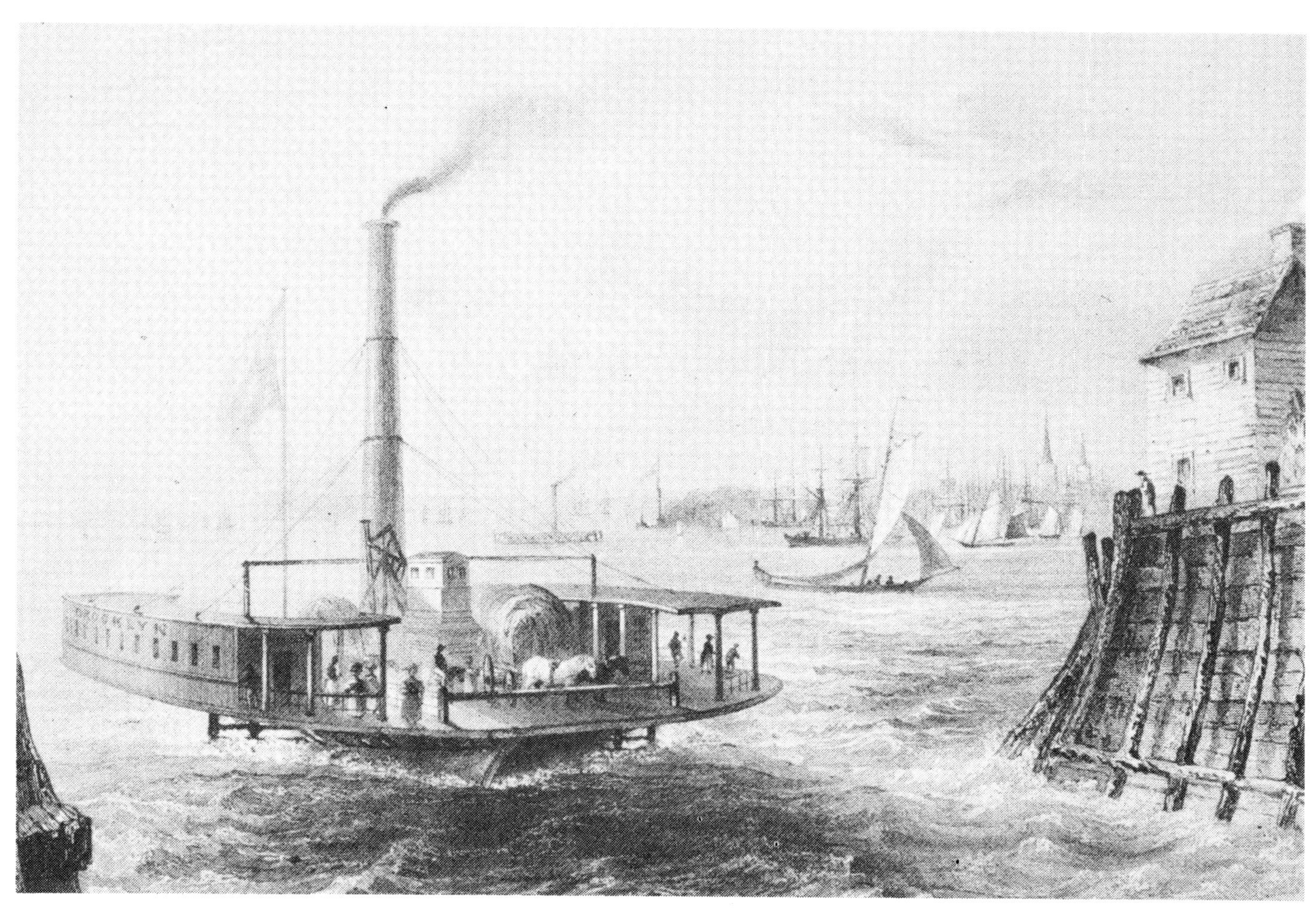

The ferry at Brooklyn, N.Y., as seen on an old engraving made about 1830. The scene reveals much of the river traffic of the day — more than 50 years before the Brooklyn Bridge was opened. (Library of Congress collection)

NAME AND SUBJECT INDEX

LIST OF ILLUSTRATIONS